LINE OF FIRE

HEROISM, TRAGEDY, AND CANADA'S POLICE

LINE OF FIRE

HEROISM, TRAGEDY, ────── AND CANADA'S POLICE

EDWARD BUTTS

DUNDURN PRESS
TORONTO

Project Editor: Michael Carroll
Copy Editor: Cheryl Hawley
Design: Courtney Horner
Printer: Webcom

Library and Archives Canada Cataloguing in Publication

Butts, Edward, 1951-
     Line of fire : heroism, tragedy, and Canada's police / by Edward Butts.

 Includes bibliographical references.
ISBN 978-1-55488-391-2

     1. Police--Canada--History. 2. Police--Violence against--Canada--History.
3. Police--Canada--Biography. I. Title.

HV8157.B88 2009   363.20971   C2009-900306-6

1   2   3   4   5   13   12   11   10   09

Conseil des Arts
du Canada

Canada Council
for the Arts

ONTARIO ARTS COUNCIL
CONSEIL DES ARTS DE L'ONTARIO

We acknowledge the support of **The Canada Council for the Arts** and the **Ontario Arts Council** for our publishing program. We also acknowledge the financial support of the **Government of Canada** through the **Book Publishing Industry Development Program** and **The Association for the Export of Canadian Books**, and the **Government of Ontario** through the **Ontario Book Publishers Tax Credit program**, and the **Ontario Media Development Corporation.**

Care has been taken to trace the ownership of copyright material used in this book. The author and the publisher welcome any information enabling them to rectify any references or credits in subsequent editions.

J. Kirk Howard, President

Printed and bound in Canada.   www.dundurn.com
Printed on recycled paper.

Dundurn Press	Gazelle Book Services Limited	Dundurn Press
3 Church Street, Suite 500	White Cross Mills	2250 Military Road
Toronto, Ontario, Canada	High Town, Lancaster, England	Tonawanda, NY
M5E 1M2	LA1 4XS	U.S.A. 14150

Mixed Sources
Product group from well-managed
forests, and other controlled sources
www.fsc.org Cert no. SW-COC-002358
© 1996 Forest Stewardship Council
FSC

To all those who serve and protect

CONTENTS —————————————

ACKNOWLEDGEMENTS ——

First, I must thank Kirk Howard, Tony Hawke, and Michael Carroll of Dundurn for thinking of me for this excellent project and entrusting it to me. I am indebted to the following individuals and institutions for assisting me in my search for information and pictures: the Library and Archives Canada; the Provincial Archives of Alberta, British Columbia, Manitoba, Newfoundland, Ontario, and Saskatchewan; the Glenbow Archives; the Moncton, New Brunswick Public Library; the Moncton Museum; the Metropolitan Toronto Reference Library; the Metropolitan Toronto Police Museum; the Victoria Police Department; the Vancouver Police Museum; the British Columbia Law Enforcement Memorial Foundation; the Royal Canadian Mounted Police Fallen Four Memorial Park in Mayerthorpe, Alberta; the *London Free Press*; the *Toronto Star*; the *Montreal Gazette*; and Steve Gibson, Jonathan Sheldan, Colette McKillop, Marie Patterson, Lynette Walton, Chris Mathieson, and Robert Knuckle. Special thanks to Norman Crane of St. John's, Newfoundland, and, as always, to the staff of the Guelph, Ontario, Public Library.

INTRODUCTION ─────────

We are all familiar with this stock movie scene: the bad guys are committing some sort of crime and the police cars roar in with sirens wailing. The cops jump out of their cars and a dramatic shootout ensues. In the course of the gun battle, one or two police officers go down. By the time the movie is over, we've forgotten about those dead policemen. They were just there for effect, like the exploding cars. They were uniforms without faces. We would never think of them as real people with families at home and lives ahead of them. But that's Hollywood, and it's the closest most people get to law enforcement stories.

Ask any group of people what the most dangerous occupation is and you will likely get a variety of replies: police officer, firefighter, high steel worker, miner, and astronaut, to name a few. The people who hold these jobs certainly do place themselves at risk, and they do so knowing that colleagues have died in the performance of those duties. Whether or not one believes the police officer has the most dangerous job, there is no denying that law enforcement is a very hazardous calling. It was dangerous for the nineteenth century North-West Mounted Police constable who rode out alone to track down a fugitive, and it remains so for the twenty-first century urban cop who knocks on an apartment door in response to a domestic dispute call, not knowing what awaits her on the other side of the door. Since 1804, when the first Canadian law enforcement officer known to have perished in the line of duty drowned in a shipwreck on Lake Ontario, hundreds more have lost their lives. Police constables, jail and prison guards, game wardens, and others have gone down in the line of fire.

What is the "Line of Fire"? That blazing gun battle between cops and robbers in which a police officer is killed might come to mind. Such tragic incidents have, in fact, happened in Canada, but here the term has a much broader definition. The antagonist in a real life police drama might not be an armed and desperate criminal, but the elements, or even a combination of the two. "Line of Fire" means any potentially deadly situation: a confrontation with an armed criminal, a patrol across frozen Arctic terrain, guard duty in a jail, or a patrol in a small boat on dark waters in the dead of night. The inescapable fact is that a law enforcement officer steps into the line of fire every time he goes on duty, and sometimes the threat doesn't evaporate with the end of the shift.

The accounts presented here come from across Canada. They have been selected from two hundred years of heroism and tragedy in Canadian law enforcement. They tell just a few of the many stories of Canadians who dedicated their lives to the service of the law, and who died in the line of fire.

1

JOHN FISK:
THE WRECK OF THE *SPEEDY*

In 1804, the pioneer community of York (Toronto), Upper Canada, was just a small collection of wooden buildings perched at the edge of the howling wilderness, on the shore of Lake Ontario. The site had been chosen as a provincial capital by founder John Graves Simcoe, in part because of the excellent natural harbour that was protected by a long peninsula. Later in the century, a storm would wash away the spit that connected the peninsula to the mainland, creating the Toronto Islands.

Lake Ontario, despite having the smallest surface area of the five Great Lakes, could be a nightmare for mariners in wooden sailing ships. Tricky crosswinds sprang up unexpectedly, and could quickly capsize a vessel. Moreover, at that time the only lighthouse on Lake Ontario (and on the entire Great Lakes system) was the Mississauga Point light at the mouth of the Niagara River. The absence of a guiding light at a strategic spot on the Canadian shore might have been at least partially responsible for the shipwreck that claimed the life of the first Canadian officer of the law known to be killed in the line of duty.

The sequence of events that led to the tragedy began in 1803. A Native known as Whistling Duck, who belonged to the Muskrat clan of the Chippewa Nation, was murdered near Lake Scugog in the eastern part of the colony. Whistling Duck's brother, Ogetonicut, accused a white trader named John Sharp of the crime. Sharp had been a soldier with the Queen's Rangers, and at the time of the murder was managing Farewell's Trading Post, at Bull Point on Lake Scugog.

Colonial authorities told Ogetonicut that the crime would be investigated, and the guilty party would be prosecuted and punished. However, a year passed and nothing happened. Then John Sharp's body was found near the trading post. He had been stabbed in the left side and his skull was bashed in. From all appearances, Ogetonicut had grown impatient with the white man's law, and had taken revenge himself. (Another possible explanation is that a different white man had killed Whistling Duck in self-defence, and that Ogetonicut murdered Sharp simply to get even with the whites.)

If the whites were slow to investigate the alleged murder of a Native by a white man, they lost no time in taking action when the situation was reversed. Shortly after Sharp's murder, the Muskrat clan travelled down to Lake Ontario on a trading mission. They camped at Gibraltar Point on the peninsula, across the harbour from York.

Courtesy Metropolitan Toronto Library

The York Gaol, Toronto's first jail, at the time that John Fisk was High Constable. Accused murderer Ogetonicut was locked in the guardhouse (inset) while he awaited the ill-fated voyage on HMS *Speedy*.

Word reached the town authorities that Ogetonicut was in the camp. A party of soldiers from the garrison was sent over to arrest him. There could have been an unpleasant confrontation, but the clan chief, Wabbekisheco, did not want trouble with the redcoats. He took Ogetonicut by the shoulder and handed him over. The soldiers took their prisoner to York and delivered him to High Constable John Fisk, who locked him up in the wooden stockade that was the York Gaol.

John Fisk was born in Wallingford, Connecticut, in 1752. During the Revolutionary War he served as an ensign in Elmore's Connecticut Regiment, which was connected to the American Continental Army. He was apparently in charge of a detail guarding British prisoners of war. He resigned his commission at the end of the war, and settled in Massachusetts, then New York, and then Vermont.

Finally, in 1801 Fisk moved with his wife Levine, and their six children, to Upper Canada. He acquired a 210 acre farm in King Township, to the north of York, along the road now known as Yonge Street. Fisk was what earlier settlers of the region called a "Johnny-come-lately Loyalist": an American who had sided with the Patriots during the war, but moved north to take advantage of cheap land, even though it meant living under the British flag.

Fisk became a prominent and influential citizen in his new community, and in April 1804, he was made High Constable of the Home District. This territory included the present counties and regions of York, Durham, Peel, Simcoe, and Toronto. There was no police force in the modern sense. In some situations, soldiers could be called upon to make arrests. Otherwise, law enforcement was the job of ordinary citizens who were sworn in as constables. Their tasks usually had less to do with fighting crime than with enforcing regulations concerning fire safety, animal control, tavern licensing, and food marketing. Unfortunately, a flood in the 1930s destroyed most of the Upper Canada court records from that period, so information on High Constable John Fisk is sketchy. We know that he was in charge of part-time, amateur constables, and was a civil representative of the Crown. It was a prestigious position, but one that Fisk would enjoy for only a few months.

The arrest of Ogetonicut caused a problem. All of the officials required for a legal trial under British law were in York, but the law stated that a trial for a capital crime had to take place in the jurisdiction where the crime had been committed. That meant the venue for Ogetonicut's trial had to be the settlement of Newcastle on the Presqu'ile Peninsula, just west of the much larger Prince Edward Peninsula. This Newcastle (not to be confused with the present Ontario town) was the administrative centre for the territory that included Lake Scugog. Because the roads were very bad, the trip would have to be made by water aboard the HMS *Speedy*.

The *Speedy* was a two masted naval schooner, fifty-five feet long, with a twenty foot bowsprit. She was built at Cataraqui (Kingston) in 1776. For a fresh water vessel she was well past her prime by 1804. In spite of extensive repairs made in 1792, the *Speedy's* hull was weakened by dry rot, and leaked so badly that the bilge pump had to be kept in constant operation.

On October 7, the *Speedy's* commander, Lieutenant Thomas Paxton, an experienced Royal Navy officer, was told he would be transporting a large number of important passengers to Newcastle. Paxton objected on the grounds that his small vessel, in such poor condition, could not safely carry so many people. Moreover, Paxton did not like the look of the weather. He thought a storm was moving in. However, Lieutenant Governor Peter Hunter insisted that the *Speedy* make the trip, and threatened Paxton with a court martial if he did not obey orders.

On board the *Speedy* that day, besides Lieutenant Paxton and his crew of five, were: Ogetonicut; High Constable John Fisk; Thomas Cochrane, the trial judge; Solicitor General of Upper Canada, Robert Isaac Dey Gray, the prosecutor; Justice of the Peace John Ruggles, a potential witness; Angus Macdonald, defence lawyer and member of the House of assembly; George Cowan, fur trader and interpreter for the British Indian Department; John Anderson, law student; and Jacob Herchmer, an officer in the York Militia. There are no definite reports of how many people were aboard the *Speedy*. Estimates range from twenty to thirty-nine. Other known passengers included Robert Baker, who was Grey's servant; John Stegman, a land surveyor for the colonial government; and two or three Natives who were to appear as witnesses for Ogentonicut. There were also two children whose parents put them aboard the schooner to spare them the rugged overland journey to Newcastle. The parents went by road, because they could not afford to pay for their own passage.

Departure from York was delayed when the overloaded schooner ran aground. Once the *Speedy* was freed, she sailed to Oshawa to pick up two brothers named Farewell, who had been John Sharp's employers. The Farewells would not board the unseaworthy *Speedy,* choosing instead to accompany the schooner in a canoe. Due to the late start and less than ideal sailing conditions, by the evening of October 8, the two vessels had gone only as far as Colborne, just west of Newcastle. They continued the voyage in darkness.

The storm Lieutenant Paxton had been expecting struck, and quickly became a blizzard. The *Speedy* was last seen fighting a heavy sea as she approached Presqu'ile Point. Allegedly, the crew fired one of her guns as a distress signal. In the absence of a lighthouse to guide the vessel to safe harbour, a Captain Selleck supposedly lit a bonfire at the tip of the peninsula as a beacon, but to no avail. The *Speedy* and all those aboard vanished with hardly a trace.

The Farewell brothers, who no doubt had paddled their canoe to shore to wait out the storm, arrived at Newcastle on the morning of October 9. They had been separated from the *Speedy* and did not know what had happened to her. No bodies were ever recovered. The only items of wreckage to wash ashore were a mast, a compass box, and a chicken coop.

The sinking of the *Speedy* was a disaster for the colonial administration of Upper Canada. The *York Gazette* reported:

> A more distressing and melancholy event has not occurred to this place for many years; nor does it often happen that such a number of persons of respectability are collected in the same vessel. Not less than nine widows, and we know not how many children, have to lament the loss of their husbands and fathers, who, alas, have, perhaps in the course of a few minutes, met with a watery grave.

The wreck of the *Speedy* also meant the end of the Newcastle settlement. The colonial government had thought that a well-publicized murder trial, followed by a public hanging, would boost Newcastle as an administrative centre. The community might even be an alternative to York as the provincial capital. That idea went down with the *Speedy*. Newcastle's harbour was declared "inconvenient," and the settlement was eventually abandoned.

The wreck of the *Speedy* remains an unsolved mystery. Was the schooner swamped, or did she run onto a notorious shoal called the Devil's Horseblock? Was the *Speedy* a victim of the Sophiasburg Triangle, an area of Lake Ontario off Presqu'ile in which magnetic forces are said to interfere with compasses? Those questions will never be answered. We know only that on a stormy night in October 1804, a ship went to the bottom of Lake Ontario, taking with it High Constable John Fisk, the first Canadian officer of the law to be killed in the line of duty. A historic plaque in Presqu'ile Provincial Park commemorates the loss of the *Speedy*.

2

CONSTABLE JOHNSTON COCHRANE: NO WITNESSES

Johnston Cochrane was born in Ireland around 1823. Like many thousands of his countrymen, he left his homeland during the Great Famine of the mid-nineteenth century that reduced the people of Ireland to starvation and poverty. He initially lived for several years in the United States, but then made his way west. By 1859, Cochrane was in the British settlement of Victoria on Vancouver Island, where he was employed as a constable.

At that time Victoria was a boomtown, thanks to the discovery of gold on the Fraser River, in what is now mainland British Columbia. Thousands of prospectors with heads full of dreams of easy riches passed through Victoria on their way to the diggings. Some stayed in town to establish businesses that catered to the miners' needs. At the onset of winter, hordes of miners would leave their Fraser River camps and descend on Victoria, swelling the resident population of about 1,500 to many times that number.

A large number of the footloose gold hunters were American adventurers who packed guns and Bowie knives. Their views on politics, law, and racial issues did not always coincide with those of the townsmen, who were mostly of British stock. Slavery, for example, was still legal in many American states, but had been abolished throughout the British Empire. This is not to say that the Anglo Saxon colonists were free of bigotry; they weren't. The prevailing attitude was that "people of colour" were inferior to whites.

Even though the letter of the law theoretically regarded all of Queen Victoria's subjects as equal, regardless of race, colour, or creed, in practice the law could be condescending and discriminating toward non-whites. This was certainly evident in Victoria, where whites mixed with Natives, Chinese immigrants, and a small number of blacks. The American element in the colony, bringing with them well-entrenched racial prejudices that were legally sanctioned at home, had little patience with *any* of the niceties of British law that said a "person of colour" was equal to a white. This was also evident in the case of Constable Johnston Cochrane.

At the time that Johnston Cochrane was a constable with the small Victoria Police Department, the most common offences were assaults, public drunkenness, disorderly behaviour, vagrancy, petty theft, impaired driving of horse drawn vehicles, and the desertion of sailors from ships. There was also a problem with livestock rustling. Often, Natives who came to Victoria to trade were blamed for the thefts of cattle, pigs, and chickens. No doubt, some of the rustling *was* done by Natives, but the white population, particularly the Americans, was unwilling to consider the possibility that some of the livestock thieves might be white. Gold rushes tended to attract a lot of riff-raff, and most of the missing animals had likely wound up in white men's cooking pots. Constable Cochrane apparently stirred up personal animosity among the Natives during his investigations of some of the thefts.

On June 2, 1859, Cochrane went to the Craigflower district of Victoria to investigate the theft of a pig. He was not armed. The suspect was a man of Portuguese descent named Joseph Lewis, known about town as Portuguese Joe. He was allegedly a butcher by profession, making him a likely candidate for the crime of hog rustling. Cochrane could not find Portuguese Joe, so he left Craigflower to return to his station. He never made it.

The next day, Cochrane's body was found in the bush near the Craigflower Road. He had been shot in the head and the mouth. By all appearances, the killer had waited in ambush. No witnesses came forward.

The crime that the *British Colonist* called a "Barbarous Murder" stunned Victoria. Vancouver Island was not California, where the wild and wooly gold camps had become notorious for their lack of law and order. Vancouver Island and the town of Victoria were British!

The police did not look for suspects among the white population. The murder *had* to have been committed by a "person of colour," or at least someone who was not of Anglo background. Racial tensions had always been simmering just below the surface in Victoria. Now, with police searching for a killer only among the ethnic minorities, it seethed to the surface. An ugly atmosphere of suspicion and intolerance gripped Victoria.

On June 3, Portuguese Joe was arrested and charged with Cochrane's murder. Ten days later he denied the charge before a magistrate. Joe said he had been sleeping at the Victoria Brewery at the time of the murder, and two witnesses supported his alibi. Joe was released with a warning to stop stealing livestock or face the consequences.

The police then arrested a man named Francois Pressci. There is little information available on this individual. His name suggests a French background, but he might have been Native, or of mixed blood. Pressci was the man who had found Cochrane's body and reported it to the police. The police knew that pretending to "discover" the body was an old ruse used by murderers to deflect suspicion, but they

The British Columbia Law Enforcement Memorial is inscribed with the names of all British Columbia law enforcement officers who lost their lives in the line of duty, beginning with Constable Johnston Cochrane, whose murder remains unsolved.

Courtesy Jonathan Sheldan. Victoria Police Department

could find no real evidence against Pressci and had to release him.

The next suspect they picked up was a man of mixed white and Native blood, named Jollibeaui. There was a belief among the whites that "half-breeds" embodied the worst traits of both races. But once again, the police could find no evidence against Jollibeaui. All they learned was that he had been involved with Portuguese Joe in "shooting game for the market."

Constable Johnston Cochrane's killer was never found. Anyone in that raw frontier community of Victoria could have committed the crime. Racism may seem to victimize only those whom it segregates and oppresses, but in truth it also burdens and demeans those who practice it; even when, like the whites in mid-nineteenth century Victoria, they are largely unaware of their misconceptions, and reflect the accepted attitudes of their peers. In such a situation, justice itself becomes a victim of bigotry.

3

THE NORTH-WEST MOUNTED POLICE: THE EARLY YEARS

Why was the wild and wooly nineteenth century American West so much more lawless than the Canadian West? All of the ingredients for the kind of anarchy that the American West became notorious for were there: white settlers moving onto Native lands, white buffalo hunters annihilating the herds with high-powered rifles, and whiskey traders, gunmen, and outlaws from Montana and the Dakota Territory crossing the border to pursue their illegal activities in Canada. Add to all that a total absence — at first — of any form of law enforcement, and the potential for disaster was explosive. In fact, a disaster was what galvanized Prime Minister John A. Macdonald's government to pass the bill that created the North-West Mounted Police. In the spring of 1873, at a whiskey fort in the Cypress Hills, a band of white hunters slaughtered over thirty Assiniboines after a drunken dispute over some stolen horses.

For about six years before the Cypress Hills Massacre there had been nobody to police Canada's newly acquired North-West Territories, and the lawless element had been left unchecked. There was even talk in Washington DC of American annexation of the Canadian West. All that changed almost overnight with the arrival of the Mounties. The redcoated constables chased out the whiskey traders, and dealt swiftly with any gunslinging riff-raff. The desperadoes learned the hard way that a Mountie was a different breed of lawman from the town marshals and county sheriffs they had known on the other side of the line. The American lawman was often an inexperienced civilian, or a hired gun little better than the troublemakers he was supposed to keep in line. He had authority over a limited jurisdiction, and was answerable to a town committee or the local electorate.

A Mountie was a well-trained member of a federal police force, answerable only to his superior officers. He had the authority to seek out and arrest criminals over the entire North-West Territories. He soon had a reputation for being relentless in the pursuit of law-breakers. The presence of the NWMP was the single greatest reason that the Canadian West had no equivalent to Dodge City, no shootouts like the one at the O.K. Corral, and no counterpart to Billy the Kid. Nonetheless, the Mountie patrolled some rugged country, populated by tough men. Every time he stepped out of a police post he was potentially placing himself in the line of fire. The NWMP did not emerge from their Old West period unscathed.

Constable Marmaduke Graburn: First to Die

When the first NWMP constables rode out onto the Canadian prairies, they were well aware that sooner or later one of them would have the unfortunate distinction of being the first to meet a violent death. The red coat that the Mountie wore was an awe-inspiring symbol of authority to resentful Natives and white ne'er-do-wells, but it would not stop a bullet. Amazingly, the Mounties chased the American whiskey traders off Canadian soil without losing a man. Nor, during those early years, was a single Mountie killed in any of the potentially dangerous incidents in which a constable had to ride into a Native camp to arrest a suspect. This was especially remarkable considering the horse stealing that became one of the Mounties' biggest problems after the whiskey traders had been sent packing.

To young Native men, horse theft was not a crime, but a sort of honourable sport. Stealing horses from a rival tribe was a means of gaining not only wealth, but also prestige and respect. However, the idea that horse stealing was honourable did not prevent the victims of a horse rustling raid from complaining to the police. NWMP constables regularly recovered stolen horses, and were resented by the culprits. Still, no angry warrior who lost face in front of his people when a constable led away horses that he had been brave and cunning enough to steal took revenge by shooting the Mountie. By 1879, five years after they had first started to police the prairies, the Mounties might well have wondered if they were leading charmed lives. For one constable, the good luck was about to run out.

Nineteen-year-old Marmaduke Graburn, born in Ontario and allegedly a former sailor, had enlisted with the NWMP only six months before he was stationed in Fort Walsh, in what is now Saskatchewan. He was one of several policemen sent out to a post called the Horse Camp, about ten miles from Fort Walsh, just inside the present-day Alberta border. The Horse Camp was a place where the Mounties rested their horses and cared for animals that were sick or injured. Local Blood warriors objected to the Mounties' corral because it was too near a trail that they used on horse-stealing raids.

On November 17, 1879, Graburn and a scout named Jules Quesnelle rode from the Horse Camp to tend to some horses in a corral a couple of miles away. Constable George Johnston, a friend who had signed up with Graburn, stayed at the camp. When Graburn and Quesnelle rode back in the evening, they stopped at the camp's garden to dig up some potatoes and turnips. A little later, as they approached the Horse Camp, Graburn realized that he had left his lariat and axe at the garden. He went back to get them while Quesnelle went on to the camp. That was the last time Quesnelle saw Graburn alive.

When Graburn did not return to the Horse Camp by morning, George Johnston sent word to Fort Walsh. Superintendent N.F.L. Crozier immediately ordered a search party.

The party was led by Jerry Potts, the legendary Scottish Métis who had scouted for the Mounties since they had first arrived on the prairies. Potts could read a trail the way that other people could read a book. He not only led the searchers to Graburn's body, but he also showed them how the killers — two of them — had ambushed the young Mountie.

Courtesy Library and Archives Canada C-1792C

Jerry Potts, the most legendary of all NWMP scouts. Potts led the search for Constable Marmaduke Graburn. By reading the trail, he was able to deduce what had probably happened to the young Mountie.

Potts found the horseshoe prints of Graburn's police mount, even though they were partially covered by snow. He followed them for a short distance, and then pointed out to his companions where the prints of an unshod Native horse suddenly came onto the trail alongside those of Graburn's horse. A little while later, Potts saw that another set of unshod hoof prints overlay the first tracks.

Potts had little difficulty reconstructing what had happened. It was an old trick, but one that an inexperienced rookie like Graburn would not expect. The first Native rider, feigning friendship, joins the prospective victim on the trail, distracting him with conversation. The second Native rider, the one who will do the actual killing, quietly moves in behind them. The victim suspects nothing, and is an easy target. Potts had no doubt about what they would find next.

Soon, Potts saw marks that told him something had startled Graburn's horse. Then a trail of blood on the snow led him to Graburn's hat. There was a bullet hole in it. Potts picked up an empty cartridge; the kind traders sold to the Natives. The men spread out to search. At the bottom of a coulee, Constable R. McCutcheon found Graburn's body. He had been shot in the back, and then again in the back of the head. Potts found Graburn's horse nearby. It too had been shot in the head, probably so that it would not return to the Horse Camp and alert the constables there that something had happened to its rider.

By this time, a Chinook had blown in, rapidly melting the snow and erasing the trail. There was nothing to do but take the body back to Fort Walsh. Jerry Potts returned to the scene of the crime the next day, but he could find no further clues. He thought the killers had probably fled to the United States.

Constable Marmaduke Graburn was buried with military honours at Fort Walsh. Commissioner James Macleod wrote in his report:

> There is no doubt the foul deed was perpetrated by two Indians, but we have not been able to fix the guilt upon the murderers. I feel sure they will be discovered … All his comrades mourned the sad fate of poor young Graburn deeply, as he was a great favourite among us all.

The only motive the Mounties could think might be behind the murder was revenge; that a Native had in some way been offended by a white man — not necessarily a Mountie — and had decided to even the score by killing any white man at the first opportunity. Whatever the reason for the killing, the guilty parties had to be apprehended. If the slaying of a policeman went unpunished, the Mounties would lose the Natives' respect. However, for six months they turned up nothing.

Early in the summer of 1880, a Blood Native named Weasel Moccasin tried to break out of the Fort Walsh guardhouse, where he'd been locked up for horse stealing. The escape was thwarted, and Weasel Moccasin told the Mounties that he had tried to run away because he was afraid of being blamed for the murder of Graburn. He said his band had been camped very near the place where Graburn was shot. Weasel Moccasin said the killer was a twenty-year-old Blood named Kukatosi-Poka, whom the whites called Star Child.

According to Weasel Moccasin, Star Child was one of the young men who objected to the location of the Horse Camp. Young warriors could no longer gain honour through battle because the Mounties forbade it, and now the Mounties were interfering with horse stealing, too. Star Child had been known to deliberately annoy the constables at the Horse Camp and Fort Walsh by begging for food, and generally making a nuisance of himself. He also might have picked a quarrel with Constable Graburn a day or two before the murder.

On the day of Graburn's death, Weasel Moccasin said that Star Child rode off, supposedly to hunt prairie chickens. He had not returned until late in the evening, and he was in a sullen mood. Weasel Moccasin thought he had been up to no good.

The next day, when Jerry Potts and some Mounties were seen nearby, Star Child became very nervous. He fled from the camp and hid in the bush for several days. Weasel Moccasin said Star Child was half frozen when he finally rejoined his band. By that time, everybody knew about the murdered Mountie. Weasel Moccasin said he accused Star Child, but the young warrior denied it.

The Bloods went into winter camp in the Bear Paw Mountains, on the American side of the border. There, where the redcoats could not come after him, Weasel Moccasin said that Star Child boasted that he had, in fact, shot the Mountie. He said he had done it in revenge for an insult he had suffered at the hands of another white man.

Weasel Moccasin gave Superintendent Leif Crozier an account of the murder that he claimed came from Star Child himself. Graburn was alone on the trail when Star Child met him. They rode together a short way and then came to some swampy ground. Graburn started to cross it first, and Star Child struck Graburn's horse. Graburn pulled his rifle from his saddle scabbard, but before he could turn around Star Child shot him in the back. The Mountie tumbled to the ground. Star Child dismounted, and fired a bullet into Graburn's head. He dragged the body into a coulee, then shot Graburn's horse.

Weasel Moccasin told Crozier that Star Child had sworn that the Mounties would never take him alive. He would stay in the safety of the Bear Paw Mountains. Weasel Moccasin added that he was risking his own life by telling Crozier these things, because if his people learned of it they would consider him a traitor.

The story Weasel Moccasin told did not fit the scenario Jerry Potts had worked out at the crime scene, and his belief that two Natives were involved. The police decided that Potts could have been wrong; the second rider on the trail could have come along sometime after the shooting. Weasel Moccasin's story had to be investigated.

By coincidence, NWMP Commissioner James Macleod was in Fort Benton, Montana, on business. Crozier contacted him with the information that a Blood named Star Child, who was hiding out in the Bear Paw Mountains, was the principal suspect in the Graburn murder. Macleod had no legal authority in Montana, so he asked John J. Healy, the Fort Benton sheriff, to go out and arrest Star Child so that he could be extradited to Canada. Healy was a former whiskey trader and the founder of Fort Whoop-Up, the most notorious of all the whiskey posts in Western Canada. The Mounties had put him out of business, so he wasn't about to do them any favours. The sheriff said he'd be glad to go after Star Child, for a reward of $5,000! Macleod had no authority to guarantee such a large sum of money, so he had to return to Canada without the suspect. The Mounties were certain that sooner or later Star Child would come home. In May 1881, he did.

The police at Fort Macleod learned that Star Child was in a Blood camp about twenty-five miles to the south. Constable Robert Patterson and two other policemen, guided by Jerry Potts, rode out. They arrived at the Blood camp at dawn. Star Child did not submit to arrest easily. He fought with Patterson, while Potts and the other constables kept a crowd of angry warriors at bay with levelled rifles. Patterson finally handcuffed Star Child, heaved him onto a horse and shouted, "Ride, boys!"

After a desperate ride, with the enraged Bloods right behind them, the Mounties arrived at Fort Macleod with their prisoner. Star Child was tossed into the guardhouse. Not a white man at the post doubted that he was Graburn's killer. None of them would have bet against Star Child's life ending on the gallows.

When Star Child went to trial on October 18, his prospects looked bleak indeed. He was a Native charged with the cold-blooded murder of a white policeman. He had no legal counsel. Six white men sat as jurors. Superintendent Crozier was Justice of the Peace, and Commissioner Macleod was Stipendiary Magistrate. The only people on the side of the accused were his fellow Bloods, and they had no trust in the white man's court.

Weasel Moccasin took the stand and repeated the story he had told Crozier. All Star Child said in his own defence was that Weasel Moccasin was a liar. Everyone present expected that the jury would take little time to arrive at a verdict of guilty.

The jury retired to deliberate. To the surprise of all, by the end of the day the six men had not reached a verdict. The following day, after hours of deliberation, the jury returned with a verdict that stunned the people in the courtroom: *not guilty*!

The foreman of the jury said that there was simply not enough evidence for them to convict the accused. The Crown's case was based entirely on Weasel Moccasin's claim that he had heard Star Child boast of killing the Mountie. The prosecution had not produced a single witness to support Weasel Moccasin's testimony. Even if Star Child had actually made the boast, there was no evidence to prove he had done the deed. Young Native warriors were notorious for bragging about things they had not actually done. Moreover, the men who had found Graburn's body had said all along that the moccasin prints they saw at the crime scene were too large to have been made by Star Child.

Star Child was acquitted. The white community accused the jurymen of cowardice, saying they had failed to convict Star Child out of fear of Blood reprisals. But several of the men on the jury were former NWMP constables, and they certainly were not cowards. On the contrary, they showed great courage in going against popular opinion by refusing to convict a Native on flimsy evidence.

No one else was ever prosecuted for Graburn's murder. The crime remains one of Canada's most famous unsolved mysteries. As he had feared, Weasel Moccasin was branded a traitor by his people. Threats were made against his life and he fled from his band, vanishing from historical records.

In 1883, Star Child was sentenced to three years in prison for stealing horses. After his release he became a scout for the NWMP. He distinguished himself in his duties and earned the praise of his commanding officer, Richard Burton Deane. In December 1889, Star Child died from that great plague of the prairie tribes, tuberculosis.

Fort Walsh, where Constable Graburn was buried, is now a national historic site. The place where Graburn was murdered is now in Cypress

Hills Park, a few miles east of Elkwater, Alberta. The coulee where his body was found is now known as Graburn's Gap. In Beechwood Cemetery, in Ottawa, the NWMP erected a memorial stone in Constable Marmaduke Graburn's honour. The inscription next to his name reads, in part: "Primus Moriri" (First to Die).

The North-West Rebellion: Casualties of War

The North-West Rebellion of 1885, in what is now Saskatchewan, was the result of the Canadian government's indifference to the plight of the Métis; people of mixed Native and French or English blood — "half-breeds," as the whites called them. The Métis were alarmed by the influx of white settlers from the east into their country. The buffalo, upon which they depended for their livelihood, had been hunted to the brink of extinction. The government did not recognize the claims of the Métis to their farms in the Saskatchewan Valley, considering them "squatters." Full-blooded Natives had been forced onto reservations, where they lived on the meagre annuities that Ottawa provided. The Métis were not eligible for even that pittance.

In desperation, they turned to the one man who they thought could champion their cause, Louis Riel. In 1870, Riel had led the Red River Rebellion against injustices similar to those that now plagued the Saskatchewan Valley. In doing so, he had become the founder of the province of Manitoba. But Riel's belligerent methods, particularly the illegal execution of a Canadian troublemaker named Thomas Scott, had forced him to flee Canada as an outlaw, and live in exile in the United States.

By 1884, Riel was a schoolteacher in Montana. The Métis delegation that met him there to seek his help did not know that Riel had spent some time in an asylum, suffering from periods of depression and delusion. Riel listened to the very legitimate complaints of the Métis, and then decided that he had a divine mission to be the saviour of his people. Riel's claim to his Métis heritage came through his maternal grandmother, who was of mixed blood.

Riel's arrival in the Saskatchewan Valley in the summer of 1884 was cheered by English and French Métis alike. He sent a petition to Ottawa, outlining the problems of the Métis people. The Conservative government ignored it. Prime Minister John A. Macdonald's only response was to send more Mounted policemen to the North-West. Riel then proclaimed a provisional government with himself at the head. His followers occupied the town of Batoche, cut the telegraph wire, took hostages, and seized private property. English speaking Métis withdrew their support, but Riel invited Native leaders to join his cause. All that stood in the way of an independent Native and Métis nation, he said, was a handful of redcoats.

The North-West Mounted Police, a "vest-pocket army," as Canadian historian Harold Horwood described the force, was never meant to be a military body along the lines of the United States Cavalry. The Mounties did not have the manpower to carry out the kind of military campaigns against Natives that the Americans had conducted in the West and the Southwest. They were policemen, trained to investigate crimes, make arrests, and generally maintain law and order. Now they would find themselves on the front line of a war.

Fort Carlton, on the south bank of the North Saskatchewan River, was the first Métis objective. It was an old Hudson's Bay trading post that the Mounties were using as a temporary station. Riel and his chief lieutenant, Gabriel Dumont, wanted to use it as a base of operations. Dumont was a skilled hunter and fighter, whom the Métis held in the highest regard; he also proved to be a clever tactician. Dumont's biggest liability would be Riel himself, who had no military abilities.

On March 25, 1885, NWMP Superintendent Leif Crozier left the settlement of Battleford with fifty constables and a seven pounder field gun, to reinforce Fort Carlton. When he arrived there, he appealed to the people of Prince Albert, the largest white settlement in the region, for assistance. Eighty militiamen of the hastily formed Prince Albert Volunteers answered the call.

Then Crozier received a letter from Riel, demanding the surrender of Fort Carlton. Riel promised to let the garrison go free and unharmed on Crozier's word of honour that they would keep the peace. He added, "In case of non-acceptance we intend to attack you ... and to commence, without delay, a war of extermination upon those who have shown themselves hostile to our rights." In his reply, Crozier not only refused to surrender, he also demanded that all Métis who had participated in illegal activities give themselves up to the police.

On March 26, a trader named Hilliard Mitchell rode into Fort Carlton from the settlement of Duck Lake, thirteen miles away. He told Crozier that he had hidden his stock of ammunition and food, but was concerned that they might fall into Métis hands. Crozier sent a patrol of eighteen men to recover the bullets and provisions, but they were turned back by a band of Natives and Métis.

Crozier was expecting further reinforcements from Prince Albert; ninety constables commanded by Commissioner Acheson Irvine, who had led the men on a gruelling journey from Regina. In the meantime, Crozier was being pressured by the civilians to teach the "half-breeds" a lesson. Deciding that he couldn't wait, Crozier assembled a company of fifty-five constables and forty-three Prince Albert Volunteers to go to Duck Lake. The men travelled on sleighs through the thick, sticky springtime snow, dragging along their seven-pounder cannon. The deep snow kept them confined to a narrow trail. Two miles from Duck Lake, the Mounties and the militia met the enemy.

Exactly how many men Gabriel Dumont had at his command at Duck Lake is not known, but they probably outnumbered the Mounties and militia by at least two-to-one. Moreover, Dumont had skillfully deployed his men in good cover, on a hill that overlooked a hollow where the Mounties were exposed. The Métis had firing positions on both sides of the column and at the front.

Two Natives approached the column, indicating that they wanted to talk. Crozier and a Scottish Métis named Joe McKay, his interpreter, met them. The conversation ended quickly when Crozier realized that the Natives were only stalling while their comrades took their firing positions.

Crozier told McKay, "We can do nothing here," and turned away. One of the Natives, an old man named Asseeweeyin, grabbed at McKay's revolver. There was a struggle, and McKay shot Asseeweeyin. That gunshot touched off the Battle of Duck Lake.

Dumont's sharpshooters poured a barrage of lead on the column.

Mounties and volunteers overturned their sleighs and dove under them for cover, then began to return fire. Twenty-four-year-old Constable Thomas Gibson, a member of the Force for just one year, was shot through the heart as he tried to help wrestle the field gun into position. The big gun got bogged down in the deep snow, and was fired only three times before a nervous gunner rendered it useless by jamming in a shell before the powder charge.

The Métis, veterans of prairie skirmishes, took full advantage of the inexperienced constables. They put their hats on sticks and propped them up just high enough to be seen. Then they moved a few feet away and drew bead on the Mounties and Prince Albert Volunteers, who rose to the bait. Constable George Pearce Arnold, twenty-five, a former U.S. Cavalry scout and a one-year member of the Force, took a bullet in the chest. He stood up, cursed at the enemy, and continued blasting away at them until he was felled again by shots to the leg and groin. Constable George Knox Garrett, twenty-four, a Mountie for three years, had a bullet pierce his lung.

By the time the shooting stopped half an hour later, nine of the militiamen and one Mountie were dead. Garrett and Arnold would die the following day in Fort Carlton. At least another dozen of Crozier's men were wounded, some of them seriously. Crozier himself had been nicked on the cheek by a bullet.

Realizing that his position was hopeless, Crozier ordered a retreat. Dumont wanted to pursue the bloodied company and finish Crozier and his men off, but Riel would not allow it. He said there had been enough killing. Four Métis (including Dumont's brother, Isidore) and one Native were dead. A few Métis had been wounded, and Dumont's scalp had been grazed by a bullet.

An hour after Crozier's defeated men reached Fort Carlton, Commissioner Irvine arrived with his reinforcements. The commissioner was furious that Crozier had allowed his "impetuosity" to overrule his better judgment. Had Crozier only waited a few hours for Irvine to arrive, their combined forces would have been enough to handle the enemy.

Irvine decided that Fort Carlton was not defendable. The stockade had fallen into disrepair, and it was surrounded by hills from which the enemy could snipe at the men inside. He had his men strip the post of every scrap of provisions, then held a funeral service for Gibson, Arnold, and Garrett, who were buried outside the wall.

Early on the morning of March 28, a fire broke out in a hospital room and was soon out of control. Irvine had the wounded loaded onto sleighs, along with the post's women and children. The company set out for Prince Albert and left Fort Carlton to burn to the ground. The Mounties and civilians reached Prince Albert that evening, without any harassment by Métis or Natives.

Most Native leaders, such as the influential Blackfoot Chief Crowfoot, chose not to take up arms against the whites. But after Dumont's victory at Duck Lake, Cree chiefs Big Bear, Little Pine, and Poundmaker decided to support the Métis cause. On March 29, the followers of Poundmaker and Little Pine approached the town of Battleford. The inhabitants fled into nearby Fort Battleford, which was garrisoned by only forty-three Mounties. The Cree did not attack the fort, but the young warriors looted the deserted town.

On April 2, Big Bear's men, led by a war chief named Wandering Spirit, descended on the community of Frog Lake. They herded the inhabitants into the church, where they were kept prisoner. Big Bear, who was off hunting, had told the warriors to take hostages, but avoid bloodshed. However, Wandering Spirit said that as war chief, he was not subordinate to Big Bear. The Cree ransacked the settlement, and found alcohol. Wandering Spirit got into an argument with the local Indian agent, Thomas Quinn, and shot him. Then the war chief told his warriors to kill all of the whites. Big Bear arrived in the village just as the warriors were carrying out the massacre, and vainly tried to stop it.

In addition to Quinn, the Cree killed eight other men, including two Roman Catholic priests. Two women and the Hudson's Bay agent were spared and taken to the Cree village as captives. Henry Quinn, the Indian agent's nephew, escaped from Duck Lake and took the news of the massacre to the nearest NWMP post, Fort Pitt, thirty-five miles away.

In command of the twenty Mounties at Fort Pitt was Inspector Francis Jeffrey Dickens, forty-one-year-old son of the great English novelist, Charles Dickens. Before coming to Canada in 1874, Francis Dickens had served with the Bengal Police in India. He was hard of hearing, spoke with a stammer, and was reputedly an alcoholic. He gained his commission in

Courtesy Canadian Illustrated News

The Frog Lake Massacre: Ignoring Big Bear's instructions to avoid bloodshed, Wandering Spirit (shown here shooting a Roman Catholic priest) and several of his warriors murdered nine helpless prisoners.

the NWMP through the patronage of Lord Dufferin, the Governor General of Canada. Dickens made a negative impression on almost everyone he met. Commissioner Irvine said of him, "I consider this officer unfit for the Force. He is lazy and takes no interest whatever in his work. He is unsteady in his habits. I am of the opinion that his brain is slightly affected."

When Dickens learned of the Frog Lake Massacre, he had good reason to expect that his post would be attacked. Like Fort Carlton, Fort Pitt had originally been a trading post, and was not constructed with defence in mind. It was surrounded by hills, and had no well. Nonetheless, Dickens put his men to work setting up barricades. He swore-in the local civilians as special constables. If an attack came, the situation would be grim. The men had only forty rounds of ammunition each. Deeming discretion the better part of valour, Dickens also had the men construct a large boat in which, if necessary, they could all escape down the North Saskatchewan River to Battleford.

By April 13, there had been no sign of the enemy, so Dickens called for a three-man patrol to scout for hostiles. The Hudson's Bay agent at the post, William McLean, argued against this. He said Dickens was sending the three men to their deaths, but Dickens would not listen. He ordered Constables David Cowan and Clarence Loasby to ride out, with young Henry Quinn as their guide.

Just two hours after the scouting party rode out, Big Bear and 250 of his followers arrived from the direction of Frog Lake. Big Bear had one of his white prisoners write a letter, which he sent to Dickens. He demanded the fort's surrender, and said he wanted tea, tobacco, and a blanket. Dickens sent him the items he requested, but refused to surrender the fort.

A second Cree messenger came to the fort with yet another demand for surrender, and a request for some clothing and kettles. Dickens gave the Natives tea kettles and some clothes. This time, however, he showed signs of wavering. He wrote in his report, "I told them that if they would go away we would leave."

On April 15, the scouting party returned and found a large Cree camp between them and the fort. They made a dash for it. Immediately warriors began shooting. Constable Lawson's horse, startled by the gunfire, threw him off. Lawson started running toward the fort, but a bullet struck him in the head, killing him instantly. As the horrified people in the stockade looked on, a Cree warrior cut out Lawson's heart and ate it. Lawson, twenty-two, had been in the Force for three years. His body was dragged off and mutilated by the Natives, and was not recovered by the NWMP until May 25.

Constable Loasby's horse was shot out from under him. He, too, began to run for the fort, and was shot in the back. He still managed to stagger forward, but a mounted warrior rode him down and shot him again. Loasby fell to the ground and lay still. Later, under covering fire from the fort, he was able to crawl to the stockade and get inside. Henry Quinn spurred his horse towards some woods and made a clean getaway.

William McLean negotiated a surrender agreement with Big Bear, since Inspector Dickens was — according to a letter written by Mrs. McLean — "so confused and excited he did not know what to suggest, nor how to act." Big Bear gave McLean his word that if the civilians surrendered to the

Cree that they would be held as prisoners, but not harmed. The Mounted Police, said Big Bear, had to abandon the fort. Wandering Spirit agreed that the women and children should be spared, but wanted to kill all of the men. This time, however, Big Bear's orders were obeyed.

The twenty-four civilians surrendered to the Natives, and Inspector Dickens and his men piled into their leaky, homemade boat for a cold, wet trip to Battleford, which they reached six days later. Henry Quinn, who was not aware that the Mounties had abandoned the fort, came out of his hiding place in the woods and was captured. Constable Loasby survived his gunshot wounds and the agonizing journey down the river. One of the bullets had gone through his body and was found in his underwear. He had it mounted on a signet ring as a memento of his brush with death. Francis Dickens retired from the NWMP in 1886, due to increasing deafness. He died of a heart attack that same year.

Prime Minister Macdonald lost no time in calling up the military to put down a rebellion for which his government was largely responsible. All across Canada, men and boys enlisted in militia units for what they thought would be a grand western adventure. Thanks to the new Canadian Pacific Railway, they could be transported to the Saskatchewan Valley quickly, even though they had to go by foot or sleigh through gaps where track had not yet been laid. Their commander, General Frederick D. Middleton, a fifty-nine-year-old British career soldier, made the entire trip in comfort, by rail through the United States.

General Middleton and his 3,000 amateur soldiers would more than have their hands full against Dumont and his Métis army of less than 1,000. But superior numbers and better armaments made victory for the Canadian army a forgone conclusion. On May 12, after the Métis had put up a heroic week long fight, their capital of Batoche fell. No Mounted policemen participated in the fight at Batoche, but they were present at another battle that took place in the dying days of the North-West Rebellion.

Before General Middleton left the assembly point of Qu'Appelle with the 800 men and artillery that he would use at Batoche, he dispatched troops to various locations to subdue renegade Natives. Middleton came from an aristocratic military family and held "colonials" in low regard.

He dismissed the NWMP as "gophers," which suggested that they crawled into their holes at the first sign of danger.

Middleton sent Lieutenant-Colonel William Otter, of Toronto, with five hundred men to drive Poundmaker's warriors away from Battleford. En route to Battleford, Otter's force was joined by about fifty Mounties, commanded by Superintendent William Herchmer. In spite of his negative opinion of the Mounties in general, Middleton seemed to have considered Herchmer a capable officer.

On April 23, Poundmaker's scouts saw the approaching army about eight miles from the settlement. The Cree set fire to the Hudson's Bay Company warehouse, and then withdrew. The next morning the inhabitants of Fort Battleford welcomed Otter's men as liberators.

Otter had carried out his orders, but now his troops and the men of Fort Battleford wanted to go after Poundmaker. Otter telegraphed General Middleton, requesting further orders. In a vaguely worded reply, Middleton told Otter to do what he thought best for the defence of Battleford. "You have sole command," the general said. Otter interpreted this as permission to hunt down Poundmaker's warriors. In fact, it was Middleton's tactic for avoiding blame in case Otter committed any blunders.

On April 30, Otter set out with 300 men, including Herchmer and his Mounties. The expedition had two seven-pounder cannons and a Gatling gun. They moved slowly, covering only eighteen miles on the first day, but Otter's scouts told him that the Cree camp was on the other side of Cut Knife Creek, only a day's march away.

Early in the morning of May 2, Otter's men crossed Cut Knife Creek and found the remains of the Cree camp. Poundmaker and his warriors were gone. Otter took his men to the top of a rise, now called Cut Knife Hill, and saw the Native camp spread out below. Some Assiniboine warriors, and about forty Métis, had joined Poundmaker's Cree. A sentinel in the camp spotted the soldiers on the hill, eliminating Otter's chance of a surprise attack.

Nonetheless, Otter sensed that a victory was practically his for the taking. As warriors hurried women and children out of the teepees and into the safety of the woods, fire from the cannons and the Gatling gun raked the camp. At first it appeared that the Cree and their allies were in the grip of chaos, but they were about to give the Canadians a hard lesson in tactical warfare. Credit for what happened has been given to a Cree war chief named Fine Day, though present-day Cree historians doubt he was the brains behind the Native defences.

Once the women and children were relatively safe, the Native fighters used the terrain to thoroughly confuse their foe. Squads of four or five sharpshooters scurried through the ravines, firing and then scrambling to new shooting positions. This left the Canadians shooting at places where they had seen puffs of gunsmoke, but that had already been vacated. The tactic also gave the impression that the Natives' numbers were greater than they actually were.

Some Mounties on horseback were nearest to the first line of Natives and Métis to open fire. Corporal Ralph B. Sleigh, twenty-seven, a four-year member of the Force, became the first casualty in Otter's command. As he dismounted, Sleigh was shot through the mouth and died instantly. Soon, two more Mounties fell wounded: Sergeant J.H. Ward and Corporal William H.T. Lowry. Ward recovered from his wound, but Lowry, twenty-eight, died the following day. Later in the battle, another Mountie, Constable Patrick Burke, thirty-three — a trumpeter and ten-year veteran of the Force — took a bullet in the stomach. He, too, died a day later. In his report, Herchmer wrote of the slain police officers, "The poor fellows deserved a better fate."

The artillery Otter had with him proved to be of no advantage at all. The wooden carriages of the cannons were rotten, and collapsed after just a few shots had been fired. The crew manning the Gatling gun could not see the enemy, and their rapid fire bullets did nothing but clip trees.

Otter might well have carried the day with a full force charge, but he overestimated the numbers opposing him. He thought there were hundreds of warriors in the bushes. In fact, there were about fifty. The rest of the men had withdrawn to the woods to protect the women and children.

After eight hours of fighting, Otter ordered a retreat to Battleford. His total casualties would be eight dead and fourteen wounded. Had the Natives been armed with better guns than their old muzzleloaders, Otter's losses might have been much higher. Poundmaker's warriors wanted to pursue the whites and cut them to pieces, but Poundmaker would not permit it. He knew what had happened on the American plains a decade earlier, after the Sioux and Cheyenne had annihilated Colonel George A. Custer's Seventh Cavalry at the Little Bighorn. The American government had waged all-out war on the plains tribes. Poundmaker now doubted the wisdom of this rebellion, and wanted it to end.

There are no records of how many casualties Poundmaker's people suffered. When Otter's men got back to Fort Battleford, they claimed to have killed at least a hundred. A white captive in the Cree camp said that the Natives had six dead and three wounded, but there may have been others whom he was not permitted to see.

With the fall of Batoche, the North-West Rebellion was all but over. Still, one more Mountie would die in the line of fire. On May 14, a five-man NWMP patrol out of Fort Battleford encountered a band of Native warriors who had not yet given up the fight. The warriors attacked, and the outnumbered Mounties fled. Constable Frank Orland Elliott, thirty-seven, became separated from the others and the warriors caught up to him. He fought bravely, but was shot several times. Elliott had been a Mountie for just two years.

Courtesy Library and Archives Canada RCMP Collection 1996-400

Chief Big Bear, under arrest following the Northwest Rebellion of 1885. Second from the left, holding the rifle, is Constable Colin Colebrook of the North-West Mounted Police. Ten years later he would be killed by Almighty Voice.

General Middleton actually praised Colonel Otter's retreat as a strategic withdrawal. But the general, who knew nothing about the West or the work of the NWMP, was highly critical of Commissioner Irvine and Superintendent Crozier. Both men resigned from the Force the following year.

Big Bear and Poundmaker served prison terms for participating in the Rebellion. Wandering Spirit was hanged for the murders at Duck Lake. Gabriel Dumont fled to the United States, but was eventually granted amnesty and returned to Canada. Louis Riel was hanged for treason in Regina. The places where Métis, Natives, and white soldiers and policemen died are now all marked as Historic Sites.

Almighty Voice and Charcoal: Native Outlaws

In all of Canada's nineteenth century "Old West" period, excluding those Mounties who were casualties of the North-West Rebellion, only four members of the NWMP are known for certain to have been killed by Natives. One young man was responsible for three of those deaths. He was also the central figure in the last armed battle between whites and Natives in North America.

Almighty Voice was a grandson of the Swampy Cree Chief, One Arrow, who served three years in prison for supporting the North-West Rebellion. He grew to manhood on the impoverished One Arrow Reserve in Saskatchewan. Almighty Voice was a crack shot with a rifle, but with the buffalo gone that skill wasn't of much use. Like the rest of the young men in his tribe, Almighty Voice lived on scanty government annuities, worked as a labourer for white ranchers and farmers, and sometimes ran errands for the NWMP at Batoche. The Mounties did not consider him a troublemaker, even though the local Indian agent complained that Almighty Voice had a habit of marrying young women of his tribe, and then casting them aside when he grew tired of them.

Then, in June 1895, Almighty Voice killed and butchered a cow. Ownership of the cow remains a mystery to this day. Nobody took notice of the cow's disappearance until October, when the brother of one of Almighty Voice's discarded wives brought it to the attention of the

NWMP. On October 22, when Almighty Voice went to Duck Lake to collect his annuity, he was arrested and locked in jail.

Almighty Voice was twenty-one years old. There is a story, for which there is no documented evidence, that a callous guard told him he would hang for killing the cow. Whether the story is true or not, Almighty Voice had been around police posts enough to know that he would be sentenced to a few months labour at the most. He just didn't want to spend any time in jail, so he made the mistake of breaking out. That offence was considered more serious than the rustling of a single cow.

The Mounties sent Sergeant Colin Colebrook, thirty-three, in pursuit of the escapee. English-born Colebrook was a fourteen-year veteran of the Force, and had been present at Big Bear's surrender at the end of the North-West Rebellion. He had a reputation for being aggressive, and complaints had been made against him for using unnecessary violence. In 1889, Colebrook had shown considerable courage when, "in a very plucky manner," as his superior put it, he arrested an American gunslinger who was wanted for murdering six men in Montana.

The relatives of Almighty Voice's ditched wives were only too glad to tell Colebrook when they had last seen the fugitive, and which direction he was going in. On October 29, Colebrook and his interpreter, a Métis named Francois Dumont, caught up with Almighty Voice a few miles south of Kinistino. Almighty Voice's fourth wife, a teenager named Small Face, was with him. She was cooking a prairie chicken when the redcoat approached the camp.

Colebrook instructed Dumont to tell Almighty Voice to surrender. Almighty Voice was armed with a double-barreled, muzzleloading shotgun. He told Dumont that if the Mountie did not go away, he would shoot. Dumont translated the threat, and warned Colebrook that the young man meant what he said.

Colebrook could not turn back just because a Cree waved a gun at him. He raised one hand in a gesture of peace, but kept the other on a revolver in his pocket. He rode slowly toward Almighty Voice. Small Face was crying and begging Almighty Voice not to shoot. Almighty Voice backed up, keeping the muzzle of his gun pointed at Colebrook. Three times he repeated his warning. Each time Dumont pleaded with Colebrook to turn back.

Then, as Colebrook said, "Come on, old boy," Almighty Voice fired. Colebrook was blown right out of the saddle, his chest and throat shredded. Dumont turned his horse around and ran for his life.

Almighty Voice allegedly told Small Face, "Now they won't leave me alone." He mounted Colebrook's horse and rode away, leaving the girl with the body. The rustler was now a murderer. The Mounties buried Sergeant Colin Colebrook at Prince Albert, with the honours due a policeman who had died in the line of duty.

News of the murder swept across the prairies. Soon Mounties and civilian volunteers were criss-crossing the countryside in search of the fugitive. They found no traces. Among the Natives the police were confronted with a wall of silence. Not even the disgruntled relations of Almighty Voice's cast-off wives would offer assistance. They had tattled on him for killing a cow, but they wouldn't hand him over to a white hangman.

Almighty Voice's father, Sounding Sky, had been in jail on a petty theft charge at the time of his son's arrest. The police released the old man, hoping he would lead them to Almighty Voice. That plan failed. The federal government put a $500 reward on Almighty Voice's head. Not a single Native made an attempt to claim it.

Weeks passed, then months, and still the killer remained at large. There were rumours aplenty: Almighty Voice had fled to Montana, he was living with Natives north of Lesser Slave Lake, he had died on the prairie. The Mounties investigated every lead, and came up empty-handed. The NWMP, hailed as the finest police force in the world, now endured criticism, and even ridicule, for its inability to apprehend a lone Cree who wasn't much more than a boy. Then, to make matters worse, another Mountie was killed by a Native.

Unlike Almighty Voice, who until the Colebrook murder had been ordinary in every way, the Blood known as Charcoal had been a warrior of renown. In his youth he had been called Bad Young Man. He had distinguished himself in raids against rival tribes, killing warriors in combat and stealing horses. His prowess had earned him the coveted Bear Knife, a symbol of the grizzly bear. This badge of courage was as prestigious to the Bloods as the Victoria Cross was to Canadians.

Now middle-aged (probably about forty), Charcoal was respected as a shaman; an elder warrior who could communicate with the spirit world. He lived quietly on the Blood Reserve along the Belly River in what is now southwestern Alberta. Charcoal had been in trouble with the Mounties just once. He had illegally slaughtered a steer to feed his starving family, and had spent a year in the Fort Macleod jail in 1883. Since then he had been, according to a police report on him, "well behaved." The Mounties knew nothing of Charcoal's status as a legendary warrior. That was about to change.

The Blood practiced polygamy, and over the years Charcoal had several wives. One was Pretty Wolverine Woman, nine years younger than he, whom he had married in 1891. In the spring of 1896, Charcoal married a teenager named Sleeping Woman. Perhaps out of jealousy, Pretty Wolverine Woman became involved in an illicit affair with a handsome young man named Medicine Pipe Stem.

Charcoal learned of the affair, and was furious. For a man of his stature, this was an unbearable humiliation. By his own code of honour, he would have been justified in killing his wife's lover, but the Mounties had forbidden such acts of retribution. Charcoal swallowed his pride and demanded that Pretty Wolverine Woman and Medicine Pipe Stem end their relationship at once. They did not.

In September of 1896, while members of the Blood Reserve were at work cutting hay for a white rancher, Charcoal caught his wife and her lover having intercourse in a shed. He pleaded with them again to end the affair, and Medicine Pipe Stem laughed at him. This was more than the proud old warrior could take. In a fit of anguish he left the shed, then went back and shot Medicine Pipe Stem dead.

While the Mounties were still looking for Almighty Voice, the murder of Medicine Pipe Stem brought about yet another manhunt in which the redcoats seemed ineffective. Charcoal seemed to have vanished into the Great Lone Land, and emerged only as a shadowy avenger who sniped at both Native and white people whom he held long smoldering grudges against. In one attack, Charcoal wounded a farm instructor named Edward McNeil. His vendetta did not claim any more lives, but all across the prairies people barred their doors and loaded their guns.

Superintendent Sam Steele, perhaps the most famous NWMP officer of that period, took personal charge of the case. The Force was under pressure from newly elected Prime Minister Wilfrid Laurier to apprehend Charcoal and Almighty Voice without delay. Laurier was actually considering disbanding the Mounted Police, and replacing them with militia units and smaller, volunteer constabularies.

On October 17, a posse of constables and Blood scouts, led by Inspector A.M. Jarvis, found Charcoal's camp in the wooded hills near Chief Mountain. They opened fire, but Charcoal escaped. The only casualty was Jarvis, whose scalp was grazed by a bullet. The Mounties captured Charcoal's horses, but that proved to be only a small setback for the old warrior. A day later, he stole the horses of two constables who were on foot in the bush, looking for him. Of course, Sam Steele was livid when he heard the embarrassing news. There was worse: the bullet that had almost killed Inspector Jarvis had been fired by one of his own men!

Steele announced a reward of $200 for information leading to Charcoal's arrest. He notified American lawmen, in case the fugitive crossed the border. He recruited cowboys, ranchers, and more Native scouts to join in the hunt. Unlike the Cree to the east, who were protecting Almighty Voice, the Bloods were anxious to have Charcoal stopped.

This was not simply a matter of wanting to get the police off their backs. Almighty Voice had killed a white man, but Charcoal had killed one of his own people. Many of the Bloods thought he had gone crazy and was liable to kill anyone, especially if he thought he had an old score to settle. There was also something else that some of the older Bloods understood: no doubt, Charcoal knew that sooner or later the redcoats would kill him. He wanted to enter the spirit world as a warrior of prestige. That meant killing someone of importance to be his herald. A chief, even one from his own tribe, would be suitable; or a white man of high rank. The older Bloods knew better than anyone else that Charcoal was a man to be feared.

Charcoal kept on the run, stealing food from farmhouses and a stagecoach station. When he had ridden the Mountie horses to exhaustion, he abandoned them and stole fresh mounts from the Blood and neighbouring Piegan Reserves. He eluded posses, and took the precaution of leaving false trails to confuse the Native scouts who were helping the white policemen. Whenever the searchers came upon one of Charcoal's camps, the ashes from his fire were cold and he was long gone.

In desperation, Steele had Charcoal's relatives rounded up and locked in the Fort Macleod jail. More than twenty men, women, and children were held on suspicion of aiding the fugitive, though there was no evidence that they had done so. Steele thought this tactic would bring Charcoal into the open.

In retribution, Charcoal attempted to bushwhack a constable at the Lee's Creek police post. When a Mountie stepped out of the cabin, a bullet pierced his shirtsleeve. The policemen quickly turned out with their guns, but the sniper was gone. The next Mountie who Charcoal encountered was not so lucky.

By the first week of November, the Piegans were as anxious as the Bloods for Charcoal to be apprehended. He had been stealing their horses at will. They also believed he was responsible for the rape of a Piegan girl who had been assaulted by a stranger. They sent out scouts, and one of them found Charcoal's trail in the snow near Beaver Creek, in the vicinity of the Porcupine Hills. The Piegans reported this to the police.

On November 5, a police party led by Sergeant William Brock Wilde set out from the Pincher Creek police post to intercept Charcoal. The posse included three Piegan scouts, one Blood, and an interpreter named Charlie Holloway. Wilde, forty-three, was a fourteen-year veteran of the force, and a former British cavalry officer. He was big, tough, and had a reputation for fearlessness. He was also a hard drinker, and a man who shared the disdain whites generally held for Natives. In 1883, Wilde had entered Mountie legend through a confrontation with the Cree Chief Piapot. In protest against the Canadian Pacific Railway being built across Cree land, Piapot had planted his village right in the railway's path and refused to move. Wilde boldly rode into the camp, dismounted, and began pulling down teepees. It was an act that represented the Canadian government's arrogance toward the Natives, but the fact that Wilde did it in the presence of armed and angry warriors singled him out as a man of considerable courage. The incident helped establish the image of the lone Mountie doing a job that would require a whole troop or cavalry in the United States.

Now the legendary Mountie and the legendary Blood warrior were about to have an appointment with destiny. They met on November 10, near a place called Dry Fork. Charcoal was in camp, cooking a meal, when the men in the posse saw him. Wilde told the others to be careful, to shoot Charcoal if he didn't surrender right away. He added, "If he's going to kill anybody, it'll be me."

Charcoal jumped onto his horse to make a run for the hills through the deep snow. The posse fired at him uselessly. They tried to give chase, but their tired horses fell back. Only Wilde, riding a strong police horse, was able to gain on the fugitive. Charcoal had a rifle hidden under a blanket. Wilde drew his revolver, though he had a rifle in his saddle scabbard. When the Mountie came within ten feet of him, Charcoal spun his horse around and fired.

The bullet struck Wilde in the left side of his body, and knocked him from the saddle. Charcoal dismounted and sang a Blood war song as he stood over the fallen policeman. Wilde moved slightly and raised his head. Charcoal finished him off with a bullet in the stomach, fired at point-blank range. Then he climbed onto Wilde's horse and rode away. Now Charcoal had his herald to the spirit world.

The other men in the posse fired at Charcoal, but he was out of range. They tried to keep up the pursuit, but their horses were spent. There was nothing left for them to do but take the body back to Fort Macleod.

Wilde was buried with full military honours. In his eulogy, Sam Steele said of Wilde: "He was one of the finest men who served in the Mounted Police; faithful, true and brave, useful in every capacity." A monument was erected in Wilde's honour in what is now Pincher Creek Memorial Park.

Ironically, if Charcoal had been captured soon after the murder of Medicine Pipe Stem, he might have escaped the death sentence. The courts of the time often showed leniency to a husband guilty of a crime of passion. But with the murder of Wilde, Charcoal had sealed his own fate; death by a bullet or on the gallows.

After a month and a half on the run, Charcoal was near the end of his endurance. He was sick, hungry, and feeling the effects of the deepening cold. On the morning of November 12, after an exhausting seventy-five mile ride, he turned up at the home of his brother, Left

Hand, on the Blood Reserve, seeking food and shelter. Charcoal did not know that for the sake of their families locked up at Fort Macleod, his brothers had made a deal with Sam Steele. They would turn Charcoal in if they got the chance.

Almost as soon as Left Hand met him at the cabin door, Charcoal sensed a trap. He turned to run, but Left Hand and another brother, Bear's Backbone, subdued him and tied him to a chair. Charcoal bitterly told Left Hand, "Now you can be a chief for catching me."

The Mounties kept Charcoal in the Fort Macleod jail under a twenty-four hour suicide watch. When he refused to eat, they force-fed him. He had all the symptoms of tuberculosis, but doctors said he was faking illness and putting on a crazy act.

Charcoal was tried for the murders of Medicine Pipe Stem and Sergeant Wilde. He was convicted and sentenced to hang. A few days before the execution, he was forced to sit for a photographer. In the resulting portrait, a hat covers up the manacles on the subject's wrists, and Charcoal defiantly refuses to look into the camera. On March 16, 1897, Charcoal was carried to the gallows in a chair, because he was too weak to walk.

The whole time that the Charcoal drama had been unfolding, Almighty Voice remained a phantom. As far as most of the whites in the Saskatchewan Valley were concerned, the young Cree was far away. Then on May 26, 1897, the Mounties got a lucky break.

Charcoal, legendary Blood warrior and killer of Sergeant William Brock Wilde, defiantly refuses to look into the camera in this picture taken shortly before his execution. The prisoner has been dressed up for the picture and has "war paint" on his face. The hat hides his manacles.

Courtesy Glenbow Archives

Napoleon Venne, a Métis rancher, saw three Cree youths slaughtering one of his steers near the One Arrow Reserve. He recognized two of them: Tupean, a brother-in-law of Almighty Voice, and Going Up to Sky, Almighty Voice's fourteen-year-old cousin. Venne did not know the third rustler, but suspected he was the young man the police had been hunting for over a year and a half. Venne rode to Batoche and informed the Mounties.

As the police later learned, Almighty Voice had been living right under their noses all along. His mother, Spotted Calf, had hidden him whenever the Mounties came calling. Almighty Voice had gone on a trapping expedition with other men, and had even been in white settlements. None of his impoverished people had betrayed him for the reward money.

On the morning of May 27, NWMP Corporal J.W. Bowridge rode with Napoleon Venne to the place where the steer had been slaughtered. While Bowridge questioned some local people, Venne spotted two male Natives running for the cover of a poplar bluff. He and Bowridge rode toward the trees. There was a gunshot, and a rifle bullet hit Venne in the shoulder. A second bullet pierced Venne's hat. The Mountie and the Métis quickly retreated out of rifle range.

The next day, NWMP Inspector "Broncho" Jack Allan arrived with a posse of policemen and civilian volunteers. The men encircled the five acre island of trees and bush. Trapped in that tangle were Tupean, Going Up to Sky, and Almighty Voice. The last "Indian battle" was about to begin.

The Mounties tried to flush the Native gunmen from the bluff. They were driven back by gunfire that wounded Allan and Sergeant C.C. Raven. Allan had ridden to Raven's rescue, and almost had his gunbelt taken by Almighty Voice. A volley of bullets drove Almighty Voice back into the trees, and the Mounties carried the wounded men to safety.

Inspector Allan and Sergeant Raven were out of the fight, so command fell to Corporal Charles H. Sterling Hockin. Thirty-seven-year-old Hockin was a former British army officer who had been with the Force for three years. He sent a Métis scout to tell Almighty Voice and his companions to surrender or he would burn them out. The Cree were defiant. They knew that the vegetation was too green to burn. Meanwhile, Natives from the One Arrow Reserve arrived. Hockin ordered them to leave, but the Cree lined the ridges to watch the battle from a distance. Spotted Calf was with them. Sounding Sky was back in jail, charged with harbouring his fugitive son.

The trio in the bluff had no food or water, and not much ammunition, but they were determined to fight. They tied a knife to a stick, and dug a rifle pit in the southwestern corner of the bluff, where the bush was thick. They fired an occasional shot to keep the police back.

Corporal Hockin could have waited for thirst and hunger to force Almighty Voice and his companions to give up, but he might have been worried that the long-sought outlaw would somehow slip through the cordon and escape. With the arrival of a few civilian volunteers from Duck Lake, Hockin now had twenty-six men in his posse. He made the fatal decision to launch another assault on the bluff.

Leaving most of his command to patrol the perimeter to prevent a breakout, Hockin personally led a nine-man squad into the bluff. One of them was Constable John Randolph Kerr, twenty-nine. He had been with the Mounties for three years.

Hockin's group made two sweeps through the trees without sighting their quarry. On the third sweep, they walked right into waiting gunsights. The Cree opened fire from the rifle pit. Hockin dropped his rifle and fell, crying, "Oh God! I'm shot." Three of his men dragged him out of the line of fire, but he would die from a bullet wound in the chest early the next morning.

The other men engaged in a shootout with the Cree. Constable Kerr fired until his revolver was empty, then turned and asked a civilian for some bullets. As Kerr reached for the ammunition he was shot in the heart and killed instantly. Ernest Gundy, the Duck Lake postmaster and a former Mountie, was also killed.

With three men down and their ammunition almost gone, the attackers withdrew, leaving the bodies of Kerr and Gundy behind. Almighty Voice took their guns and coats. There is evidence that suggests that Tupean may have been killed in the gunfight during the early stages of the stand-off.

The next morning the police were reinforced by militia who brought along a seven-pounder cannon. Before evening, NWMP Commissioner John McIllree arrived with twenty-four Mounties and a nine-pounder field gun. Now more than one hundred men encircled the poplar bluff. Escape was impossible for the trapped Natives. By that stage it would not have taken very long for thirst and hunger to force them out, but McIllree decided instead to give his gunners some "excellent practice."

The outcome was never in doubt. The police bombarded the bluff with cannon fire. Occasionally, the outlaws and Mounties duelled with small arms, but there were no more casualties among the police or the volunteers. Almighty Voice shouted insults at the police, while off in the distance his mother sang a Cree death song.

The gunners for the seven-pounder soon ran out of ammunition, but the nine-pounder continued pounding the bluff throughout the night and into the morning of May 31. At 10:00 a.m. the shelling stopped. No taunts or gunshots came from the bluff. The besiegers waited four hours.

At 2:00 p.m. a police party cautiously approached the battered island of trees and brush. They found Tupean's body just inside the edge of the trees. He had been shot in the head. In the rifle pit they found the bodies of Almighty Voice and Going Up to Sky. Both had been killed by cannon fire. The last "Indian" battle was over.

The North-West Rebellion, the mysterious murder of Constable Graburn, and the stories of Almighty Voice and Charcoal are all Canadian tragedies. The policemen who died with their boots on, in the line of duty, have been honoured as heroes, but they were also victims. They had been thrust out onto a wild land by a government with little real understanding of the people who already lived there. The Mounties' job had been to impose a foreign concept of "law and order" upon indigenous peoples with their own codes of honour and behaviour. Perhaps the wonder is that the number of the dead was so low.

4

THE MANITOBA PROVINCIAL ─────── POLICE: FOUR OFFICERS DOWN

Richard Power: A Terror to Evil-Doers

The North-West Mounted Police were not the only officers who made life difficult for bad men in the Canadian West. Even before the Mounties arrived on the prairies, the newly formed province of Manitoba organized a small, but effective, police force. The Manitoba Provincial Police began in 1870 with nineteen men. It was operated out of an old Winnipeg post office that was converted to a police station and courthouse. A log house behind the building was used for a jail. The force was poorly funded, so the officers had to provide their own firearms. They had no standard uniform. Within a few years, the department dwindled to a mere eight men. Some constables were dismissed for inappropriate behaviour, such as public drunkenness, others resigned to seek better paying employment.

In 1874, Richard Power, a twenty-three-year-old who had become an original member of the force at the age of nineteen, was made Head Constable — the equivalent of Chief of Police. The rapid decline in the force's numbers was only part of the reason for this young man's promotion to such a position. Even before joining the MPP, he had allegedly served as a scout for the United States Cavalry. He was also a lieutenant in the Winnipeg militia. Power's contemporaries described

Archives of Manitoba N271

The Manitoba Provincial Police (and dog) pose for a group photo at Rat Portage, 1883. Four MPP officers died in the line of duty, including Chief Richard Power.

him as "a fine looking man, magnificently proportioned, every inch a soldier with the courage that nothing could daunt." Power wore a Colt .45 with a nine-inch barrel, and a gunbelt that was always full of cartridges. Local newspapers called Power "a terror to evildoers." In a few short years, Power had shown himself to be a courageous and enthusiastic policeman. Some thought he might have been *too* enthusiastic. He had once been sharply reprimanded for shooting a Native during an arrest.

By the time Power took command of the Manitoba Provincial Police, Winnipeg had been incorporated as a city and had its own police department. That left the rest of Manitoba under the eyes of Power and his tiny department. Power strategically placed men in the more populous settlements outside Winnipeg; towns like Selkirk and Kildonan. He kept a few men with him at his headquarters in Winnipeg. Most Manitoba communities had to depend on special constables — civilian volunteers — to keep the peace. If there was any real trouble, Power could send one of his constables out to see to the matter. The policing situation in rural Manitoba was not unlike that of rural Ontario and other points east.

Manitoba, especially the country along the American border, was woefully under-policed, but the situation was same on the other side of the international line in the Dakota Territory. There was a sheriff in Pembina, just over the border, and another many miles away in Fargo. For those lawmen, just looking after their towns was a full-time job. They didn't have the resources, or manpower, to go chasing after the desperadoes who roamed the plains and hills of the Dakota country. Rustlers, gunmen, and other men on the dodge had only to keep out of the sheriff's way to avoid arrest. With so much open country, that was not a hard thing to do. Moreover, American lawmen were often unwilling to apprehend fugitives wanted in Canada, unless there was a reward involved.

Nonetheless, Power seems to have developed a good working relationship with the sheriffs in Dakota. In October 1873, a Métis named Gilbert Godon killed a man in a drunken brawl at Red River, and then fled to the Dakota Territory. The following June, Godon got into another saloon-wrecking brawl in Pembina, and was tossed into the local jail. The sheriff there held onto Godon until Power could go down and pick him up.

One of the outlaw gangs operating along the border was a band of horse thieves, led by a man named Edward Couture. His bunch had a hideout south of Pembina, within easy striking distance of the border. Under the cover of night they would slip across the line to raid farms and ranches in Manitoba. The outlaws would drive the stolen horses down into the Dakota Territory and sell them off. Quite likely, as they squandered their ill-gotten gains in the saloons of small Dakota towns, the outlaws enjoyed a good laugh at the inability of American and Canadian law officers to interfere with their business.

Early in September 1874, Chief Constable Power received a message from F.T. Bradley, Justice of the Peace and Customs Officer in Emerson, a Manitoba village just across the line from Pembina. Bradley had information that one Edward Martin, a rider with the Couture Gang, was heading north to visit relatives in Manitoba. On the morning of September 7, Power rode out of Winnipeg accompanied by a constable named Heusons. Power was sure Martin would come along the stagecoach road that followed the meandering course of the Red River. Forty-three miles south of Winnipeg, the two policemen stopped at a stagecoach station called Scratching River (now Morris, Manitoba). Darkness had fallen, so they left their horses with a farmer and settled in to watch the road. They did not have to wait long.

Edward Martin soon rode into view, astride a stolen horse. With him was a fellow horse thief named Charles Garden. The two Manitoba policemen took the outlaws completely by surprise and without gunplay. Power grabbed Martin's horse by the bridle, and Heusens seized Garden by the leg. Power told the pair to dismount, and they meekly obeyed.

Because it was late, Power decided to keep his prisoners at the stagecoach station overnight, and then take them to Winnipeg in the morning. He told Garden to help Constable Heusens take care of the horses. Then he began walking Martin toward the station building. But Edward Martin had no intention of going to jail.

At the doorway of the station, Martin suddenly wheeled around and threw himself at Power, knocking him off balance. The outlaw pulled a revolver and fired at Power from point-blank range. Amazingly, the bullet missed! Before Martin could cock the weapon for a second shot, Power recovered his footing and grappled with the desperado. By now they had tumbled through the door and were inside the station.

When Charles Garden heard the shot, he bolted for the station house. Constable Heusens was right on his heels. Garden burst into the room in which his partner was struggling with Power, and knocked a lantern off a table. The room was thrown into darkness. Garden pulled a hunting knife from his boot and turned to meet Heusens. He might as well have tried to fight a grizzly bear with a toothpick. Constable Heusens was a big, muscular man, and his one thought was for the safety of Chief Constable Power. Heusens tossed the knife-wielding Garden aside like a rag doll. Then he groped in the darkness, trying to go to Power's aid.

Martin managed to fire off two more wild shots. The bullets hit no one, but the sound of gunfire put Garden to flight. The terrified outlaw hauled himself up from the floor where Heusens had thrown him, and ran into the night.

Power finally had a chance to pull his big Colt .45. At that moment, Power could have blown Martin to kingdom come, and no one would have blamed him. Instead, he told Martin to drop his gun. Facing that small cannon, the outlaw did as he was told.

Power left Heusens to watch Martin while he went after Garden. In the darkness he heard a noise from the direction of the corral. He briefly caught sight of a figure running away. Power fired a shot, and heard a stifled groan of pain. He didn't bother to go searching for the fugitive in the dark. If Garden had been hit, he wasn't likely to get very far.

The next morning the two officers found blood on the ground near the corral. Power sent Martin back to Winnipeg in Heusens' charge, then rode out after Garden. He trailed the outlaw to a settler's shack where the horse thief had sought attention for the bullet wound in his leg.

Power took Garden to Winnipeg in a wagon. He had a doctor treat the wounded leg, then locked Garden in the Winnipeg jail, where Martin was already a reluctant guest.

The capture of Martin and Garden would have worried Ed Couture; not so much because of the loss of two riders — saddle tramps like them were a dime a dozen — but because Martin and Garden might be made to talk, one way or another, about the activities of other gang members. However, Martin, who evidently had some skill with locks, decided that he didn't want to stay in a Canadian jail.

On the night of October 1, Ed Martin and a prisoner named Charles Bigeral broke out of the Winnipeg jail. Charles Garden was left behind, probably because of his bad leg. Power didn't learn of the escape until the following morning. He found that Martin had picked a total of five locks to get himself and Bigeral from the cells to the street.

A known Couture gang member named Rogers had been seen in Winnipeg, loitering near the jail. Power was certain he had been awaiting the escapees with horses and a change of clothes. He knew he wouldn't have much chance of catching the fugitives before they crossed the border, so he telegraphed information of the jailbreak to sheriffs in the Dakotas and Minnesota. On October 23, Martin and Rogers were arrested by American lawmen near Glyndon, Minnesota. The deputies also recovered several stolen horses that the outlaws had with them. The other escapee, Bigeral, had long since split from the others, and was not found.

Ed Martin was locked in the jail in Moorhead, North Dakota, to await extradition to Canada. The sheriff put him in leg irons and had an extra lock put on his cell door, but this horse-rustling Houdini was not ready to accept the idea of a long prison term. He knew that he would be kept under close watch for a while, but that sooner or later the guard would be relaxed and he would get his chance.

The opportunity came months later, on the night of May 5, 1875. Martin easily picked both locks on his cell door, and then used the keys he found in the sheriff's desk to get out of his leg irons. Instead of boldly walking out to the street, where he might be recognized, Martin cut a hole in a wall, crawled out to an alleyway, and escaped.

Ed Martin was now a wanted man on both sides of the border. He headed for the Canadian line, but was caught at Sioux Falls, South Dakota. This time, an American court sentenced him to a long prison term. Martin's days of stealing horses in Manitoba were over.

That was also the end of the line for the Ed Couture Gang. American and Canadian police now had enough evidence to round up the rest of the horse thieves. Couture himself was arrested and taken to Winnipeg, where he stood trial on June 14, 1875. He managed to escape jail, but his gang was finished.

Chief Constable Richard Power was responsible for bringing many outlaws and killers to justice. One was a thief and gunman named Edward Daniels. Daniels had participated in shootouts in the booming gold rush town of Deadwood, North Dakota, when men like Wild Bill Hickok walked its streets. He had also kept a journal of his escapades. Most of Daniels' criminal colleagues would have considered him a fool to keep a written record of his lawless ways, but Daniels apparently never thought that his tell-tale diary would fall into the hands of the law. Moreover, since he wrote only for himself, there is no reason to believe his accounts are not factual.

By the time that Power cornered him in a settler's cabin near Kildonan in 1879, Daniels was wanted for theft, horse stealing, and escaping custody. Daniels actually "got the drop" on Power; he had his gun aimed and cocked, but when he squeezed the trigger, the only sound was a click. A misfire! Daniels tried to go for a second gun, but by that time Power had hauled out the big .45 with the nine-inch barrel. Once again, Power could have shot the outlaw, but he didn't. Ed Daniels was on his way to jail. His own diary helped to convict him.

Many an American frontier sheriff lived with the knowledge that one day he might wind up dead on a dusty street, riddled with outlaw bullets. Lawmen in Canada lived with the same nagging fear. Chief Constable Richard Power was among those whose sterling careers ended in tragedy, but it was not a bullet from a gunslinging desperado that brought Power to the end of his trail.

Mike Carroll was not a big man physically. However, by 1880, when he showed up in Port Arthur (now part of Thunder Bay), Ontario, looking for work with the Canadian Pacific Railway, he had a reputation as a tough guy. Carroll was put to work on a stretch of the line between Port Arthur and Rat Portage (now Kenora, Ontario). He was soon in jail for robbing his fellow workmen.

While Carroll was serving a term in the Rat Portage jail, the police there learned that he was wanted for a long list of crimes back east, and was an escapee from Toronto's Central Prison. For a man who had broken out of that formidable jail — as well as several other slammers — the small log jailhouse in Rat Portage was no challenge at all. Carroll escaped and fled west.

Mike Carroll could have quietly joined the ranks of the anonymous drifters who were now moving out to Canada's Big Lonely, but he was a braggart who couldn't resist boasting of his exploits to anyone who would listen. The Manitoba Provincial Police soon learned that a fugitive from Ontario had been shooting his mouth off in Selkirk, northeast of Winnipeg. An MPP detective named McKenzie tried to arrest him there, but Carroll managed to get away, with the detective's bullets whistling past his ears.

Carroll's big mouth still gave him away wherever he went, and the police soon tracked him down. They locked him up, and told him they were sending him back to Ontario to face charges. That journey would include a boat trip across Lake of the Woods. Carroll vowed to police that he would never be taken back to Ontario alive. If he had to, he would drown himself and his police guard in the lake. That threat turned out to be prophetic.

Early in July 1880, Richard Power and Detective McKenzie took Carroll to Rat Portage. Magistrate C.J. Brereton sentenced the outlaw to two years in prison, but instead of sending Carroll to Toronto's Central Prison, the judge ordered him taken back to Winnipeg.

On July 8, Carroll was signed into the Manitoba Provincial prison in Winnipeg. Guards there wanted him fitted with a ball and chain, but the request was refused. On July 23, while working with a woodcutting gang, Carroll made a break for it. Dressed in his prison uniform, he was seen running toward the bridge (then under construction) across the Red River between Winnipeg and St. Boniface.

Chief Power was sick in bed when he was told of the escape. Nonetheless, he got dressed, strapped on his big Colt, and led the search for the outlaw. He and a constable named J. Bell tracked Carroll across the unfinished bridge to a haystack near the railway, just outside St. Boniface. Carroll surrendered without a fight, and Power commandeered a railway handcar to take them back to St. Boniface.

By then it was midnight, and the ferry to Winnipeg was out of service. A man in a rowboat offered to take the policemen and their prisoner across the river. Power stepped into the small boat first. Then he offered a hand to Carroll, who was handcuffed. Carroll put a foot on the gunwale. Suddenly the boat overturned, spilling both Power and Carroll into the river. Neither man came up.

Both bodies were found the next day. Carroll drowned because his hands were bound. According to the newspaper reports of the time, Power was weighed down by his big Colt and his ammunition belt. The officers remembered Carroll's earlier threat to drown himself and his escort in Lake of the Woods, rather than go back to prison. As Chief Constable Richard Power was buried with full military honours, his men could only wonder if Mike Carroll had actually capsized the boat deliberately.

Charles Rooke: Death on a Routine Call

Richard Power was the first MPP officer to be killed in the line of duty, but not the last. Charles Rooke, a native of Surrey, England, came to Canada in 1895, and served five years with the NWMP. In 1905, at the request of the provincial government in Winnipeg, he organized a squad called the Manitoba Mounted Police to put a stop to horse rustling along the American border. The worst band of horse thieves was known as the McGraw Gang. Rooke's riders not only broke up the McGraw Gang and the other rustler bands, but recovered most of the stolen horses. They did the job so quickly and thoroughly that there was no further need for the Manitoba Mounted Police, and the squad was disbanded. Rooke then joined the MPP and was stationed in the settlement of Dauphin.

Over the next few years, Constable Rooke won the respect and friendship of most of the people in the Dauphin area, many of whom were immigrants from Eastern Europe. Around 1911, however, he began to have trouble with John Baran, a Galician who had homesteaded near Dauphin. Baran was a bully and a lout. He didn't bother to work his land, and if it wasn't for the moose meat he brought home, his wife and children would have starved. Baran was reputed to be skilled at crafting things with his hands, but he didn't have enough ambition to make a trade of it. His home was a miserable shack. Even Baran's Galician neighbours despised him.

One day Mrs. Baran showed up in Dauphin with two of her children in tow, looking for help. She had fled from her husband after he'd beaten her, but had left her other two children in his dubious care. In sub-zero weather, Constable Rooke rode thirty miles to the Baran homestead. He arrested Baran for assault, and took charge of the half-starved children. They were eventually taken in by the Manitoba Children's Aid. Baran did some jail time, and then left Dauphin.

Two years later, he returned with a woman named Annie Chizyk and a boy about two years old. If the child was Baran's was never known, but once again the problem of non-support arose. A Dauphin magistrate sent Baran a summons, but Baran did not respond to it. The magistrate therefore issued a warrant for Baran's arrest. When one MPP constable was unable to serve the warrant, the magistrate gave the job to the reliable veteran, Charles Rooke.

On January 26, 1913, Rooke set out for the Baran homestead in a sleigh driven by John Tomski, an English speaking Galician. Rooke had agreed to let Tomski talk to Baran before he made an arrest. They arrived at the shack at noon, and knocked on the porch door. Annie Chizyk appeared at a window and said Baran was not home.

Knowing Baran from previous encounters, Rooke was sure that the woman was lying. He stepped past Tomski and entered the porch, then started to open the cabin door.

Three bullets smashed through the rough wooden door. Two whistled harmlessly away, but the third struck Rooke in the chest, just above the heart. Startled though he was, Tomski dragged Rooke off the porch and away from the cabin. He had to leave the constable on the ground while he ran to the nearest farm for assistance.

The farmer helped Tomski carry Rooke back to his house. Tomski then drove nine miles to the nearest house with a telephone and called the police station in Dauphin. A doctor hurried to the farmhouse in a sleigh and saw that there was little he could do for the wounded man there. He wrapped Rooke in blankets, put him in his sleigh, and took him to the little Dauphin hospital.

Meanwhile, the police in Dauphin organized a six-man posse. They also called MPP headquarters in Winnipeg. Deputy Commissioner John McKenzie and Detective John Parr headed for Dauphin. Before they arrived, the posse set out for the Baran homestead. The shadow of tragedy was about to grow darker.

On the morning of January 27, the posse cautiously approached Baran's cabin. There did not seem to be anybody around. Suddenly there was a roar as flashes of gunfire came from the window. The posse responded with a volley of bullets, riddling the small cabin. Then they waited.

There was no more shooting from the window, so the men rushed the cabin. When they burst through the door, there was Annie Chizyk on the floor, bleeding from gunshot wounds to her chest and waist. On a bed lay the little boy, killed by a bullet that had pierced his body. Baran was gone.

The men took the wounded woman and the dead child back to Dauphin, where they met McKenzie and Parr. The MPP officers immediately set out after Baran. They caught up with him on a trail just five miles from his cabin.

Baran surrendered without a fight. He said that Annie Chizyk, and not he, had shot Constable Rooke. At first, Annie supported the story, but later said that it was not true — she had lied out of fear of Baran.

Baran was held in the Dauphin jail on the non-support charge while police investigated the shootings and awaited developments on Rooke's condition. A coroner's jury absolved the posse of any blame in the death of the child and the wounding of Annie Chizyk. The men had been fired upon without provocation, and were not aware that the woman and child were in the cabin. The incident, "while regrettable, was purely accidental, under the circumstances."

On the morning of February 3, Charles Rooke died. That same day, Baran was charged with murder. His trial was held at Portage la Prairie, on March 6.

Baran's lawyer argued that his client was defending his property, and did not know that Rooke was a police officer. But a friend of Baran's testified that Baran had told him that he would shoot any police officer who tried to arrest him. The jury took less than two hours to reach a guilty verdict. Before he was sentenced, Baran confessed to shooting Rooke. On May 20, 1913, Baran was hanged in the Portage la Prairie jail.

Alex McCurdy and James Uttley: "There's No One Like McCurdy"

In February 1920, the MPP was reorganized. Among other new duties, the department became responsible for enforcing provincial morality laws, including the Manitoba Temperance Act. Since breaches of the Act resulted only in fines it was unusual for officers to encounter serious trouble, so they did not carry guns. One establishment that more or less openly defied the Temperance Act was the Stockyards Hotel in St. Boniface. Because St. Boniface was outside Winnipeg city limits, it was beyond the jurisdiction of the Winnipeg Police Department. However, the hotel had still been raided five times by the St. Boniface police and the MPP.

The MPP's senior morality officer was Alexander McCurdy, fifty-nine. He had arrived in Manitoba from the east more than thirty years earlier, and had been a resident of Winnipeg for fourteen years, working as a contractor in the construction industry. McCurdy had long been an advocate for social and moral reform. He was appointed Chief Morality

Inspector for Manitoba in 1918. McCurdy did not like guns, and refused to carry one. A fellow officer said of him, "He would rather be shot himself than shoot another man."

At one o'clock, on the morning of November 11, 1920, Alex McCurdy led a raid on the Stockyards Hotel. With him were Constables James Uttley, Jack Dineen, A.W. Miller, and Fred Cawsey. What should have been a routine inspection became a bloody tragedy.

When the officers entered the hotel, McCurdy sent Miller, Cawsey, and Dineen to the restaurant on the ground floor to look for liquor. Then he and Uttley went to check the upstairs rooms. They opened the door to room number eight, and saw a man and a woman in bed "in an undressed state." Acting according to the prevailing code of decency, McCurdy and Uttley withdrew from the room so the man and woman could put on their clothes; a simple act of courtesy that turned out to be a deadly mistake.

When the officers returned to the room, the man was in his underwear and he had a pistol in his hand. As soon as they entered, he opened fire. One bullet hit McCurdy in the arm, staggering him. As McCurdy fell, the gunman fired another shot that went right through his head. Uttley hurled himself at the man and grappled with him, managing to knock the gun from his hand, but somehow the man got his hands on a second revolver. As the two men wrestled, the gun went off. The bullet smashed into Uttley's chest, piercing a lung and severing his spine. Uttley collapsed to the floor, paralyzed!

Dineen, Cawsey, and Miller heard the shots and ran up the stairway. In the upstairs hallway they encountered the gunman. The man aimed his weapon at Cawsey and pulled the trigger, but the gun misfired. Cawsey ducked into a bathroom. The man fired at Dineen, who was wounded and fell. As Miller made a hasty retreat, the gunman fired three more bullets into Dineen's back. The killer raced down the stairs, and Cawsey dragged Dineen into the bathroom.

While Miller fled from the hotel to get help, the gunman and a man known as Curly O'Neil forced Joseph Biernes, the hotel owner, to drive them away from the scene of the crime in his car. O'Neil held a gun to Biernes' head while the other man pulled on some clothes that he'd grabbed after shooting Uttley. After dropping the men off near the

Canadian National Railway yards, Biernes drove straight to the Winnipeg police station. When constables searched his car they found eight .38 calibre bullets and three spent shells on the back seat.

McCurdy, Uttley, and Dineen were taken to the St. Boniface hospital. At 8:10 that morning, McCurdy died. Uttley clung to life for five days. He was able to tell investigators what had happened in room number eight, before dying on November 16. Uttley's last words were, "I'll stand by Alex McCurdy as long as I live. There's no one like McCurdy." McCurdy left behind a widow, and Uttley a widow and an infant son. Jack Dineen, shot three times, survived.

The woman who had been in the room with the killer was a chambermaid named Christina Johnson. She was apparently more upset about the newspaper story that said she was naked when the officers first entered the room than she was about the shootings. She told the police she knew nothing about the man, except that his name was James Brown.

Investigators soon learned that "James Brown" was actually James Buller, an Ontario-born hoodlum with a long criminal record, and an equally long list of aliases. Buller was a bank burglar and confidence man, who had done prison time in Saskatchewan after a shootout with the Regina police. He had also been jailed in Calgary and Vancouver. The MPP issued a warning that Buller usually carried two guns, and was an extremely dangerous man.

The MPP suspected that Buller had been involved in an armed bank robbery in the town of Winkler on October 13, 1920. That was a well-planned job, in which the bandits had not only cut the telephone and telegraph wires to the town before hitting the bank, but had even tied down the community fire bell. As the robbers sped out of town, a local blacksmith tried to raise an alarm. One of the bandits blasted him in the legs with a shotgun.

Police in Moose Jaw, Saskatchewan, arrested Curly O'Neil, and he was jailed for assisting Buller in his escape. O'Neil was well-known on the horse-racing circuit, and had a criminal record. Investigators also learned that a man named Patrick "Paddy" Joyce had helped Buller skip across the border into the United States. The police believed that when McCurdy and Uttley surprised Buller in the Stockyards Hotel, the outlaw mistakenly thought that they were after him for the Winkler bank robbery.

For almost a year, Canadian detectives tried to track down the killer of Alex McCurdy and James Uttley. The trail took them as far away as Mexico, but always led to a dead end. The Manitoba government put a reward of $2,500 on Buller's head, but he remained elusive.

Then, in the middle of October 1921, the MPP was notified by the Chicago Police Department that James Buller and Patrick Joyce were dead. They had been shot by policemen while sitting in the back seat of a Ford. The official report said that the officers had fired in self-defence, but there was speculation that the killings were part of a gangland vendetta. The Chicago policemen applied for the $2,500 reward, but the Manitoba government paid only $1,000. No reason was given for this reduced reward payment.

Shortage of funds had always been a major problem for the MPP. In 1932, with the entire country tumbling into the depths of the Great Depression, Manitoba could not afford to maintain its own provincial police force. The MPP was absorbed by the RCMP. The four officers who had been slain in the line of duty while serving in the MPP remain heroes of the vanished police force.

5

JOSEPH STEADMAN: ——————
MURDER IN MONCTON

Joseph Steadman was a long-time member of the small police force in the town of Moncton, New Brunswick. He was, in fact, its first official marshal (chief).

In December 1879, shortly after a tight-fisted town council had laid-off the community's lone night policeman as a cost-saving measure, a shoe store on the main street was burglarized. A man named Thomas Warren informed Steadman of the break-in. Suspicious, Steadman decided to keep an eye on Warren. Before the day was out, he saw Warren spend a silver dollar that was listed among the stolen items. Steadman confronted Warren, who immediately confessed to the robbery. The crime proved to the town council that Moncton needed a constable on night patrol, and the speedy solution of the robbery showed Steadman to be a resourceful and observant policeman.

Still, Joseph Steadman had a checkered career with the Moncton police department. In 1884, the municipal government suspended him for three months, possibly for being too lenient in enforcing the Scott Act — a law that forbade the sale of alcoholic beverages. When Steadman was reinstated, he was no longer marshal. As a constable he often drew night patrol duty, and would do his rounds with his dog at his side. In spite of his fall from grace, Joe Steadman remained very popular in the community.

In the 1890s transient men — at that time called "tramps" — were a fact of life in Canada. Most of them were young men who criss-crossed the country by whatever means possible, including hopping freight trains. The majority were searching for work, or travelling from one seasonal job to another, but others were thieves. These criminals, operating individually or in gangs, saw towns like Moncton, with their small police departments, as places of opportunity. A mobile crook could drift into town, burglarize a home or business, and be on the road and far away before local police knew anything about it. Their activities gave a bad name to the honest transients, who were often hauled into police stations for rough questioning while the real culprits were miles away. Such a crime led to a violent confrontation between a tramp and Constable Steadman.

In the summer of 1892, a large number of transients trekked through New Brunswick; some heading for Halifax; others for Montreal, Toronto, and the West. Not all of them were looking for work. First, the Sackville Post Office was hit. Thieves robbed it, and then set it on fire. In late July, burglars struck the W. Wilson & Co. Store in Chatham. They blew the safe with dynamite, and got away with $250 in cash and a hoard of coins that included several Mexican silver dollars.

In the days following the crime, Moncton newspapers carried articles that included descriptions of the loot. A local resident read the story and told Moncton Chief of Police Charles Foster that he had seen two men in possession of Mexican silver dollars. He knew them only as Jim and Buck, and said that they had been in a "hotel," which was actually a brothel, run by a Mrs. Donnelly and her daughters. As far as the informant was aware, the two were still there. Because Mexican coins weren't often seen in circulation in Canada, Chief Foster concluded that Jim and Buck must have been connected with the Chatham robbery.

On the night of August 1, Foster quietly approached the brothel at the head of a posse consisting of Constable Joseph Steadman, another policeman named Scott, Special Constable Charles Colborne, and a civilian named Alexander McRae. Foster had a feeling that the suspects were armed and would not be taken easily. He'd told his men, "We've got an ugly job on hand tonight." When they reached the brothel, Steadman asked Foster how he intended to handle it. Foster replied that he was going in the front door. The veteran Steadman said, "If you do, you won't come out alive." Steadman's words would prove prophetic.

Foster sent Steadman to a door at the side of the house. Scott and Colborne went to watch the back. Foster took the front door himself, with McRae backing him up.

When the men were in position, Foster entered the front door with a pistol in one hand and a billy club in the other. Inside were Mrs. Donnelly, her daughters Selina and Maggie, her son Thomas, and two men named Ira German and John Dryden. With them were the suspects, Jim and Buck.

As soon as the police chief came through the door, Selina cried, "Foster is here! The cops is round the house!" Buck pulled a revolver and shouted "Hi Jim!" to his partner, who also yanked out a gun. Both men rushed to the side door and burst through. Buck ran right into the arms of Constable Steadman and grappled with him. Jim fired two or three shots, but kept on running. He disappeared into the darkness.

Around the corner of the building, Scott and Colborne heard gunshots. Scott ran to the side door and saw Steadman struggling with Buck. Steadman seemed to be in distress, but he did not release his hold on Buck until Scott slugged the man to the ground with his billy. Then Steadman staggered a few steps and gasped, "My God, boys, I'm shot!" He collapsed and was carried to the Park Hotel. Chief Foster sent for a doctor, but it

Town Hall Building, Moncton, New Brunswick, circa 1895. Chief Charles Foster (fourth from right) and Constable Scott (second from right) were present the night Constable Joseph Steadman was killed.

Courtesy Moncton Museum Collection

was no use. Constable Joseph Steadman, forty-four years old, was dead. He left behind a wife and a young son.

Buck was handcuffed and hauled off to jail. In addition to the bruises he'd received from Constable Scott, he had a bullet in his leg. There would be some argument as to whether the slug came from his own gun or from Jim's. None of the officers involved in the raid had fired a shot.

The local press described Buck as "brutish and rough looking," with small eyes, high cheekbones, and an unshaven face. He was about thirty years old, and of average stature at five foot seven, and 150 pounds. Buck covered his face every time a photographer tried to take his picture, and he refused to tell the police his real name. Confronted with the charge that he had killed Constable Steadman, Buck replied, "I did not do it."

Officers searched the yard where Buck and Steadman had fought. They found a Smith and Wesson revolver. Two of the gun's chambers had been fired. Police had already seen gunpowder marks on Buck's clothing.

Outside of the jail where Buck was locked up, a small crowd gathered. A few people called for a lynching, but no attempt was made on the jail. Nonetheless, two constables stood guard at the door. Meanwhile, Steadman's faithful dog found its way to the Park hotel and tried to enter the room in which its master's body lay.

An inquest was held the next day, and the coroner's jury formally charged Buck with murder. A police committee authorized a reward of $250 for information leading to the arrest of the man they knew only as Jim. The police believed Buck and Jim were members of a gang of thieves who had been responsible for numerous felonies in the province.

Constable Steadman's funeral procession was the largest ever seen in Moncton, up to that time. The pall bearers were members of the Orange Order, which was a significant political force in those days. As Steadman's widow and son listened, several of Moncton's leading citizens delivered eulogies. Said one, "As an officer he was fearless and bold in doing his duty, and his affable manner in the performance of such won for him many friends."

The tragic death of a small-town policeman did not go unnoticed in Montreal, which was then Canada's largest city. The *Montreal Gazette* stated on August 5, 1892:

The killing of Constable Steadman at Moncton is another reminder that the policeman's lot is not a happy one. Canada is happily comparatively free from affairs of this kind, though they occur with a frequency that lets people know how useful the blue coat and the baton are, and how serious is the work their wearers are engaged in.

Police and civilian volunteers scoured the town and countryside in search of Jim. Buck, wracked by nerves as he paced his cell and pondered his future, frequently asked the guards if they'd had any news of Jim. He told Foster he would help the police in anyway he could to find Jim, if that would save his own neck. He confessed that he and Jim had been members of a five-man gang, but he still refused to tell police his real name.

At that time it could be very difficult for a police department to positively identify an individual who was a stranger in town. Many transients, even those who were not criminals, did not travel under their own names. They used nicknames like Buck, Slim, Mac, or Butch. Not many people carried identification papers. Fingerprinting was virtually unknown. Communications between the many police departments and other law enforcement agencies across Canada, and the United States, were disjointed at best, even with such modern technology as the telegraph, the telephone, and photography. A dogged investigator could take months to track down the identity of an uncooperative suspect. Often, a police department simply could not spare the man-hours, or the cost to its budget.

Chief Foster finally received a telegram from the Montreal Police Department. A detective there had read Buck's description and believed that he was Buck Whelan, a man who was "well known in Montreal as a very desperate character." Buck Whelan's partner, the detective said, was a notorious burglar named Jim Christie.

Buck denied this. He finally told Foster his real named was Robert Olsen. He said he was an American, a son of Norwegian immigrants who had settled on a farm in Minnesota. However, Foster learned that just hours before the shooting of Steadman, Buck had told Thomas Donnelly that he was a sailor from St. John. A former Moncton policeman accused

Buck of being the thief who had burglarized the Dorchester Post Office four years earlier. Of course, Buck denied that too. Whoever "Buck" really was, the Moncton police entered his name in their books as Robert Olsen. Quite likely he was American, and perhaps he even had been a sailor; his arms were covered with tattoos of American flags and eagles.

The search for Jim continued, and police doubled the reward to $500. Passing tramps were picked up for questioning and then released. A farmer, out late at night looking for some missing cows, was detained; as was a young man in Sussex who had gone to town to buy a suit for his wedding. Police there had thought his behaviour "mysterious." Most Monctonians believed Jim was miles away, but others suspected he was still hiding in town. They were reluctant to open their doors if someone knocked after dark. Police received numerous tips from people all over New Brunswick who claimed to have seen the wanted man, but the leads all proved false.

One man who decided to join the hunt for the elusive Jim was Peter Carroll, a detective with the police department in Pictou, Nova Scotia. Known as Peachy to his friends, Carroll was something of a legend in Nova Scotia. His biographer, N. Carroll MacIntyre, wrote that Carroll had been described as "a one man vigilante committee, bounty hunter, bootlegger and 'damn good detective.'" By 1892, Carroll had already been chief of police in Pictou and Yarmouth. He was also a seasoned mariner who had been "Round the Horn," and had even talked a disgruntled crew out of committing mutiny.

Detective Carroll took the train to Moncton and engaged a local man named Wilbur Delancey as a guide. He promised Delancey half of the reward if they found Jim. The two went to Kent Junction, then to Coal Branch. There they met a farmer who told them that a tramp had broken into a farmhouse near Bass River the night before. Bass River was about nine miles away, and the farmer took them there in his wagon.

The farmer whose house had been robbed said the thief had taken some food, a razor, and a pair of boots. He'd gone out to his barn and found a stranger asleep in the loft, wearing his boots. He'd awakened the man, who immediately pulled a gun. The farmer pointed Carroll in the direction that the stranger had taken.

One of the stolen boots the man was wearing had had a repair made to the heel with four horseshoe nails, leaving a print that was easy to follow. The trail led to another farmhouse, about three miles away.

Carroll told Delancey to wait by the gate while he went into the house. The door was open, so Carroll walked right in. Two men were sitting by the stove. It was clear to Carroll that the man in shirtsleeves was the farmer who lived there. The other man, who looked like a tramp, he correctly guessed was Jim. Carroll asked the man his name.

"Thomas Moore," Jim replied. He said he lived on a farm a few miles away. Carroll asked the farmer if that was true.

"No," the farmer said. "He just came in here about an hour ago and asked for some food."

Carroll told the farmer to go out and tell some men who were waiting in a wagon to come into the house. As the farmer left, Jim reached into a pocket and started to pull out his gun. The pistol wasn't halfway out before Carroll seized Jim's wrist with one hand, and smashed him in the head with the other.

Jim fell to the floor, but did not let go of the gun. Carroll jumped on him and pounded him into unconsciousness. By the time Delancey ran into the kitchen with his revolver drawn, Carroll had Jim handcuffed. They took the prisoner to Coal Branch railway station, where Carroll wired the Moncton police that he had captured Jim.

Carroll took his prisoner to Moncton. Like Buck, Jim refused to tell the police his real name. He said only that he was from Toronto, and that he "had always been used to city life." Newspaper reporters who spoke to him judged that, unlike Buck, Jim was well-educated and well-read. In fact, Jim was from New York, and had once been a school teacher.

The prisoners were transported to the Westmorland County Gaol in Dorchester. There, a grand jury brought in a true bill for murder against Buck, and indicted Jim on seven counts, including discharging a pistol at Steadman. Both prisoners pleaded not guilty. When the Attorney General asked Buck if he was ready to stand trial, he replied, "About as ready as I can ever get."

Buck's trial began on September 13. His defence counsel was D. Grant. Attorney General Andrew Blair (who was also premier) prosecuted for the Crown, and Judge John James Fraser, a former premier of New Brunswick, presided. The most damaging testimony against Buck came from Detective Carroll. When the policeman brought Jim in, he stayed the night in the jail and overheard a conversation Buck and Jim engaged in late at night, when they undoubtedly thought everyone else in the building was asleep.

According to Carroll, Jim said, "Olsen, Olsen! Hi, Olsen, is that you?"

Buck replied, "Yes. Is that you, Jim?"

"Yes," Jim replied. "Yes, everything is quiet. I had a hard time since I saw you last."

Buck said, "Yes, and I had a hard time of it since I saw you last."

Then Jim said, "Why didn't you shoot low? I always told you to shoot low. We will have to take our chances. You made a hell of a job of it."

Buck responded, "Perhaps you would have done the same if you were in my place. When I fired that shot I thought I would get clear, but the other policeman knocked me stiff with a club."

"There's only one thing we can do now," Jim said.

"What's that, Jim?"

"We will have to take our chances."

Buck said, "Your chances are all right, Jim."

Jim replied, "It's a pity I didn't fix the big fellow (Carroll), but he was too quick for me."

Buck said, "He gave you a pretty good smashing up."

"Yes," Jim said.

As Carroll gave his testimony, Buck derided him from the prisoner's box. In his cross-examination, Grant asked Carroll if he had been drinking that night. The detective said he'd had only three or four glasses of sherry.

William Wilson, owner of the store in Chatham that had been robbed, took the stand and identified the silver coins that had been in Buck's possession at the time of his arrest. The surviving officers from the raid on Mrs. Donnelly's establishment gave their accounts of the events of the night of August 1. The testimonies of Mrs. Donnelly and her family did nothing to shake the general belief that Buck had fired the fatal shot.

In his lengthy summation, Grant first pointed out that Chief Foster had no warrant when he went to the brothel to arrest Buck and Jim. Therefore, he said, Buck had the right to resist unlawful arrest, and the charge of murder should be reduced to one of manslaughter. Grant also asked the jury to consider the fact that the bullet in Buck's leg had not yet been removed. Why not? Could it be because the officers actually *did* discharge their firearms that night, and the slugs that struck both Steadman and Buck were in fact police bullets? That possibility would nullify the Crown's case.

Grant added yet another scenario. When Constable Steadman grappled with Buck, he was armed with a billy club. Was it not possible that during the struggle, Steadman's billy had struck the trigger of Buck's revolver, causing it to fire the bullet that killed the officer?

Grant was grasping at straws. Blair demolished the defence counsel's points in his rebuttal. He said that Foster and his men did not need warrants, because they went to the brothel on reasonable suspicion that wanted criminals were there.

> We have these people properly under suspicion and we have an officer going there properly to effect their arrest. I do not know any other way a careful officer would start to work to arrest such desperate men as these men proved themselves to be. What other course could they take but to surround the house?

Buck knew he was suspected of the Chatham robbery, Blair said, and when Selina Donnelly announced Chief Foster's arrival, he knew that the police were on to him. Rather than submit to arrest, Buck chose to resist. The result, said Blair, was the murder of Constable Steadman. That none of the officers fired a shot had already been well-established, and it would have been impossible for Steadman's billy to have pressed the trigger of Buck's gun, because it was too thick to fit into the trigger guard.

After a short deliberation, the jury found Buck guilty. However, Judge Fraser postponed passing sentence until after Jim's trial which began on September 19. Many of the witnesses from Buck's trial were again called upon to testify.

However, Blair brought in one new witness. A boy named Henry James had been arrested for a minor offence and had been sentenced to a short stay in the Moncton jail at the time that Jim and Buck were being held there. Foster had put James to work doing odd jobs in the building. James testified that on the morning of August 23 he was about to sweep a hallway around a corner from the cells, when he overheard Buck talking to Jim. According to James, Buck said:

> My God, I am sorry I shot him now. I almost cried after I heard the people say how good a man he was, but I could not help it. I went to point the revolver to fire and in doing so some one hit me on the head which made me drop my revolver quite a piece. I intended to raise my revolver again, to shoot over his shoulder but I got another clout on the head that made me drop my revolver just as I was going to pull the trigger.

Buck added that he wished he had pointed the gun at Foster the moment he saw him.

Detective Carroll returned to the stand to tell how he had apprehended Jim — who by this time was also suspected of a robbery that had occurred at Molus River — a few days after the Steadman shooting. Carroll said that when he took Jim to Moncton, he warned him that anything he said could be used against him in court. In spite of the warning, Jim admitted that he had fired four shots as he ran from the Donnelly place. Now he was afraid that he, not Buck, had shot Steadman.

Carroll said he told Jim that the bullet taken from Steadman's body was a .32, the same caliber as Buck's revolver. Jim's gun was a .38. Carroll testified that upon hearing this, Jim seemed to be greatly relieved and said, "Thank God I didn't shoot him. God help Buck."

Jim's lawyer, R.B. Smith, said he knew his client was a bad character, but he did not think that there was sufficient evidence for him to be found guilty of the charges against him. To the surprise of all, Smith called Buck to the stand to testify in Jim's defence. It wasn't a good tactic. Buck identified himself as Robert Olsen. He said he'd been "paralyzed drunk" the night of the shooting. Then he brought a new, mysterious person into the story. Buck said he and Jim had been expecting to meet another man in Moncton. That man had arrived on the train on August 1, and was in the yard of the Donnelly house the night of the shooting. Buck could not, or would not, identify the man. Nor would he answer questions about his own activities prior to the shooting.

Jim was found guilty of four of the seven charges against him. Judge Fraser sentenced him to twenty-five years in the Dorchester Penitentiary. He upbraided Jim as: "One of a band of robbers, burglars and murderers who are travelling throughout the length and breadth of this land committing crimes."

Given the opportunity to make a statement before he was taken away to prison, Jim said that the real killer of Constable Steadman was the mysterious "third party" whom Buck had spoken of. Nobody bought that story. Buck was sentenced to be hanged on December 1. Grant's plea for a new trial was denied.

A gallows was constructed at the Westmorland County Gaol and hidden from the public's "vulgar gaze" by a twenty foot high wooden wall. The day before the execution, Buck was told that there was no hope of a reprieve. "Perhaps it is all for the best," he said. "I believe if I had got clear, it might have been worse for me in the future. Nobody can tell. I intend to die like a man if I have to go."

Buck received a letter from Jim, in which his former partner-in-crime urged him to ask God's forgiveness and "Forget the world and fix your heart on eternity." In fact, guards brought Jim from the penitentiary to the jail to bid Buck farewell personally. Jim said, "Goodbye, old fellow. Bear up."

Buck replied, "Take care of yourself up there." Allegedly, Jim tried to convince the authorities that *he* had actually shot Steadman, but no one believed him.

Among those who visited Buck in his final hours was Police Inspector C.M. Hanscom, from Boston. He suspected Buck and Jim of involvement in the burglary of a cottage owned by the wealthy Vanderbilt family in Bar Harbor, Maine. Neither Jim nor Buck would confess to this crime, but after interviewing them, Hanscom was convinced that they were professional criminals who had worked under a variety of aliases in both Canada and the United States. He said they probably travelled with "tough looking rigs" to give the impression that they were ordinary tramps. Hanscom noted a small mend at the bottom of Buck's hip pocket. He said that was quite likely caused by the constant wearing of a handgun.

At 9:30 a.m. on December 1, Buck was delivered into the hands of John Radclive, Canada's official hangman. At the time, Radclive was not using the traditional "drop" gallows. Instead, he employed a device of his own invention that reporters called the "jerk 'em up gallows." The condemned man was yanked up into the air when the hangman released a heavy weight attached to the rope around the victim's neck. Radclive claimed this guaranteed a broken neck, and a quick, painless death.

After a brief prayer, Buck said, "Let her go; God have mercy on my soul." Radclive pulled a cord, and Buck's body shot up four or five feet. Half an hour later the body was cut down. The bullet in Buck's leg was finally removed. It was a .38, from Jim's gun.

Buck had gone to his death as Robert Olsen, but there was still speculation as to his real identity. The Montreal police had a photograph of the man who had been hanged for the murder of Constable Steadman. They said he was Buck Whelan, allegedly a nephew of James Whelan, the man who had been hanged for the assassination of Thomas D'Arcy McGee. They said Buck's partner was Jim Christie, who was wanted for burglary in Quebec and several New England states. Jim did not live to breathe free air again. After a failed escape attempt, he was transferred from Dorchester to the Kingston Penitentiary. There, yet another escape plot involving Jim was thwarted. Guards beat Jim so badly that he was sent to the prison hospital. From there he was transferred to the ward for the insane, where he died.

In 1997, in Fredericton, a memorial was erected in honour of all New Brunswick peace officers who lost their lives in the line of duty. On August 26, 2001, a memorial service was held there for the first of them to be killed on duty, Constable Joseph Steadman.

6

MICHAEL TOOHEY: ──────────
A KILLER FROM TEXAS

When Marion "Peg-Leg" Brown arrived in Canada in 1898, he already had all of the necessary ingredients to become an American Wild West outlaw legend. He was a gunslinging desperado with a criminal record and several murders to his credit. But unlike well-known gunmen Billy the Kid, John Wesley Hardin, and Doc Holliday, Brown never had a chronicler to "write him up" for the American pulp press.

Born in San Saba, Texas, in 1873, Brown was of mixed white and Mexican parentage. In his youth he worked as a cowboy, but when he was nineteen, Brown lost the lower part of his left leg in an accident. He subsequently wore a peg-leg made of elm.

No longer able to work as a cowboy, Brown turned to crime, using the alias Thomas Allen. He allegedly killed four men in Texas. In May 1898, he was convicted of burglary and jailed in Georgetown, Texas.

Within a month of his incarceration, Brown escaped, taking a jail guard's gun and watch. Texas lawmen were soon hot on his trail. In a gunfight, Brown killed a marshal and wounded a deputy. He escaped a posse by jumping onto a moving freight train with bullets whistling around him. Brown must have spent the next couple of weeks living the hobo life; riding the rails and begging for, or stealing, food. Sometime in June he crossed the border into Ontario. Like many American desperadoes on the lam, Brown thought that Canada would be a safe haven. On the evening of June 24, Brown rode a freight train into the railyards of London. The Texas badman, who had been overlooked by the hack journalists in his own country, was about to make news in Canada.

At about 7:00 p.m. James Ross, an elderly watchman for the Grand Trunk Railway, saw a man with a peg-leg walking along the tracks. Railway employees always had to be on watch for tramps seeking free rides, so Ross confronted the man and told him he was trespassing on GTR property. The trespasser, who was later identified as Brown, could have just walked away and avoided trouble. Instead, he pulled out a small club and struck Ross on the head, knocking the old man out cold.

Workmen from an adjacent lumberyard found Ross and carried him to their shanty. When Ross regained consciousness he told them what had happened. One of them notified the London Police Department. Three constables named Monohan, Morgan, and Rowell arrived in the patrol wagon. Ross told them his assailant had a peg-leg and was wearing a black felt hat.

The constables began to search the railyards and neighbouring streets. Morgan encountered Constable Michael Toohey, who was walking his beat in the town's east end. When told of the assault, Toohey guessed that the suspect might head for the Canadian Pacific railyards, so he went in that direction.

Michael Toohey, thirty-nine years old, a married father of three, had been with the London Police Department since 1887, and was well-liked by his fellow officers. Toohey was a veteran copper, who had dealt with a lot of tramps in his eleven years of service. But Peg-Leg Brown, Texas desperado, was not the typical down-on-his-luck hobo, riding the rails as a migrant worker.

Some boys told Toohey they had seen a peg-legged man at the corner of Ontario and Elias streets, which indicated that he was indeed going to the CPR yards. The boys showed him the unmistakable tracks Brown left in the dirt. Toohey evidently anticipated trouble, because he did the nineteenth century equivalent of "calling for backup"; he told a boy to run and fetch help. Then Toohey went looking for his man.

There were no eyewitnesses to what happened next, but several people saw Brown in the vicinity before and after the incident. They reported hearing Toohey shout, "Hold on there!" followed by two gunshots.

There must have been a scuffle when Toohey attempted to arrest the suspect, because Brown lost his hat. Then he pulled a gun and shot Toohey twice. The first bullet struck a silver watch in Toohey's left breast pocket. The impact probably staggered the policeman. Brown's second shot hit Toohey in the forehead, above his right eye, tearing into his brain and killing him on the spot.

Minutes after the shooting a pair of soldiers found the body. Toohey's service revolver was still in his holster. Nearby lay a black felt hat. The murderer had escaped into the darkness.

The brutal slaying of the popular constable shocked the small city of London. Toohey was the second London policeman to be murdered in the line of duty, the first being Detective Harry Phair, who was shot in 1892. Many people believed that in Toohey's case, supernatural forces were at work, and that he was a victim of the infamous Donnelly Curse.

Michael Toohey was from Biddulph Township, near London. The town was the scene of a feud between the so-called Black Donnellys and their neighbours that had climaxed in a massacre eighteen years earlier. On the night of February 4, 1880, a vigilante gang murdered five of the Donnellys in cold blood. No one was ever brought to justice for the crime, even though the names of the men who had committed the atrocity were known. According to local lore, the families of all the vigilantes were cursed. One version of the story says that Johanna Donnelly, the matriarch of the clan, damned the murderers before she was beaten to death. In another story, it was her son William, who had survived that bloody night, who had called upon dark powers for the vengeance he did not get in court. Michael Toohey was related to one of the vigilantes. Several of the men who had Donnelly blood on their hands did, in fact, meet with untimely deaths, so there were people who said that the curse had caught up with Constable Toohey.

Curse or no curse, there was now a killer to be tracked down. At that time industrial and agricultural accidents often resulted in the amputation of limbs, so a man with a peg-leg was not an unusual sight.

The London police picked up several such men for questioning, and then released them. In the following weeks, as the search for the killer spread across Canada and the United States, dozens of peg-legged men were rounded up as possible suspects.

Meanwhile, Brown was making his way across Southern Ontario, walking when he had to, stealing horses or riding freights when he could. He got handouts of food from farmers who did not know that he was running from the law. On June 27, Brown begged a meal at the farm of Malcolm Campbell in Brooke Township, near Owen Sound. While he was eating, three local constables came to the front door: Philip Fuller, Duncan Gillies, and John Shaw (who also had a peg-leg). They asked Campbell if he had seen a one-legged tramp. When Brown heard Campbell reply that a tramp with a peg-leg was sitting at his kitchen table, he jumped up and hurried out through another door. He had a gun in his hand, and he shouted that he would not be taken alive.

Fuller had a rifle, but Shaw and Gillies were unarmed. Brown and Fuller exchanged a few shots, and one of Brown's bullets nicked Fuller's shirtsleeve. Brown warned the constable to stay back, telling them he was better armed than they were. When he heard Fuller call to his companions that he was out of ammunition, Brown laughed, "You ain't got no more cartridges." Then he fled into the woods. Wary of Brown's gun, the constables did not chase him. Instead they circled the woods, hoping to surprise him when he came out. But the killer managed to slip by them and escape.

As news of the murder of Constable Toohey spread, Canadian authorities learned that their suspect might be one Marion Brown of Texas, recently escaped from the Georgetown jail. According to the Texans, Brown was one mean *hombre*. A $500 reward was offered for information leading to Brown's arrest.

For weeks following his escape from Campbell's farm, nothing was heard of Peg-Leg Brown. Every lead the police had turned out to be a dead end. At some point, Brown crossed back into the United States, possibly on a lake boat or a freight train. Then he made his way to the west coast. He evaded police until the evening of September 24, when he was spotted by a sharp-eyed U.S. Marshal named Abraham Lincoln Dilley.

Marshal Dilley was a tough character who had been a cowboy and a rancher, and had earned a reputation as a very capable lawman. He had read about Brown in a detective magazine, and by sheer chance he saw a man who matched the fugitive's description at a theatre in Yakima, Washington. Dilley arrested Brown at gunpoint, and tossed him into the Yakima jail.

The marshal had his eye on the reward money, but he knew that the extradition process was notoriously slow. Rather than tell Brown that he was under arrest for a murder in Canada, and give him an opportunity to fight extradition, Dilley told him that he was charged with selling liquor to Natives. Two weeks after the arrest, Brown was taken by train to New Westminster, British Columbia. He was over the border before he knew what was happening. A Detective Nickel of the London Police Department was waiting to charge him with Toohey's murder.

On October 11, escorted by Dilley and Nickel, Brown boarded a train for the long ride back to London. The policemen handcuffed him and took away his wooden leg. Even so, as the train crossed Manitoba, Brown managed to get free of his handcuffs in a failed escape attempt. Nickel would later say of Brown: "Of all the men I have ever handled, Brown is the worst. He is not only possessed of phenomenal strength, but he can talk as smoothly as any gold brick swindler and at the same time act like a man who would not do the slightest harm."

The officers and their prisoner arrived in London on October 15, and Brown was lodged in the fortress-like Middlesex County Courthouse and Gaol. At the preliminary hearing on October 21, Brown pleaded innocent to the charge of murder. His lawyer, Mr. McPhillips, argued that Brown had been falsely arrested and that the extradition treaty between Canada and the United States had been violated. But courts of the day sometimes sidestepped the finer points of the law, and the judge committed Brown to stand trial on March 22, 1899.

The trial lasted seven days and was a sensation. Among the witnesses that the prosecution brought forward were two Texas deputies, Thomas Basham and William Smith. These men were well acquainted with Brown and positively identified him. They also identified the black felt hat that had been found beside Toohey's body as his.

Courtesy London Free Press

Marion "Peg-Leg" Brown, the killer of Constable Michael Toohey. This illustration appeared on the front page of a London newspaper the day Brown was hanged for the murder.

Lawyer McPhillips had no witnesses to call for the defence, and he did not put Brown on the stand. Instead, he made a passionate speech, describing his client as an innocent man in a foreign country, who was being framed by the Crown because the police could not find the real killer. "Not one man" McPhillips said, "could show positively that the man who fired the shot at Toohey was Brown."

McPhillips' oratory moved Brown to tears, but it did not have the same effect on the members of the jury. They took less than two hours to reach a guilty verdict. Brown was condemned to be hanged on May 17, 1899. That sentence was duly carried out by hangman John Radclive.

Ironically, the tragic story of Marion "Peg-Leg" Brown and Constable Michael Toohey, which became an episode in the tale of the Donnelly Curse, spawned yet another "curse" legend. Brown protested his innocence to the very end. As he was being taken to the gallows, he allegedly cursed the Middlesex County Gaol, vowing that his ghost would haunt the place. Every year on the anniversary of his execution, it's said that the ghost of Peg-Leg Brown can be heard clumping along the corridors of the old London Gaol.

7

THE LOST PATROL: ————————————
DEATH IN THE ARCTIC

At the turn of the twentieth century, Canada's federal government had jurisdiction over hundreds of thousands of square miles of the Arctic. This included all of the lands and waters of the Yukon Territory and the North-West Territories (now the Northwest Territories and Nunavut). The vast domain was sparsely populated by Natives and a handful of whites, with a few remote outposts that passed for communities. To establish the rule of law, and to secure Canadian sovereignty — especially in the face of American whaling fleets freely operating in Canadian waters — the government set up police posts in a number of isolated centres of trade and transportation. The North-West Mounted Police had done a superb job of maintaining order during the Klondike Gold Rush, which began in 1897. It was largely because of the Mounties that the Canadian gold rush was not marred by the violence and anarchy that were so evident during gold rushes in American frontier regions such as California, the Dakotas, and Alaska. The Canadian government was optimistic that the North-West Mounted Police (renamed the Royal North-West Mounted Police in 1904) would be an effective custodian of the country north of the Sixtieth Parallel.

The lonely police posts strung across the Arctic expanse were connected to each other — and to the outside world — by a network of trails that crossed some of the most inhospitable country in the world. A journey along one of these Mountie patrol trails was not for the faint of heart. The trip was physically, mentally, and emotionally demanding, as well as being downright dangerous. There was very little margin for error, and not much help for a man who fell ill or was hurt. Many a trail-hardened, experienced civilian outdoorsman accompanied a Mountie patrol as guide or trailbreaker, only to vow at journey's end that he would never do it again. Yet every year the constables patrolled a total of more than one hundred thousand miles of Arctic and sub-Arctic trails, carrying out a host of official duties as they trudged, mushed, canoed, and rode from one speck on the map to the next.

Most of the hardships that the men endured on these wilderness patrols did not make it into the laconic official reports submitted by the commanding officers. They would have made for repetitive (though heroic) accounts of brutal cold, howling blizzards, torrential rains, tortuous terrain, clouds of voracious blackflies and mosquitoes, frostbite, snow-blindness, and hunger. The important thing was that a patrol was completed successfully, regardless of the obstacles. One patrol, however, became an epic in the saga of the Mounted Police and the North. This was a story, not of triumph over an Arctic gauntlet, but of tragic failure. As author and historian Dick North so succinctly states in his definitive book on the subject, *The Lost Patrol: The Mounties' Yukon Tragedy*, the story is "where legend and reality become one."

The stage upon which this drama unfolded was the 475-mile trail between Dawson City, the mecca of the Yukon Gold Rush, and Fort McPherson, a small post in the North-West Territories, on the Peel River, about seventy-five miles south of present-day Inuvik. The RNWMP had a post in Forth McPherson, which was the principal link to another police post on Herschel Island. This island in the Beaufort Sea was a little over three miles off the Yukon coast, and despite being Canadian territory, it was a centre for the American whaling fleet. The Mounties on Herschel Island could have sent out reports with American whaling ships, but it was not considered prudent to entrust foreigners with official Canadian documents, especially since the bulk of those documents dealt specifically with the activities of the whalers themselves. Therefore, it was important for Hershel Island to be connected to Dawson City through Fort McPherson.

The route that the Mounted Police blazed, with the help of local Loucheux Natives, began eighteen miles down the Yukon River from Dawson City, at the mouth of the Twelve Mile River (now called the Chandindu River). Sixty-four miles up the Twelve Mile River the route crossed Seela Pass, went down the Blackstone River and across a divide to the Little Hart River, down the Hart River, and then up Waugh Creek. The route then crossed another divide, and went down the Little Wind and Wind rivers to the Peel River. There was a cutoff that took the route up Mountain Creek and across a thirty-seven mile portage to the Trail River, before striking the Peel again for the final seventy mile run down to Fort McPherson. Much of this route would have been all but impassable in summer, but in winter it was negotiable by dogsled. The time it took to get from Dawson City to Fort McPherson depended largely on the weather and trail conditions. Usually it took about thirty days. The longest patrol took fifty-six days.

The first Mountie patrol to travel the Dawson City to Fort McPherson trail was led by Constable Harry G. Mapley in the winter of 1904–05. With him were three other officers, plus a Native guide and two Native trailbreakers. The patrol encountered no unusual difficulties, although Mapley was of the opinion that the Mounties could have done without the "civilians," by whom he meant the Natives. Some of his successors would share that belief. With the exception of the winter of 1917–18, when there was no patrol, the Dawson City to Fort McPherson patrol continued until the winter of 1920–21, after which it was no longer necessary. Every patrol but one started out from Dawson City, since that community was in a much better position to supply and equip the men than Fort McPherson was. The single patrol that started out from Fort McPherson was that of the winter of 1910–11. That was the one fated to meet with disaster.

The officer assigned to lead the 1910 patrol was Inspector Francis Joseph Fitzgerald, a man who had packed a lifetime of adventure into his forty-one years. Born in Halifax in 1869, Fitzgerald lied about his age when he joined the NWMP in 1888. He easily passed the tough Mountie training program at their school in Regina.

Courtesy Alberta Provincial Archives

Inspector Francis Joseph Fitzgerald, leader of the Lost Patrol.

By the time gold fever swept the world in 1897, Fitzgerald had served with distinction at several posts in western Canada. He was one of a hand-picked team of Mounties under Inspector J.D. Moodie, assigned to survey an overland route from Edmonton to the Yukon River. This back door road to the goldfields covered about 1,200 miles, most of it uncharted and known only to Native hunters.

Moodie's party left Edmonton on September 4, 1897, and did not reach the Yukon River until October 24, 1898. The men encountered every difficulty imaginable: bad weather, muskeg, impassable underbrush, unreliable guides, shortages of food for men and dogs, sickness, and injuries. Their trail-blazing expedition made the adventures of some of Canada's better known explorers look like romps in the woods. The trek was all the more remarkable because these men were police officers, not explorers. Corporal Francis Fitzgerald proved himself to be so resourceful and reliable that Moodie quickly acknowledged him as his right-hand man. At the successful completion of the expedition, Fitzgerald was promoted to sergeant.

With the outbreak of the Boer War, Fitzgerald joined the Second Canadian Mounted Rifles in January 1900, and went to fight in South Africa. He returned to Canada a year later, and was discharged from the army in January 1901. Fitzgerald immediately resumed his career with the NWMP. In the spring of 1903 he was ordered to travel to Herschel Island (which did not yet have a police post) to investigate American activities there, and to determine if a post would be required.

For Fitzgerald, just getting to Herschel Island from his posting at Maple Creek, Saskatchewan, involved an arduous journey. En route he visited Fort McPherson for the first time, and found it a dreary place. Had Fitzgerald found no need for a police post on Herschel Island, the Mounties might well have abandoned Fort McPherson.

However, Herschel Island — which was even more desolate than Fort McPherson — did require a police presence. The American whalers had built storehouses and dwellings there, and there were rumours that the United States planned to annex the island. The Americans were paying no duty on the goods that they got from the Natives in trade. Moreover, they were debauching the Natives with liquor. Fitzgerald quickly put a stop to the whiskey peddling, but he could do nothing about collecting duties until he was sent tariff schedules.

Fitzgerald was responsible not only for Herschell Island, but also for an area covering about 40,000 square miles. He was, in addition to being the senior police officer, the health inspector, customs agent, diplomat, and eventually even mining inspector. He had two constables to assist him, but no communication with the outside world besides the annual patrol from Dawson City via Fort McPherson. Fitzgerald, therefore, had to make decisions concerning laws and regulations on his own. That involved everything from settling disputes between white whalers and Natives, to being on the lookout for a suspected murderer. As always, Fitzgerald carried out his duties capably and efficiently, winning the praise of his superior officers. In 1910, while visiting his mother in Nova Scotia, he received the news that he had been promoted to the rank of inspector, which is the equivalent of a lieutenant.

Soon after he returned to Herschel Island that year, Fitzgerald received orders to command the Dawson City to Fort McPherson patrol. This was the first — and only — time that the patrol would be done in reverse, from Fort McPherson to Dawson. Fitzgerald had all the qualifications to lead the expedition. He was a tough, smart officer, with years of hard Arctic experience and a genuine affinity for life in the wild. Moreover, he had been over part of the trail once already. In the winter of 1905–06, on a return journey to Herschel Island, he had been with Harry Mapley's second patrol. This was the patrol that had taken the longest time to complete, because Mapley diverged from the established route. He went southeast from Dawson to Mayo, then cut north and joined the original trail at the confluence of the Wind and Little Wind rivers. The journey certainly enhanced Fitzgerald's wilderness experience, but the use of the different route would cause him confusion five years later.

December 21, 1910, was an ominously dismal day as the Mountie patrol prepared to leave Fort McPherson. The temperature was -21°F (-29°C), and a strong north wind was blowing. Three sleds, each with a five-dog team, were drawn up in front of the Hudson's Bay trading post. The bulk of the cargo on the sleds was food: mostly moose meat, caribou meat, bacon, and fish. On the trail, men and dogs alike had to consume enormous amounts of food (especially fatty food) to keep up body heat in the face of the brutal cold. The Mounties heading out on long patrols usually took enough food for thirty days, but they always expected to shoot game along the way and buy meat from Natives whom they met on the trail. The loads on the sleds also included extra clothing (especially spare mukluks, socks, and mittens), a tent, sleeping bags, cooking utensils and other camping gear, candles, tobacco, and a .30-30 carbine.

One of the men travelling with Inspector Fitzgerald was ex-constable Sam Carter, age forty-one. Carter had joined the Mounties just a few weeks before Fitzgerald, and had retired from the force earlier that year. Carter had been part of the 1906–07 patrol from Dawson City to Fort McPherson, and was now Fitzgerald's official guide. However, Carter had never made the trip from Fort McPherson to Dawson, and there were crucial differences in going in the opposite direction that could cause confusion.

Fitzgerald had decided not to take any Natives, in spite of it being proven repeatedly that even the very best white woodsmen could not equal the skill of the Loucheux guides. In addition to his trust in Carter, Fitzgerald had a map that had been drawn for him by Special Constable Hubert Darrell, who had been over the trail twice. However, the map was missing some essential details. Darrell was an almost legendary northerner who had walked from the shores of Hudson Bay to the Beaufort Sea. Ironically, he would later mysteriously vanish without a trace, somewhere near the mouth of the Anderson River.

The other two constables in Fitzgerald's company were Richard O'Hara Taylor and George Francis Kinney. Taylor, twenty-eight, was a Scot and a former White Star Line ship's officer. He had been with the Mounties since 1905. American born Kinney, twenty-seven, had served with the American army in Cuba during the Spanish-American War, and then spent four years with the infantry in the Philippines. He had cowboyed around the American West for a while before joining the MWMP in 1907. Neither Taylor nor Kinney had much Arctic experience.

Having four men and three sleds meant that one man would always be free to walk ahead and break trail. Usually the first few miles of a long trip were relatively easy, because of trails already broken by other traffic in and out of the settlement. Fitzgerald's men had tough going right from the start, because there had recently been heavy snows and no trappers had been going into or out of Fort McPherson. Patrols leaving from the Dawson City end of the trail would have a horse and sleigh break trail for the first fifty miles or so. The men leaving from Fort McPherson did not have that luxury.

Fitzgerald's patrol was doomed, but because the inspector kept a diary, we know what happened out on the trail. The teams made a respectable fifteen miles on the first day, in spite of mist off the Peel River that limited visibility. The men spent the first night in an abandoned cabin. The troublesome mist continued for the second day, but the men covered eighteen miles before stopping to make camp.

Over the next couple of days the patrol made good time, in spite of a heavy snowfall. On Christmas morning they reached a cache of fish that had been placed for them by the Trail River. The temperature dropped to -30°F (-34°C), but the going was easier because a party of Natives had gone ahead of them and broken the trail.

On December 26, the Mounties met a band of Native families and camped with them. These people told Fitzgerald he was on the wrong trail. Fitzgerald hired a man named Esau George to guide the patrol across the portage that would take them back to the Peel River. With George leading, and the rest of the Natives following, the Mounties spent the next few days slogging through extremely deep snow that exhausted the dogs. On New Year's Day they reached a cabin on Mountain Creek, four miles from the Peel River. The temperature had dropped to -51°F (-46°C).

Fitzgerald would have been wise to keep George on as a guide all the way to Dawson City. His patrol had actually been lost when it encountered the Natives. They still had almost 300 miles to go, and were already well behind schedule. At that point the sensible decision might have been to return to Fort McPherson, but Fitzgerald felt that the worst of the trip was behind them. He still had faith in Carter, and in his own knowledge of the trail from five years earlier. He paid Esau George $24 for his services, and the Natives went their own way.

For the next few days, strong winds, deep snow, and difficult terrain slowed Fitzgerald's patrol. The temperature continued to drop, so that -51°F was not the daily low, but the average. This was cold that was not just uncomfortable, it could kill! Cold of that intensity caused the moisture in a man's breath to freeze on his face, trees to burst with a sound like gunshots, and the steel head of an axe to shatter like glass. For a man guiding a dogsled, the mist from the breath of the labouring animals could block visibility as effectively as a blanket of fog. The fierce winds that Fitzgerald's men frequently encountered blew away the mist, but the wind chill reduced the temperature to -110°F (-79°C).

After a horrific week, in which they endured weather conditions worse than any previous patrol had experienced, Fitzgerald's men camped six miles below the confluence of the Wind and Little Wind rivers. They had made only nine miles that day, and the temperature had sunk to -64°F (-53°C). Then nature played a cruel trick.

On January 9, the temperature shot up to a balmy -22°F (-30°C). Once again, Fitzgerald thought the worst was over. The trail ahead would be better, and even though food was running low, they would soon enter a timber belt where they could find moose and caribou. Or so Fitzgerald hoped!

For the next three days, as the men travelled up the Little Wind River, the relatively mild weather continued, though a strong wind made the going tough for the dogs. The next important link on the trail was a stream that is now called Forrest Creek. Because the entire Little Wind River was in overflow, Fitzgerald and Carter missed the mouth of that stream.

At midday on January 12, the men stopped for lunch. Fitzgerald sent Carter to look for the creek, not realizing it was at least eight miles behind them. When Carter could not find the stream, Fitzgerald made a fatal decision. Instead of facing the fact that once again they were lost, he chose to go on, rather than turn back. The patrol now had enough food for nine days.

They travelled up the Little Wind River until it became so small that Fitzgerald finally knew that they had passed Forrest Creek. He and his men now began a fruitless search up and down the Little Wind and its tributaries, looking for the trail. On Friday, January 13, with the temperature at a beautiful -12°F (-24°C), they came upon a stream that Carter though was Forrest Creek. They went four miles up the stream, before concluding that it was the wrong one. The men mushed their teams back to the Little Wind and made camp. They were about seven miles upstream from the creek they were now desperate to find.

On January 14, gale force winds kept the men in camp. Another day lost, and more of the dwindling food supply consumed. The following day, with the temperature now dipping to -39°F (-39°C), they pushed sixteen miles up another stream before they realized they were mistaken again. The frustrating search continued the next day, when the men went six miles up yet another nameless stream. The temperature dropped to -43°F (-41°C).

By January 17, Fitzgerald knew that his patrol was in serious trouble. The temperature had risen to -23°F (-30°C), but gale force winds once again shrieked down on them. Even so, the men could not afford to waste time sitting in the shelter of their camp. Their food supply was now dangerously low. The men went out in different directions to search for the trail. They didn't find it. Fitzgerald wrote in his diary that they were down to ten pounds of flour, eight pounds of bacon, and some dried fish. He had decided to turn back to Fort McPherson. "My last hope is gone," he wrote. At the end of this entry he added, "I should not have taken Carter's word that he knew the way from the Little Wind River." One can only wonder what other words were spoken between Fitzgerald and Carter that were not recorded in the diary.

On January 18, the men began the journey back to Fort McPherson. They knew they were in a race with death, and that a determined effort and large measure of good fortune would be necessary for them to win that race. The effort was certainly there, but fortune had turned its back on them. The men encountered no Natives or white trappers who might share food with them. There was no game for them to shoot. The men hoped they would have a relatively easy time travelling on their back trail: the trail that they had already broken through the snow. Back trails were sometimes visible for weeks, but the Mounties found that for most of their route heavy snowfalls had obliterated their back trail. That meant that the trail had to be broken all over again, taking precious time.

On the night of January 18, the Mounties killed and ate one of their dogs. They tried to feed some of the meat to the other dogs, but the animals would not eat it. The next day they killed another dog, and this time the dogs ate the meat. The men would continue butchering and eating their dogs until there were only five left.

If the mild weather had stayed with them, the men might have had a chance. On January 20, a gale blew up, bringing a wind chill factor of -50°F (-45°C). On January 22, the temperature plunged to -64°F (-53°C). The day after that, strong winds made travel impossible. When the temperature did rise, heavy mist reduced visibility so much that the men could not travel for fear of wandering away from the trail.

Dog meat provides poor nourishment. Fitzgerald and his men weakened and probably began to suffer the effects of scurvy. They lost weight and were affected by frostbite. Skin began to peel from their faces. As inevitably happens when mental capacity is worn down by physical privation, accidents began to happen. On January 24, as the patrol struggled along the Wind River, Carter and Taylor broke through the ice and were soaked from the waist down. In such bitter cold, getting wet was like the kiss of death. The men had to stop and build a fire so the two could dry out. Days later, Fitzgerald himself went through the ice. One of his feet froze before the men could start a fire.

As the ailing, starving Mounties drove their dogs on, and sought the strength to just keep putting one foot in front of the other, it must have seemed as though every devil the Arctic hell could summon was laying in wait for them. Rivers that should have been frozen over were open, forcing long, time-consuming detours. The men became ill after eating a dog's liver, and had to keep walking even as they doubled over with retching. They came across an abandoned prospector's tent, but there was no cache of food.

On February 3, Fitzgerald's men reached the Trail River after an ordeal that would have paled the hearts of the Mountie recruits in Regina. Forty-five days had passed since they'd left Fort McPherson. They still had to cover one hundred miles of ice and snow to get back there. Fitzgerald thought they could make it, if only the weather would be good to them. It wasn't.

The temperature stood at -26°F (-32°C) when the men started down the Trail toward the Peel, but it quickly dropped to -52°F (-46°C). The Mounties and the last few dogs dragged themselves the last miles to the Peel River. There, about seventy miles from Fort McPherson, they lost the race with death. Fitzgerald made the last entry in his diary on February 5.

On February 20, Esau George and his group arrived in Dawson City. He told RNWMP Superintendent A.E. Snyder about guiding the Fitzgerald patrol back in December. He said the Mounties were lost when he met them, having somehow strayed from the established trail.

The Fitzgerald patrol was already long overdue, and this news from Esau George increased Snyder's concern. However, he could not send out a search party without permission from headquarters in Regina. The Canadian telegraph line was down, so Snyder had to route his message through the American telegraph system. This took time, and Snyder did not receive authorization from Regina until February 27.

The following day, a relief patrol set out, led by Constable W.J.D. Dempster, and including Constable J.F. Fyfe, ex-Constable F. Turner, and a Native guide named Charles Stewart. Those men also experienced difficulties on the trail. They encountered overflowing rivers, and on the third day out Turner's feet were frostbitten, making the rest of the trip a painful ordeal for him.

Dempster was sure that Fitzgerald, an experienced Arctic traveler, had probably run into trouble and turned back to Fort McPherson. Nonetheless, he tried to make haste in case the patrol actually was in difficulty somewhere on the trail. On March 12, he found one of Fitzgerald's camps near the junction of the Wind and Little Wind rivers.

Over the next two days his patrol passed three more, no more than five miles apart. Dempster realized these were camps from Fitzgerald's outward journey, and the retreat back to Fort McPherson.

On March 16, the relief patrol came to a cabin by Mountain Creek. There they found a sled, dog harnesses, and other items that had been discarded. They also discovered the remains of a dog that had been slaughtered. This was the first evidence that Fitzgerald's men had run out of food.

As they continued to follow the trail of the Lost Patrol, Dempster's party could see that they were on a long detour instead of the established route. On March 20, they reached a cabin on the Peel River, about five miles below the mouth of the Trail. Inside they found two packages. One contained the official dispatches Fitzgerald had been carrying. The other was a thirty-pound bag of mail. There was also a pile of dog bones on the floor.

As Dempster's patrol continued down the Peel the next day, they found more evidence that, bit by bit, told the story of a tragedy; an abandoned tent and stove, cast off dog harnesses, and, finally, another abandoned sled. Then Dempster saw a blue kerchief tied to a willow on the riverbank. He walked over to it and saw the remains of a small camp. A camp kettle contained scraps of moosehide (used for ground lashings on sleds) that someone had evidently tried to cook.

Nearby were two bodies; George Kinney and Richard Taylor. It was evident that Kinney had died first, because his hands were carefully folded across his chest. Taylor had shot himself with the carbine. His face was unrecognizable. There was no sign of Fitzgerald or Carter. Dempster guessed that the two younger men had been unable to go on, so the older men had left them in hope of making it to Fort McPherson and sending back help.

The relief patrol covered the bodies with brush, and then hurried down the trail, hoping against hope that they might find Fitzgerald and Carter still alive. On March 22, at a site just twenty-five miles from Fort McPherson, they came upon the two men — dead! Carter's hands were folded across his chest, and his face was covered with a handkerchief. Fitzgerald had performed this last act of dignity before he had expired. In

Fitzgerald's pocket there was a scrap of paper, on which he had written his will with a piece of burnt wood, bequeathing all he owned to his mother in Halifax. All four men probably died between February 12 and 15, 1911.

The bodies were taken to Fort McPherson and buried in a common grave with full military honours. Constable Dempster returned with his patrol to Dawson City, making the trip in a record nineteen days. He reported the disaster to Superintendent Snyder, who broke the news to the outside world.

The story of the Arctic tragedy made dramatic headlines around the world, and not all of the newspaper accounts were accurate. One said the men had been killed in a snowslide. Ironically, the four deceased Mounties had been chosen to be among the officers representing the RNWMP at the coronation of King George V that summer.

The story of the Lost Patrol has become an enigmatic legend of the Canadian North; a tragedy that should not have happened. Much of the blame has fallen on Inspector Fitzgerald. He should have taken along Native guides, say his detractors. He should have turned back earlier, but didn't because he was too proud and stubborn. Others hold Carter responsible for getting the patrol lost in the first place.

However, some Arctic experts say that the patrol was poorly planned, and was bound for misfortune even before the men left Fort McPherson. Their food supply, mostly meat and flour, had no vitamin C content, leaving the men susceptible to the debilitating effects of scurvy. Four men were not enough for a three-sled patrol, as that left only one man at a time to do the exhausting job of breaking trail.

The patrol's single gun, a high-powered carbine, was good for bringing down moose and caribou. But to stalk large game a hunter would have had to get well away from the dogs, whose presence frightened animals off. Fitzgerald did not have a man to spare to send on hunting sorties. A small gauge shotgun, a light caliber rifle like a .22, and snares would have enabled the men to supplement their food supply with small game, such as rabbits and birds. The men of the Lost Patrol had neither light guns nor snares.

The RNWMP learned valuable, if costly, lessons from the horrific fate of the Lost Patrol. Future patrols were always accompanied by

Native guides. Food caches were established at key points along the trail. The route between Fort McPherson and Dawson City was blazed so thoroughly that the greenest Mountie recruit could have followed it. New men underwent a two-week training course at Dawson City before leaving for Fort McPherson. The tragedy of the Lost Patrol was not repeated.

8

JULES FORTIN AND DANIEL O'CONNELL: A BAG OF RUBBER BOOTS

At just about any other time, a double police murder in a major Canadian city would merit banner headlines on the front pages of newspapers. But on May 9, 1910, the death of King Edward VII on May 6, and the succession of King George V, had pushed everything else to the inside pages. Nonetheless, the slaying of two Montreal police officers stunned the country; and the cause of the tragedy was a bag of stolen rubber boots.

Timothy Candy, thirty-seven, was a Liverpool Irishman who had come to Canada in hope of finding a better future than what was available to him in England. He had left his wife and children in Liverpool, and expected to send for them when circumstances permitted. Two weeks before the incident that would change his life forever, Candy was hired as a watchman in the warehouse of the Ames-Holden Company, which manufactured rubber boots. His position required him to carry a revolver.

Candy decided to supplement his income by helping himself to the stock in the warehouse. He stole six pairs of boots (total value $18) and went around to stores trying to sell them. On the evening of May 6, he was in a second-hand shop on St. James Street, trying to convince proprietor James Cowan to buy the boots. At the same time, an off-duty policeman,

Constable Daniel O'Connell, was taking a stroll along St. James. He was not in uniform and was not armed.

Cowan suspected that the boots were stolen, and did not want to buy them. Candy left the store, and Cowan followed him, intending to go to another shop to buy a cigar. He was an eyewitness to what happened next.

When Candy left the shop he came face to face with O'Connell, a five-year veteran of the Montreal Police Department, who was immediately suspicious of a man carrying a bag full of boots. The constable asked Candy where he got the boots, and was not satisfied with the answer. He took Candy by the arm and said he would have to go with him to Number Six Station, which was a short distance away. Candy resisted, and the two began to struggle.

Just then, Constable Jules Fortin passed by on the St. James streetcar. Fortin was in uniform, but was not armed because he was just returning to Number Six Station from an errand. Fortin had been with the department only ten months. He had recently been off work with an injury, after a man he was arresting slashed his arm with a broken bottle. Now he saw a fellow officer having difficulty with a suspect. Fortin jumped off the streetcar to assist his colleague.

With two policemen to contend with, Candy seemingly gave up the struggle. He started off with them, toward the station house. Neither officer had searched him for weapons. They had reached Chanoillez Street, when Candy suddenly pulled his revolver and pointed it at the officers. There was a scuffle in which Candy lost his hat. He fired a shot, putting a bullet into Fortin's brain and killing him instantly. Candy fired again and O'Connell collapsed with a slug in his stomach. Candy fled the scene, leaving behind his hat and the bag of rubber boots.

A Sergeant Chartrand was sitting at his desk in Number Six Station when he heard two gunshots. He rushed out immediately, calling other officers as he did so. He came upon the scene of the shooting and found twenty-five-year-old Jules Fortin already dead, and Daniel O'Connell, thirty-one, seriously wounded. Several people had seen the shooting and gave the police a description of the suspect: a short, thick-set man with a heavy grey-brown moustache, wearing a gray shirt. O'Connell was taken to Notre Dame Hospital where he died on May 9. He was able to tell police what had happened and describe the man who had shot him and Fortin. O'Connell left a wife and seven children. Fortin was unmarried.

After shooting the two policemen, Candy hurried to the Ames-Holden warehouse and punched the time clock at 9:26 p.m. This was about five minutes after the shooting, and nineteen minutes before his starting time of 9:45. Candy hoped that his punched time card would provide him with an alibi. When his shift was over, he told his employer that he was quitting his job. He said he'd had a message from his wife; she was ill and wanted him to return to Liverpool.

The following day, newspaper coverage of the crime included a description of the boots that the killer had been trying to sell. Someone at the Ames-Holden Company read it, and realized that the boots were their merchandise. A quick inspection of the warehouse revealed that some stock was missing. The manager informed the police.

Officers went to the company to question employees. They were told of Timothy Candy, who had punched in minutes after the shooting, had been in possession of a gun, and who had suddenly quit. Employees identified the hat the police had found at the crime scene as his.

The police found Candy at his boarding house. He seemed very nervous when they questioned him, and he could not give a satisfactory account of his whereabouts the previous evening. Then, to the officers' astonishment, Candy's landlady reported that he had told her all about the shooting. Later, several second-hand shop owners identified Candy as the man who had tried to sell them a bag full of rubber boots.

Candy wasn't in custody for long before he made a full confession. He said he had not intended to shoot the constables. He claimed that he had pulled the revolver to scare the officers so that he'd have a chance to escape. The shot that killed Fortin, Candy said, was an accident. The gun had just gone off. Then O'Connell tried to take the gun away from him, and it discharged again. Candy's tearful explanation that the whole thing had been accidental did not sway the coroner's jury at an inquest held on May 10. They reached the following verdict:

> We find that Jules Fortin died in the city of Montreal
> on the 6th May, instant, from a bullet wound at the

hands of Timothy Candy, and Daniel O'Connell died on the 9th of May also from a bullet wound inflicted upon him by the same Timothy Candy, who is to be held criminally responsible.

Candy was tried on September 12, and found guilty. He was sentenced to hang on November 18. There was no recommendation of mercy from the jury. Ironically, Daniel O'Connell's widow made a plea for the life of her husband's killer. She said she did not want Candy's wife and children to endure the kind of loss she and her children had suffered. Mrs. O'Connell considered it her Christian duty to request that the death sentence be commuted to life imprisonment. Ottawa did not agree.

On the morning of November 18, Timothy Candy walked to the gallows in the yard of the Montreal jail, maintaining what the press described as "a wonderful composure." This would be Montreal's last public hanging. Fifty people had official invitations to the execution, but from beyond the jail walls about five hundred people looked on from windows and rooftops. Newspaper columnists lamented that many of these were "women and children of tender years."

Hangman Arthur Ellis made a quick, clean job of it. Candy was pronounced dead ten minutes after he dropped. The case remains tragically unique in the annals of Canadian crime. Three deaths, over a bag of stolen rubber boots!

9

VANCOUVER POLICE ———————
DEPARTMENT: THREE HEROES

In the history of the Vancouver Police Department, eleven officers have been killed by gunfire. All of the deaths have been tragic, and all of the stories deserve to be told. The three that appear in this chapter have been chosen for specific reasons. One of the murders resulted in a double hanging, one of the officers was a Victoria Cross recipient, and one of the victims was a Chief of Police.

Constable James Archibald: Two for the Gallows

On July 29, 1912, a convict named Herman Clark escaped from California's Folsom Prison, where he'd been serving a twelve-year stretch for burglary. Clark was the son of a lawyer and grandson of a judge, but had made up his mind that he preferred living on the wrong side of the law. He fled California for Seattle, and eventually made his way across the border to Vancouver. Clark became involved in a drug-smuggling operation, which was probably how he met local hoodlums Frank Davis, William Hamilton, and Joseph "Blackie" Seymour. With his new partners, Clark went back to his old stock-in-trade: burglary.

Vancouver Police Constable James Archibald was shot three times at point-blank range while arresting two suspected burglars. His killers were hanged.

The gang pulled several robberies. Then, on the night of May 27, 1913, Clark and Davis broke into the office of the Hastings Shingle Mill on Powell Street. They stole a small amount of money and some other property. The two thieves left the building and were crossing a vacant lot on their way to Blackie Seymour's shack, when Clark stopped to light a cigarette. The flame of the match caught the attention of a police officer walking a beat alone.

Constable James Archibald, twenty-seven, had been with the Vancouver police for a year and a month. Due to a sudden outbreak of burglaries in the neighbourhoods he patrolled, he'd been advised to keep a sharp eye for anything suspicious. At about 1:30 a.m. on the morning of May 28, he saw a flash of light in a vacant lot. Archibald shone his flashlight and saw two men. He approached them with his revolver drawn and asked what they were doing there at such a late hour. Clark said they were just looking for a place to sleep. That answer didn't satisfy Archibald, so he decided to search the suspects.

In order to frisk the men, Archibald put his gun back in its holster. He patted Clark down first, and immediately found a small crowbar known as a "jimmy," a tool commonly used by burglars to break into homes and businesses. Constable Archibald knew at once that the two were criminals. He reached for his gun again, but it was too late. Clark and Davis were also armed. One (or both) of them shot Archibald three times at point-blank range, killing him on the spot.

At first the murderers panicked and ran away. Then they returned to get rid of the evidence. They dumped the body in some bushes, after taking the constable's gun and flashlight. These they hid in a mud hole, along with their burglar tools. However, they carelessly left behind a homemade, black cloth mask.

The following morning when Constable Archibald did not report in to his station, the police began a search. After they found Archibald's body, a tip led two detectives named Levis and Tisdale to Blackie Seymour's shack. Inside they discovered the material from which the mask had been cut. Clark, Davis, Seymour, and Hamilton were all charged with murder.

Though Seymour and Hamilton had not been present when Archibald was killed, they could nonetheless be convicted as accomplices, carrying a possible death sentence. To save their own hides they agreed to give King's evidence, thus gaining immunity from prosecution. They also tipped the police on where to find Davis and Clark's guns.

The two accused were tried together before Justice Morrison on November 6. Each had been claiming all along that the other had done the shooting. They stuck to their stories at the trial. The jury found both men guilty, and Morrison sentenced them to hang on May 5, 1914.

The defence counsel immediately launched an appeal, partially based on a technicality. Judge Morrison had neglected to put on the traditional black cap before pronouncing the death sentence. The appeal was denied.

Officials still hoped that one of the condemned men would confess to the shooting, because there was a chance that the other man would have his sentence commuted to life imprisonment. However, Clark and Davis each insisted to the bitter end that the other man was the killer. Hangman Arthur Ellis executed them together at the New Westminster Gaol on the appointed day. The truth was lost forever on the gallows. Clark's body was shipped to his mother in California. Davis's family would not claim his remains, so the body was buried in an unmarked pauper's grave in Vancouver's Chinese Cemetery.

The Vancouver *Daily Province* published a poem, "James Archibald — Hero, Vancouver Police Force," by an anonymous author honouring the slain constable. Its literary merit may be suspect, but there can be no doubt that the spirit in which it was composed reflected the feelings of the community for a police officer who had been senselessly murdered.

A wreath for "James Archibald-Hero of Peace"
Who answered when "Duty" did call-
For a moment the tumult of Vancouver cease-
As in Silence we follow his pall.
Then! — a cheer for our policemen — their children
and wives,
Of such men our Vancouver is proud.
When "Duty" doth need it, they'll give up their lives
For the careless and confident crowd.

Malcolm MacLennan: Fallen Chief

On Prince Edward Island only one police officer has been killed in the line of duty: Constable George B. Mullally, of the University of Prince Edward Island Security Police, was killed in a car accident in 1973. But another native of Prince Edward Island became Chief Constable (Chief of Police) on the other side of the country, in Vancouver. He was one of the few Canadian police officers to reach such a high position and then

Courtesy Sgt. Stephen Gibson, Vancouver Police Museum

lose his life in the line of fire.

Malcolm MacLennan arrived in Vancouver around 1897. He joined the police department in 1901, and rose steadily through the ranks "by sheer merit," as one newspaper account put it. In 1914 he became Chief of the Vancouver Police Department, a force of 250 personnel in a city of one hundred

Vancouver Police Chief Malcolm MacLennan was an advocate for such enlightened ideas as the establishment of a drug addiction treatment centre. He was killed in a shootout with a man reputed to be a "dope fiend."

thousand. MacLennan was described as, "a man of huge stature, and generous as he was big. He sympathized always with the underdog, and was a constant advocate of the 'second chance.'"

MacLennan was indeed a police chief whose ideas were very liberal for the time. In his day, policemen were expected to work seven days a week. MacLennan gave his men two days a month off. He also worked to get them a raise in pay. At that time, police wages were notoriously low, making officers targets for corruption.

Of course, Chief MacLennan's work on their behalf made him very popular with his men. But his enlightened policies went beyond labour issues. MacLennan was the first Vancouver police chief to accept a person from a visible minority onto the force. A Japanese Canadian named Raiichi Shirokawa joined the department in 1917. Unfortunately, the Japanese community suspected him of being a police spy and pressured him into quitting.

MacLennan also argued for the establishment of a drug treatment centre in Vancouver. At that time people with narcotics problems were called "dope fiends" and were regarded as criminals. This was not only because they often stole to feed their addictions, but also because the very act of being addicted was seen as a chosen form of anti-social behaviour. MacLennan believed these people would benefit more from medical aid than from jail, but the nineteenth century attitude that alcoholism and drug addiction were symptoms of weak moral character prevailed, and MacLennan's arguments were ignored. Ironically, one of the "dope fiends" who MacLennan wanted to help would seal his fate.

Bob Tait, an American, and his prostitute girlfriend Frankie Russell, were both known to the Vancouver police as drug addicts. The police would have taken a dim view of the fact that Tait was black and Russell was white. In those days there was little tolerance for mixed-race relationships.

Tait and Russell lived in an apartment above a grocery store at 522 E. Georgia Street. On March 20, 1917, their landlord, Frank King, went to the apartment and demanded four months back rent that they owed him. Tait threatened King with a shotgun, swearing he would blow King's brains out. At least, that was the story that King told the police when he called them. Frankie Russell would later claim that King and a hired thug had barged into the apartment and were the first ones to utter threats.

Detective Ernest Russell (no relation to Frankie), and Constables John Cameron and Duncan Johnston responded to King's call. Accompanied by King, they went to the apartment door, knocked and called to Tait to open up. Without warning, Tait fired a shotgun blast through the door's window. The four men were sprayed with buckshot, shattered glass, and wood splinters. Russell received facial wounds, but was not seriously injured. King and Cameron each had eye injuries that resulted in permanent partial blindness.

The policemen and the landlord quickly withdrew to the street. They flagged down a passing car whose driver took the wounded to hospital. Russell dashed to the nearest police phone box and called for help.

Before police could secure the area, Tait began shooting indiscriminately from an upstairs window. In addition to the shotgun, he was armed with a rifle and a pistol. One of his bullets struck eight-year-old George Robb. The boy died within an hour of reaching hospital. According to the newspaper reports, he had been on his way to the grocery store to buy candy.

Police soon surrounded the building. Tait refused to come out and surrender, putting the officers in a stand-off situation. They decided to send for Chief MacLennan, who had taken the day off to host a birthday party for his ten-year-old son.

As soon as he was notified of the situation, MacLennan hurried to the scene. He made the fatal decision to storm the apartment in which Tait had barricaded himself. Ordinarily, the Chief of a large city police department is not expected to place himself in the line of fire, but MacLennan held to the principle that he would not send his constables into a dangerous situation that he would not risk himself.

MacLennan led the assault on the apartment, armed with a large fire-axe to chop through the door. He did not have a gun. When the police gained entry to the apartment, they found themselves in a darkened room. The darkness was instantly split by flashes of gunfire as Tait, who had fortified himself in a bedroom, opened fire on them.

A fierce gunbattle erupted, as the police returned fire with their revolvers. But Tait was too well-protected in his improvised bunker. The officers ran out of ammunition and had to retreat again. When they reached the street, they realized to their horror that Chief MacLennan was not with them.

By this time, Malcolm MacLennan, age forty-four, lay dead on the apartment floor, with part of his skull blown away. His men did not know that. They hoped he had only been wounded, and was still alive. In those days it was not uncommon for police to use dynamite to force a gunman out of a barricaded position, but in this case the officers were concerned about MacLennan.

For the next four hours, police sharpshooters sniped at the windows to keep Tait down. Officers tried to rush the apartment again to rescue the chief, but Tait's gunfire drove them back, though there were no further casualties. In one of the exchanges Tait was wounded. After a while, Tait's rate of fire diminished as he used up his supply of bullets and shells. Officers were finally able to get back into the apartment and remove MacLennan's body.

The police were about to use sulphur pots to smoke Tait out of his hole, when they heard one more shot. Tait had committed suicide with a shotgun blast to the head. It was just past 11:00 p.m. Over a hundred shots had been fired. About twenty minutes later, Frankie Russell surrendered, unhurt, after the police threatened to use dynamite if she didn't come out. She would face charges as Bob Tait's accomplice, but would escape being sent to jail or the gallows as an accessory to murder. Chief Malcolm MacLennan, a son of Prince Edward Island, was given a hero's funeral in Vancouver, thousands of miles from his birthplace.

Constable Robert McBeath: Twice the Hero

Robert McBeath was born in Kinlockbervie in Sutherlandshire, Scotland. He was only sixteen years old in August 1914, when the Great War broke out, but he lied about his age and joined a Scottish regiment, the Seaforth Highlanders. Three years later, at the age of nineteen, he was a battle-hardened veteran with the rank of Lance-Corporal.

On November 20, 1917, the Seaforth Highlanders were engaged at Cambrai, France, in the bloody Battle of the Somme. The Highlanders' advance had been bogged down under the murderous fire of several German machine gun nests, and the Scots were taking heavy casualties. McBeath volunteered to silence the enemy guns.

Single-handedly, armed with only a Lewis gun (a type of machine gun) and a revolver, McBeath attacked the first machine gun emplacement and killed every man in its crew. Then, under the covering fire of a tank, he knocked out four more machine gun nests, one-by-one. The German soldiers thought they were being attacked by a large British force, and hastily withdrew to the security of a dugout. Heedless of his own safety, McBeath went in after them. One German soldier showed fight, and McBeath shot him dead. The rest, three officers and thirty soldiers, surrendered to Lance-Corporal McBeath.

Robert McBeath was awarded the Victoria Cross for his heroic actions, becoming one of the youngest men to receive the British Empire's highest military honour. When he returned home from the war he was given a hero's welcome. His neighbours presented him with a silver tea service, and the Duke of Sutherland gave him the title to a farm.

McBeath was grateful for these honours, but he decided that Canada held better prospects for the future. He sold the farm, and he and his new bride, Barbara MacKay, emigrated in February 1918. They went to Vancouver, where McBeath joined the British Columbia Provincial Police. A few months later he transferred to the Vancouver Police Department.

In the early morning of October 9, 1922, McBeath was on Granville

Courtesy Sgt. Stephen Gibson, Vancouver Police Museum

Vancouver Police Constable Robert McBeath in the uniform of the Seaforth Highlanders. The Scottish-born recipient of the Victoria Cross survived the horrors of the First World War, only to be gunned down by a drunk driver on Vancouver's Granville Street.

Street in downtown Vancouver, with Detective R.S. Quirk. The tragic events of that autumn night were later related by Quirk to a reporter for the Vancouver *Sun*.

> It was about 02:30 hours when Constable McBeath and I were at Granville and Davie Streets. We conversed for a few minutes when our attention was attracted by the loud honking of an auto horn and the erratic manner in which the car was swerving from curb to curb as it came north on Granville Street. McBeath went into the road and signalled the driver to stop but the driver attempted to avoid the officer and we both jumped onto the running boards. People in the car were Marjorie Earl and Fred Deal. We succeeded in getting him to stop the car and McBeath took the negro to the patrol box while I remained with the woman. I heard a sudden roar behind me and saw McBeath and the negro struggling. As I went to McBeath's aid I saw the flash of a gun. It was pointed directly at my breast but I swung it aside just as it went off and the bullet passed through my hand. A second shot struck me in the side of the head as I grappled with the man and I fell. There was another shot and McBeath fell on top of me. As I tried to crawl out from under McBeath the man who had moved off some distance fired again. I guess that was the bullet that went through the shoulder of my coat. I rolled McBeath on his back and fired at the negro. Then I followed him a little way and we again exchanged shots. I could not keep up and went back to McBeath.

Detective Quirk was able to stop a passing motorist, who took him and McBeath to St. Paul's Hospital. Within minutes of their arrival McBeath died from a bullet wound just below his heart. In a matter of hours, the police tracked down the gunman and arrested him. They also found the murder weapon, which he had discarded during his flight from the scene of the crime.

Fred Deal, the black man in custody, was a thirty-year-old railway porter who was originally from Florida. Marjorie Earl, who was passed out in the car from intoxication when the incident occurred, was a middle-aged white woman from Kentucky. She was known to Vancouver police as the keeper of a bawdy house. Deal had been living with her. She owned the car he had been driving, and the gun he had used to shoot the officers.

War veterans who had been decorated with the Victoria Cross were held in high esteem, so news of McBeath's murder made the front pages of major newspapers across Canada. His funeral was one of the largest in Vancouver history. Banks and stores were closed. Thousands of people turned out to watch the procession of pipe bands, civic dignitaries, policemen, firemen, war veterans, Masons, and members of Scottish-Canadian societies. McBeath's widow rode in a hearse. The open casket, draped in the Union Jack, was set out for public viewing at the Vancouver Police Station. At its foot was a wreath in the shape of the Victoria Cross. Robert McBeath went to his grave as a hero of the British Empire.

As far as most of the white citizens of Vancouver were concerned, Fred Deal was gallows bait. The fact that he was drunk when he killed McBeath would carry little weight with a jury. Only a few years had passed since the murder of Chief MacLennan at the hands of a black "dope fiend." White Vancouverites generally believed that black men like Fred Deal used dope to seduce white women like Marjorie Earl, though there was no evidence that Deal had ever used narcotics. On October 9, an editorial in the *Vancouver Daily World* stated: "If Vancouver were south of the Mason Dixon line there would be a lynching today." The author went on to state that even though British justice frowned upon lynch-law, Deal would "surely hang at the end of a hempen rope by due process of law, after his guilt has been formally established in court."

Mayor Charles E. Tisdall and Chief of Police James Anderson initiated a crackdown to "secure the conviction or deportation of idle and degenerate men and their paramours ... all vagrants of every description: poolroom loafers, drug fiends, bootleggers, and so on."

In a hastily arranged trial, held within a month of the shooting, Deal was convicted and sentenced to be executed on January 26, 1923. However, there were people in Vancouver, particularly in the black community, who believed that there were extenuating circumstances that the jury had not considered, and that racism had played a part in Deal's sentencing and conviction.

Among those demanding a re-trial was a black woman named Nora Hendrix. A former vaudeville dancer from Tennessee, Nora worked in Vancouver as a laundress. Her husband, Ross, had once been a "special constable" with the Chicago Police Department. Nora was the grandmother of the 1960s rock star Jimi Hendrix.

Nora Hendrix was a founder of the Fountain Chapel Church, which was the Vancouver chapter of the African Methodist Episcopal Church. Largely through the efforts of Nora and other church members, Fred Deal was granted another trial. Once again he was found guilty, but this time of the lesser charge of manslaughter. There was evidence that he had been beaten up while in police custody. There would be further allegations that he had pulled his gun because Constable McBeath and Detective Quirk were roughing him up. Deal was sentenced to life imprisonment. After sixteen years he was deported to Florida, where he died a few years later.

Exactly what happened that October night on Granville Street will probably never be known. Police officers of that period were often heavy-handed with drunks, and attitudes that we would now call racist certainly existed in police departments across Canada. We do not know what Robert McBeath's feelings toward racial minorities were. Nor do we know why Fred Deal was carrying a gun.

Robert McBeath's grave can be found in Vancouver's Mountain View Cemetery. On the monument, his name is misspelled; "MacBeath." A Vancouver Police marine vessel has been named the *R.C. McBeath VC* in his honour. In his hometown of Kinlochbervie, a housing development is named after him. Constable McBeath's Victoria Cross, and other medals, can be seen at the Regimental Museum of the Queen's Own Highlanders near Inverness, Scotland.

10

DEPUTY SHERIFF JAMES MCKAY: A HYPNOTIC SPELL

In the largely French Canadian region of Steep Creek on the North Saskatchewan River, about twenty-six miles east of Prince Albert, Saskatchewan, almost everybody was afraid of "Doctor" Joseph Gervais. Ever since August 1917, when he and his two teenaged companions moved into an isolated house overlooking the river, a reign of terror had existed in the district, which was still a wild place with no telephones and poor roads. Dr. Gervais, Victor Carmel, and Jean-Baptiste St. Germain (aged sixteen and eighteen when they arrived at Steep Creek) stole whatever they wanted. They carried guns wherever they went. A local man named James Sugar disappeared without a trace, and people were sure the Steep Creek Gang had something to do with it. Another man, Adolphe Lajoie, died when his cabin suddenly went up in flames. The police had investigated that fire, and decided that it was accidental, but the police didn't know about Dr. Gervais and the Steep Creek crime wave. People were afraid to tell them. They feared Gervais' hypnotic powers. Some even said he had the evil eye.

Gervais, Carmel, and St. Germain were all from Montreal. Gervais claimed to have studied hypnotism there and in Chicago. He also said he had used his powers to cure Carmel of tuberculosis. When the Canadian government passed the Military Service Act in 1917, which gave it the legal power to conscript men into the army, Gervais convinced Carmel and St. Germain to go west with him. He said the war in Europe had nothing to do with French Canadians, and the government couldn't draft them if it couldn't find them.

Gervais evidently intended to establish a hideout for draft-dodgers, who would make up a bandit gang with him as leader. In the spring of 1918, another teenager, Joseph DeFond of Shawinigan Falls, arrived at the Steep Creek lair. However, after a few months, young DeFond returned home, "in bad health, due, it is said, largely to the experiences he encountered with Gervais." It was later revealed that Gervais used Carmel "for the most disgusting immoral practices," leading to speculation about just what kind of "experiences" DeFond had suffered.

In the bluffs of the riverbank, Gervais had the young men dig an underground bunker and tunnels, as well as a series of "battlefield" type trenches. This, he said, was where all the young Quebecers who came west to escape conscription would hide. He had the bunker stocked with food, weapons, and ammunition.

Gervais was so certain of the local people's fear of him and his hypnotic powers that he was brazenly open about his robberies. On one occasion, Gervais went to the farm of a man named Phillips, about three miles from his own place, and shot a steer. Gervais then went to the home of his neighbour, Peter Desmoreaux, and told him to hitch up his wagon, go and load the carcass on it, and take it to Gervais' place. When Desmoreaux refused, Gervais pointed a gun at him and told him to do as he was told or be shot. A startled Desmoreaux cried, "Man, do you not see my wife is with me? Surely you would not shoot me!"

Gervais cursed and snarled that he would wipe out the whole family if Desmoreaux didn't obey. The frightened farmer quickly complied. The police wouldn't learn of this incident until much later.

Gervais decided that his gang needed a wagon, so he offered to buy the one Desmoreaux had, promising to pay him $150 for it. Desmoreaux probably thought he had no choice but to agree to the deal, and Gervais drove off in the wagon. But when some time passed and Gervais did not pay, Desmoreaux overcame his fear and made a complaint at the sheriff's office in Prince Albert. The sheriff gave a writ for $150 to

Deputy Sheriff James McKay to serve on Gervais. If Gervais did not pay the money, McKay would seize the wagon.

On Friday, November 15, 1918, McKay drove out to the Gervais house. He knew nothing about the draft dodgers. Gervais was not home when McKay arrived, but Carmel and St. Germain were watching from a dugout. When they saw a deputy sheriff get out of the car and start to walk toward the house, they immediately assumed he was coming to arrest them as draft dodgers. The boys drew their guns and fired. McKay staggered when he was hit. He grabbed hold of a tree to keep from falling. The gunmen fired again, and McKay fell to the ground. One of the boys walked over to the fallen deputy and told the other that the man was still breathing. His companion said to put another bullet into McKay to finish him off, which he did. McKay left a wife and a young daughter.

When Gervais returned and saw what had happened, he told the boys to dump the body in the river. Then he had them dig a hole big enough to bury McKay's car. They were not aware that Peter Desmoreaux's young son had been watching them, and had seen everything.

By Monday, when McKay had not returned home and had not reported for work, the sheriff's office notified the Saskatchewan Provincial Police. Sergeant Stanley Kistruck of the SPP headed for the Gervais place with a warrant and a posse that included several soldiers. Kistruck entered the house and found Gervais sleeping. He awakened him and began to question him about McKay. He also asked about the two young men, who were believed to be staying in his house. Gervais replied that McKay had not been on his property, and he knew nothing about two young men.

Meanwhile, Kistruck's men were searching the property. Corporal Charles Horsley, a soldier from Clinton, Ontario, approached the entrance of a dugout that was partially concealed by brush. Suddenly shots rang out. Horsley tumbled down a six foot embankment at the edge of the river. He was dead. A soldier and an SPP constable climbed down to retrieve the body.

Sergeant Kistruck was not certain how many gunmen were holed up in the dugout, or how well they were armed. He decided to go back to Prince Albert with Gervais in custody, and return with reinforcements. He left men behind to watch the dugout.

Kistruck returned the following day with a larger force. The men rushed the dugout, only to find it abandoned. It was stocked with guns and ammunition, and enough food to last three months. Kistruck was now certain that only two men had been in the dugout. He guessed that they must have slipped out during the confusion following the shooting of Horsley. The police questioned residents of the Steep Creek area and found that people were afraid to talk about Dr. Gervais. However, they did get an eyewitness account of McKay's murder from the boy who had seen it. They also unearthed McKay's car.

The search for Victor Carmel and Jean-Baptiste St. Germain ended at 10:30, on the morning of November 24, when police tracked them to the farm of Charles Young on the bank of the North Saskatchewan River, six miles east of Prince Albert. The fugitives, exhausted and starving, were hiding in a haystack. They had thrown away their rifles, but were still armed with handguns. Police officers surrounded the haystack and told the pair to surrender or they would open fire. The young killers crawled out of the hay and threw down their guns.

At first, the young desperadoes refused to say anything to the police. Then Carmel made a statement that would make the case unique in Canadian judicial history: He claimed that he and St. Germain committed the crimes while under Dr. Gervais' hypnotic influence.

At that time, hypnotism was widely believed to be a practice not far removed from the dark arts of the occult. Many people believed that an expert hypnotist could make an innocent person do almost anything. For that reason, the court decided to try Dr. Gervais and his young companions separately.

When Dr. Gervais went to trial in May 1919, his principal defence was that he had not shot anybody, and had not even been present when McKay was murdered. But there was no escaping the fact that he had strongly influenced the youths who did the shooting, had armed them and harboured them after McKay's murder. He had helped them try to conceal the crime, and he shared the blame for Corporal Horsley's murder because of his refusal to cooperate with Sergeant Kistruck. At one point during the trial, when his attorney asked him if he wanted to take the stand to testify in his own behalf, Gervais "simply stared in a dazed fashion at the lawyer and made no answer." On May 10, the jury took less than an hour to find him

Courtesy Saskatchewan Archives Board #R-B1566

Prince Albert Gaol, Prince Albert, Saskatchewan, circa 1905. "Doctor" Joseph Gervais, Victor Carmel, and Jean-Baptiste St. Germain were hanged here on October 17, 1919, for the murder of Deputy Sheriff James McKay.

guilty of being an accomplice to murder, which was punishable by death.

A week later, Carmel and St. Germain were tried. The notion that these young men had allegedly been under the hypnotic power of Dr. Gervais made the trial something of a sensation. But when it was all over, the members of the jury refused to accept the idea that a hypnotist could make an unwilling person commit murder. Trial judge Justice Brown broke down in tears as he sentenced Carmel and St. Germain to hang with Dr. Gervais.

With no hope of escaping the hangman, Dr. Gervais confessed that he and his companions had murdered Adolphe Lajoie, and then set fire to his cabin so that the death would appear to have been accidental. Gervais said he wanted Lajoie's land and when Lajoie wouldn't agree to sign it over to him, Carmel shot him in the head. Police exhumed Lajoie's bones and found a bullet hole in the skull.

Dr. Gervais tried to cheat the executioner by hanging himself in his cell with bedsheets, but the attempt failed. On October 17, 1919, Gervais, Carmel, and St. Germain were hanged together in the Prince Albert Gaol. The body of Deputy Sheriff James McKay was never recovered.

11

FRANK WILLIAMS: "THE ____ WAS GOING TO SHOOT ME"

In the third week of November 1918, Toronto was still euphoric over the end of the long, bloody conflict then known as the Great War. The fighting in Europe had ceased with the Armistice of November 11. The front pages of Toronto's major newspapers were crowded with stories about the surrender of German U-Boats to the Royal Navy, and the last Canadian soldiers to die in the final hours of the war. On November 20, however, the newspapers' editors had to make room on the front pages for a story unprecedented in Toronto's history; an account of the killing of a city policeman in the line of duty. No Toronto police officer had been slain while upholding the law since the city was incorporated in 1834. This story would turn out to be just the first chapter in a bizarre saga that finally ended on the gallows.

At age twenty-four, Acting Detective Frank Williams was the youngest detective in the Toronto Police Department, and one of the youngest officers on the force. A farm boy from the town of Clinton, Ontario, Williams had joined the department in October 1914, when he was just twenty. At that time, patriotic fervor was sweeping across Canada, and thousands of young men signed up for the Canadian Expeditionary Force. Many Toronto policemen left the force to do military service. Some,

Courtesy Metropolitan Toronto Police Museum

Acting Detective Frank Williams, right, was the first Toronto police officer to be slain in the line of duty since the city was incorporated in 1834. He was shot in November 1918, while arresting robbery suspect Frank McCullough.

like Williams, chose to remain at home. This had nothing to do with being faint-hearted. Constables were still needed to police Canadian streets. Criminals did not take a holiday just because there was a war on.

Frank Williams' fellow officers dubbed him "Noisy" because of his loud laugh. He became a popular figure with the newsboys, merchants, and other people he encountered every day. One of Williams' superior officers said he was a "remarkably keen constable." For most of his short career, Williams worked out of the Claremont Street station in Toronto's west end. On November 1, 1918, he was promoted to the rank of Acting Detective. The word "acting" meant that the promotion was a temporary one. Williams would have eventually had to relinquish the position to an officer returning from the war, since all policemen who had joined the army were guaranteed their old jobs back when they came home. Nonetheless, Williams got the promotion because he had shown what his superiors called "initiative and detective ability."

The sequence of events that would seal the fate of young Frank Williams began late in the afternoon of November 19, when two men who would later be identified as Frank McCullough and Albert Johnson, drove up to Madam May's clothing store at 372 College Street with a buggy load of clothing and furs. They tried to sell the goods to proprietor George May at prices he thought suspiciously low. Certain the merchandise had been stolen, May made up an excuse to go to the back of the store and then phoned the police station on Claremont Street.

The police had already received reports about stolen furs and clothing, and Acting Detective Williams was one of the officers looking for anyone trying to sell such goods. The call from George May was a break he'd been waiting for. Williams and Constable Walter McDermott got into the police department's "emergency car" and sped to 372 College. It was about 5:00 p.m.

When Williams and McDermott arrived at the clothing store, the suspects were gone. However, George May had recognized their buggy as a rental from Cross's Livery Stables, located on King Street, near the intersection with Bathurst. The two policemen hurried to the livery, hoping to catch the suspects when they returned the rig. McDermott parked the car across the street while Williams went inside.

William Cross, the owner, lived with his wife in a house next door to the stable. He was unhitching some horses in a laneway that separated the two buildings when Williams arrived. He told the detective that he had rented a buggy to two men, and they fit the description of the men who had been at Madam May's. They had not yet returned the rig. Williams said he would wait for them. Then he made the mistake that would cost him his life. He went across the road and sent Constable McDermott back to the station. Why Williams did that has never been satisfactorily explained. As a rookie detective, perhaps Williams wanted to impress the brass by bringing the culprits in single-handed.

William Cross thought it peculiar that Williams sent McDermott away. He told Williams that the suspects were "rather burley men for him to handle." He asked the officer if he was sure he wouldn't need help. Williams laughed and said if he needed help, he would call Cross. Then he went into the office at the back of the stable to await the suspects.

At 6:20 p.m., McCullough and Johnson pulled into the livery and stepped down from the buggy. Cross went out and engaged them in conversation. As the three were discussing the rental fee, Williams quietly came out of the office and approached them from behind. They did not know that Williams was there until he suddenly grabbed both by the collar, announced that he was a police officer and told them they were under arrest.

One of the suspects asked, "What's the fuss?" Williams hustled both men toward the office door and shoved them inside. According to Cross, the suspects went with Williams "as quietly as two children would go." After the detective and his prisoners disappeared into the dark office, Cross stayed outside to unhitch the horse from the buggy. A few minutes later he heard two or three shots.

Cross rushed into the office and saw Williams struggling with McCullough, who had a gun in his hand. When Johnson saw Cross he immediately bolted through another door, and was never seen again. That night a conductor found Johnson's coat and vest on a King Street streetcar.

McCullough had Williams pinned up against the wall. Williams had a grip on the wrist of McCullough's gun hand. In his other hand, Williams had a billy club, which he used to strike McCullough several times. Williams carried a gun, but had no opportunity to draw it.

As Cross looked on, the struggling men staggered out the door and onto the driveway, still grappling. Cross reported later, "They got out there, and were scuffling around back and forward, both were hanging on to one another. I could see a gun flying around."

Williams shouted to Cross to help him. Cross got behind McCullough, put an arm around his neck, and pulled him back. That gave Williams a chance to use his billy more effectively, and he struck McCullough hard on the head. McCullough sank to his knees, groaning, "I'm through." For a moment it seemed that the fight was over.

Suddenly, McCullough sprang to his feet and attacked Williams, warning Cross to stay away or he'd kill him. As McCullough and Williams grappled, Cross grabbed McCullough again. A shot rang out. Then two more. A bullet grazed the liveryman's wrist, leaving a welt. Cross managed to twist McCullough's arm, forcing him to drop the gun. Another blow from Williams' billy sent McCullough to the ground, on his hands and knees. Then Cross heard Williams gasp, "For God's sake get a doctor. I'm shot." Williams collapsed against the side of a wagon. Two bullets had pierced his chest, one of them severing an artery near his heart.

Mrs. Cross heard the shots and ran out of the house to get help. She saw Constable Henry Holmes at the intersection of King and Bathurst, directing traffic. Mrs. Cross shouted that there was a fight going on. Holmes jumped on his bicycle and raced to the livery stable as a small crowd gathered at the driveway entrance.

William Cross had a hold on McCullough, but when he saw that Williams had been shot, he released him so that he could run to his office and phone a doctor. Right away, McCullough leapt to his feet and ran down the driveway, right past the startled Holmes. When Cross saw McCullough make a run for it, he shouted, "That's the man! Get him!"

Holmes immediately began to chase McCullough on his bicycle as the suspect ran east along King toward the Bathurst intersection. A newsboy named Herbert Jenkins dashed across the street toward the commotion, and seemed to trip McCullough, sending him crashing to the ground. Before McCullough could recover, Holmes snapped handcuffs on him. Back at the livery, Frank Williams died as Mrs. Cross cradled his head in her arms. He was carried inside the stable where, a few minutes later, a doctor pronounced him dead.

With the help of a military policeman who happened upon the scene, Constable Holmes dragged his prisoner back to the livery. From Williams' body the constable took the detective's unfired automatic pistol. In the driveway he found the revolver that the suspect had dropped; five rounds had been fired. McCullough was sitting on the bumper of a truck, holding his battered head in his hands while the military policeman watched him closely. Holmes asked him why he had shot Williams. According to the *Toronto Globe* McCullough answered, "Well, he was arresting me and I shot him. The _____ was going to shoot me, but I shot him."

The following day, in a city still elated with the victorious end to the war, flags were at half mast in honour of the first Toronto policeman to fall in the line of duty. As arrangements were made for the body to be taken home to Clinton for burial, newspaper reporters wrote sensational accounts of the fight at the livery stable. Said the *Daily Star:*

> Acting Detective Williams met his death discharging his duty in one of the most courageous fights that a police officer was ever called upon to face. Although outnumbered two to one, and overpowered by two men much bigger in stature than himself, Williams proved himself to be a man, and with one bullet in his body, hung onto McCullough and wrestled with him until McCullough shook him off.

Herbert Jenkins was singled out for praise for using a "schoolboy trick" to trip up McCullough so that Holmes could nab him. The newsboy (who was actually a young man in his twenties) said that he hadn't really tried to interfere with McCullough, but had collided with him unintentionally. But even though he was an accidental hero, Jenkins was very much affected by the tragedy.

> Williams was quite a friend of mine. He spoke to me on his way down to the livery, saying that he was out on detective duties. I heard someone say that shots had been fired, but I knew nothing of what had happened until one of my newsboys came in and told me that a man had been shot down at the livery. I ran down at once, and to my horror saw that the victim of the tragedy was my friend. Detective Williams was dead when I arrived, and I was not able to sleep last night after seeing him lying dead in the livery kitchen.

By strange coincidence, about a year earlier a very similar crime had occurred. Acting Detective Jack Stewart had been shot (not fatally) on the City Hall steps while escorting two fur thieves to court. The suspects had been arrested in Madam May's clothing store.

The man now sitting in a Toronto jail facing a murder charge called himself Frank McCullough. His real name was Leroy Ward Fay Swart, and he had been born in the tiny community of Westville, New York, in 1892. At fourteen, Swart ran away from home. According to his own account, he fell in with tramps who taught him to steal. A burglary conviction landed him in the Missouri State Penitentiary. He was released in October 1914, about the same time that Frank Williams was joining the Toronto Police Department.

Swart enlisted in the United States Army. He would later tell a colourful yarn about being shot in the leg in Mexico during the U.S. Army's pursuit of Pancho Villa. In fact, Swart was stationed in Fort Adams at Newport, Rhode Island. On March 24, 1917, when it appeared certain the United States would be drawn into the war, he deserted. He fled to Canada, arrived

American hard case Frank McCullough was wanted by the United States Army for desertion at the time of his fatal encounter with Acting Detective Frank Williams.

Courtesy Metropolitan Toronto Public Library

in Toronto in early April, and adopted the alias of Frank McCullough.

For awhile McCullough worked at a munitions factory. Soon, however, he returned to his thieving ways. McCullough did a year in the Burwash Penitentiary for burglary and assaulting a constable with a whiskey bottle. He was paroled in June 1918. Canadian authorities were not yet aware that Frank McCullough was an American, with a criminal record in the United States.

In the few months between his release from Burwash and his fatal encounter with Detective Williams, McCullough did work at a few legitimate jobs, including that of bread deliveryman, but those jobs were just covers. McCullough had gone right back to burglary. He would break into any business that might have merchandise he could sell illegally: a furniture company, a cigar store, and a doctor's office, to name a few. He even rifled a railway car for a load of silk.

Around the beginning of November, McCullough met the young man he knew only as Albert Johnson. The pair went to Ottawa and looted a large number of coats and furs from a clothing store. They sent the merchandise by train to Toronto, and stored it in McCullough's boarding house at 177 Palmerston Avenue. His landlady, Mrs. Gladys Mytton, was apparently in cahoots with McCullough and Johnson. Following the shooting, she was arrested when police found more than $2,000 worth of stolen merchandise on her premises. The variety of items included in the loot indicated that Frank McCullough would steal just about anything. Stashed throughout the Mytton house were handkerchiefs, cigarettes, coats, silverware, ketchup, blouses, and underwear.

McCullough was first interviewed by Inspector George Kennedy and Detective Bartholomew Cronin. He said he was twenty-six years old and American by birth. Though the officers warned him that anything he said could be used against him in court, McCullough admitted to shooting Williams. However, he claimed the shooting was unintentional and an act of self-defence.

McCullough claimed he did not pull his gun until after Williams had started beating him on the head with a billy club. Furthermore, he said he was pleading temporary insanity. He said he had a tendency to lose control of himself when hit on the head. McCullough said the blows he had taken from Williams' billy had addled his brain and caused him to shoot.

McCullough admitted buying the gun from a trainman in Parry Sound for $20. He would give no information whatsoever on Albert Johnson, or anyone else connected with the burglaries or the sale of stolen goods. "I refuse to tell, because I am in trouble now," he said. "I am done for and it is no use getting another party ten years. I am no snitcher."

At the coroner's inquest McCullough was not represented by counsel, and had to question witnesses himself. There was a major contradiction between the testimonies given by William Cross and Constable Henry Holmes. Cross said he picked up McCullough's gun and Williams' billy club from the driveway and gave them to Holmes. However, Holmes said he found Williams' billy club in the detective's pocket. McCullough picked up on this discrepancy, which was clearly an error on Holmes' part, to emphasize his claim that Williams had been beating him. "I had no intention of shooting that man," he insisted.

Still, the statements McCullough had made to Kennedy and Cronin worked against him. Moreover, the fact remained that he had been carrying a gun. As far as the coroner's jury was concerned, a man with a criminal background did not put a loaded gun in his pocket unless he expected to use it. That, in their opinion, made the killing of Frank Williams premeditated murder.

Realizing that he was now officially bound over to be tried for murder, and would face the death penalty if convicted, McCullough suddenly lost any inhibitions about being a "snitcher." He confessed he had lied about buying the gun from a trainman in Parry Sound. He said he had actually bought it from a Toronto youth who had assisted him and Johnson in a burglary. The young man was promptly arrested.

McCullough then confessed to a string of burglaries in which he'd been involved. He took police to numerous locations where he had disposed of the swag, and helped to recover large quantities of stolen goods. All the while, McCullough was working his charm.

McCullough was a hoodlum, to be sure, but he had a charisma that seemed to make people like him. He was well-spoken, and he could spin an entertaining yarn. Before long, the very officers who held McCullough responsible for the slaying of their colleague were calling him by his first name, and telling reporters that he wasn't such a bad fellow, once you got to know him. In *No Tears to the Gallows,* the definitive study of the Frank Williams murder case, author Mark Johnson states: "It was McCullough's personality that was so subtly powerful and attractive. In the events that followed, he showed himself to be cocky but sensitive; reckless but thoughtful; brutal but polite; dangerous but affectionate." McCullough had a "consummate ability to manipulate others."

McCullough's case was taken by Thomas Cowper Robinette, a very successful criminal lawyer who agreed to defend McCullough *pro bono.* Robinette knew that the case would receive a lot of publicity and would be a challenge. The trial began on January 21, 1919. Justice Hugh Edward Rose presided. Peter White, K.C., prosecuted for the Crown.

Robinette fought hard to keep any mention of the robbery charges against McCullough out of the testimony, but without success. He damaged William Cross's credibility as a witness when he tripped him up on the matter of where Cross had been when the first shots were fired. Robinette suggested those shots could have been fired by Albert Johnson. The lawyer also revealed that Cross himself had a minor criminal record.

During his examination of Detective Bart Cronin, Robinette pounced on a discrepancy concerning the statement that McCullough had given the police at the time of his arrest. The blunder by a principal Crown witness was large enough for Robinette to take the risk of putting his client on the stand. In McCullough's version if the events, Albert Johnson shot Williams. McCullough said he had shouted at Johnson,

"Quit that, you damn fool!," and wrestled the gun away from him. Then Williams, who might already have been shot, attacked him with the billy club while Johnson ran away. That was when Cross entered the stable. McCullough said that after the fight spilled out into the driveway, Cross grabbed him, and that caused the gun to discharge again. He had not intentionally pulled the trigger.

This was a completely different version of events from the one McCullough had given previously. When Robinette asked him to explain that, McCullough responded that he wasn't sure what he had said during the questioning by Cronin and Kennedy. He said he was in a dazed condition at the time. He swore he was not in the habit of carrying a gun, and that he'd had no intention of doing Williams any harm.

McCullough's performance — if it was such — altered his role in the tragedy from that of a calculating, pistol-packin' outlaw, to one of an unfortunate (if not quite innocent) man who had actually tried to *save* the officer from the real murderer. All that remained was to convince the jury. They might convict McCullough on the lesser charge of manslaughter, which did not carry the death penalty. Or they might even decide that he was guilty of nothing more than burglary and selling stolen goods.

Crown Prosecutor White had other ideas. In his cross-examination of McCullough, he brought the jury's attention back to the defendant's criminal background, with special emphasis given to McCullough's assault on a constable with a whiskey bottle. Not exactly the conduct of a man concerned with the well-being of a police officer.

White then took McCullough and the jury through a careful examination of the Cronin-Kennedy interview. He scrutinized each question and answer, all the while asking McCullough to explain his recorded responses. The prosecutor cleverly lured McCullough into revealing that he was not as "dazed" during that interview as he claimed to have been; that his answers to the officers' questions were, in fact, purposefully thought out.

Up until this point, McCullough had appeared cool and confident. When he realized that White had tricked him, he began to lose his composure. White could see that McCullough was getting nervous, and he was aware that the man had a short temper, so he pressed him. "You knew, and had the consciousness in your mind that you were leading a life of crime and that society was organized against you?"

McCullough replied, "Yes, sir."

"You realized that?"

"Yes, sir," McCullough repeated.

Then White asked, "And nothing to protect yourself?"

McCullough showed his fists and snapped, "That is all, sir!"

White said he had no more questions. It was a dramatic moment to end the cross-examination, with McCullough sitting in the box with his fists raised, defiance on his face, and the anger in his voice still ringing in the jury members' ears.

The two lawyers made their final addresses to the jury. Robinette pleaded with them to convict McCullough of nothing greater than manslaughter. "This is not murder," he said. "Get that into your heads at once."

White argued that the crime was "nothing but" murder. He asked the jury, "Are you going to say to policemen, 'Do your duty, but if you are killed in the discharge of your duty, we will let the man off because of weakness or a sentimental feeling we have for him?'"

In his instructions, Justice Rose would not give the jury the option of a conviction of manslaughter. They must either find McCullough guilty of murder, or they must acquit him. For the man in the prisoner's box it was all or nothing!

The jury retired, and during the hours that followed, McCullough joked and laughed with Detective Cronin and his guards. At 8:30 p.m., the jury returned with a verdict. "We find the prisoner guilty!" Justice Rose sentenced McCullough to hang on May 2.

McCullough was lodged in the death cell of Toronto's Don Jail, which by 1919 was already over fifty years old and notorious. It was overcrowded, understaffed, and had a history of management that was corrupt, incompetent, or both. As a condemned man, McCullough was kept under a "death watch" to ensure that he did not escape or cheat the hangman by committing suicide. In the meantime, Robinette lost his bid for an appeal, so he went to work on having the death sentence commuted to life imprisonment.

Losing a case did not sit well with Thomas Robinette, especially one so well-publicized. He would go to great lengths to gain a commutation, even if it involved some chicanery. Robinette knew that public opinion could play a large role in influencing such official decisions, so he started with the media. He announced to the press that he was going to Ottawa to appeal for executive clemency. He told reporters that Frank was bearing up well and was very hopeful. Robinette said that in spite of the verdict, there were a lot of "doubts" in that trial. The Crown's evidence, he said, was not conclusive. The jury had doubts about convicting McCullough of murder, and would have settled for manslaughter if Justice Rose had given them that option. Arthur Hill, the foreman of the jury, agreed with this and fully supported the quest to have the sentence commuted.

Robinette went behind Justice Rose's back and tried to influence the acting minister of justice, Hugh Guthrie. Guthrie wrote to Rose, saying he would be pleased to receive "any additional statement that you may see fit to make in elucidation of the facts of the case." But Rose had no intention of seeking clemency for McCullough.

To build up public sympathy for the condemned man, Robinette described how Frank broke down and wept when he spoke of his mother. Robinette described how the tears flowed down Frank's face when he said that his greatest sorrow was for his mother, whom he called one of the best mothers in the world.

Robinette actually did locate Frank's mother, now a widow living in Youngstown, Ohio. He wrote to her and asked if she would come to Toronto to visit her son. The lawyer thought that nothing would play on the public's sympathies like the story of the heartbroken mother, seeing her doomed son behind bars. But the widow Swart hadn't seen her wayward son Leroy in thirteen years, and wanted nothing to do with him. If he had murdered a policeman in Canada, he could expect no help from her. Moreover, she wanted no more communication from Robinette, because any connection with Frank McCullough — as her son now called himself — could cause problems for herself and her daughter.

Of course, Robinette said nothing to the press about this. He kept up the pretense that the condemned man had a loving mother in the United

States, wringing her hands and weeping over his terrible fate. He even told the *Toronto Daily Star* that the McCulloughs were a well-known and prominent business family in Ohio.

While Robinette was trying to save McCullough's life through legal channels, the prisoner in the death cell was causing problems at the Don Jail. The man officially in charge at the jail was Frederick Mowat, the Sheriff of Toronto. He was an incompetent who had gained his cushy position through his father, Sir Oliver Mowat, a former premier of Ontario. Sheriff Mowat's office was not even in the jail, but at city hall. Daily administration of the jail was in the hands of the chief turnkey, Henry Addy, a man with whom Mowat did not get along.

The first problem to arise was finding men for the twenty-four hour "death watch." The jail was already short staffed, so Addy asked Mowat for three additional guards. Mowat sent him two city hall employees; Sam Follis and Alfred Amory. These men had done death watch duty before, and they took the two daytime shifts. The much-despised night shift went to Ernest Currell, a returned soldier who, like so many veterans of the Great War, came home to unemployment and poverty. Currell had been shot in the right hand and suffered from sciatica. He had a pregnant wife and three small children, one of whom was sick. Currell would be paid three dollars a shift to spend the long nights all alone with silver-tongued Frank McCullough.

Regulations stated that the only visitors allowed to see a prisoner in the death cell were his lawyer, a doctor, and a clergyman. Anyone else required written permission from the sheriff. Just two days after McCullough's conviction, that rule was put to the test.

Doris Mytton, sixteen-year-old daughter of McCullough's landlady, Gladys Mytton — the woman who had been arrested for receiving stolen property — showed up at the Don Jail asking to see Frank. Henry Addy would not let her in. When the girl persisted, Addy told her she would have to get permission from the sheriff. He thought Mowat would send the teenager home. To Addy's astonishment, Doris returned with a permit signed by Mowat. This was a breach of regulations because Doris was not even related to McCullough. The incident increased the friction between Mowat and Addy, and caused a rift among the jail's staff. Addy was responsible for the regular employees, but the men on the death watch felt they were answerable only to Mowat.

After the Doris Mytton incident, Addy stopped sending unwanted visitors to the sheriff's office. He simply told them they could not see McCullough, and that was that. One such visitor was a mysterious, well-dressed young woman who arrived at the jail with a small package she wanted to give Frank. Addy sent her away, but he didn't realize that more trouble was brewing.

The Mytton family belonged to the Western Congregational Church, as did death watch guard Alfred Amory. The Sunday after her visit to McCullough, Doris gave Amory a letter for Frank. Against regulations, Amory passed the letter on to the prisoner. In it, Doris advised McCullough to request a visit from her pastor, the Reverend R. Bertram Nelles. Frank did, and soon had the clergyman designated as his spiritual advisor, with the right to visit him daily.

Reverend Nelles undoubtedly wanted to save McCullough's soul from damnation, but there would also be considerable publicity for his church if he could convert so notorious a sinner. McCullough exhibited deep remorse for his wrongdoings, and convinced Nelles that he was not guilty of murder. Before long, Nelles was leading his congregation in special prayers for McCullough's salvation. Then the young women of a Bible study group associated with the Western Congregational Church began sending McCullough gifts of cookies and fresh eggs. These were smuggled in by Amory. Young people in Nelles' congregation held "letter bees" in support of a campaign to have McCullough's sentence commuted. They were also the first to circulate petitions requesting executive clemency. They collected more than 20,000 signatures in Toronto and communities as far away as Ottawa.

Newspaper reporters told their readers how Frank passed the time in his cell doing physical exercises, reading his Bible, and working on his drawings and paintings. Surprisingly, Frank's artwork showed a degree of talent. On March 26, the Toronto *Evening Telegram* displayed his picture of a British battleship on the front page. Torontonians began to see McCullough, and not Frank Williams, as the victim in the whole sorry affair. Even Justice Rose wrote in his report to Ottawa, "I have never been thoroughly convinced in my mind that the prisoner did, at any time, intend to shoot Williams."

Meanwhile, more gifts were getting through to McCullough, thanks to the three men on the death watch. Unlike other inmates, McCullough didn't have to endure the wretched fare from the Don Jail's kitchen. He enjoyed roast chicken, fresh bread, fruit, fish and chips, bacon and eggs, sandwiches, candy, and pies. To the chagrin of the regular guards, Frank shared chocolates and cigars with the death watch.

A death cell prisoner was not supposed to have utensils of any kind. McCullough had a kettle, a teapot, a coffee pot, a toaster, and a frying pan. He had a deck of cards, also forbidden. Sam Follis even provided McCullough with a cupboard where he could keep all of this contraband hidden from the regular guards.

Henry Addy complained to Sheriff Mowat about the unorthodox goings-on, but to no avail. The regular guards were further annoyed that the death watch men engaged in horseplay with McCullough in the corridor outside his cell, as though they were in a "playhouse," as one guard put it. When a guard named Harry Denning inspected McCullough's cell while Alfred Amory was called away to the telephone, Frank made sure to tell the death watch men that Denning had trespassed on their territory. Follis and Amory angrily told Denning to mind his own business. Denning suggested to Addy that the death watch men be dismissed. Addy passed the complaint on to Mowat, who told him to "be a little lenient."

Aside from all that, McCullough was a model prisoner. To Reverend Nelles' great satisfaction he became a full member of the church and a "brother in Christ." Frank's only other breach of the rules was to stand on a chair so that he could reach one of the barred windows of his cell. When ordered to get down, he would complain that he only wanted to get a little fresh air.

The death cell had three high windows. One of them looked out upon Riverdale Park, beyond the jail's stone walls. When McCullough climbed up to that window, he was not just taking the air. On several occasions witnesses saw a young woman standing in the park, looking up at McCullough's window, waving to him and tossing him kisses. Frank responded in kind. Whenever guards or police approached this woman, she ran off. She would turn out to be the same mysterious woman whom Addy had refused to admit to the jail.

With May 2, the scheduled date of his execution rapidly approaching, McCullough seemed to be as cheerful as ever. Observers thought that odd for a man who had just a short time to live. Some of his Christian admirers felt McCullough had resigned himself to his fate and took joy in the belief that he would soon be with the Lord. Others thought he had the utmost confidence in Robinette and all the people who were striving to get executive clemency. But McCullough no more wanted to spend the rest of his life in prison than he wanted to hang. Sometime early in the morning of April 16, in the midst of a severe thunderstorm, Frank McCullough escaped from the Don Jail. He was the first condemned prisoner to break out of a Canadian jail.

At five o'clock on the morning of April 16, the night guards on duty in the Don Jail heard the alarm from the corridor where the death cell was located. They hurried there and found a groggy and embarrassed looking Ernest Currell sitting all alone in the cell, in his underwear. He had a piece of paper in his hand. Two bars of the window McCullough liked to climb up to for a breath of air had been sawn through, and were lying on the window ledge. The Toronto *Daily Star* would call the escape "the most sensational in the history of the [Toronto] police."

Henry Addy, Sheriff Mowat, Detective Bart Cronin, and W.W. Dunlop, the provincial inspector of prisons, were all awakened and summoned to the jail. There was no question as to how McCullough had made his escape. After cutting out the two iron bars, he had lowered himself onto the narrow top of a wall below the cell window. His boots had left marks on the side of the building. McCullough had crawled along the top of the wall to the main wall that surrounded the jailyard. Then he had jumped about eighteen feet to the ground, and was free.

Currell said he had relieved Follis at ten o'clock the night before. Then, he claimed, McCullough had drugged him. He said McCullough had given him a cup of coffee, and soon after drinking it he passed out. He did not awaken until five in the morning. When he saw that the bars had been cut and McCullough was gone, he immediately rang the alarm. The paper Currell had in his hand was a note from McCullough:

Currell, old man,

I am sorry, but it had to be done. Now do not you be scared, for it isn't your fault, for I doped your coffee with a sleeping powder of Veronal and so you see kid they cannot blame you. I am leaving the paper wrapper in which I had the stuff so that you can have the evidence if necessary. If you do not want this note shown to them, why lay the paper on the floor and somewhere where you will be able to accidentally find it. You understand, I got the stuff I am using from a friend who came here as a prisoner on purpose and managed to slip it to me.

Wish me luck. I am sorry but you know life is sweet, old man.

So long
Frank

Addy and Cronin read the note; then Cronin arrested Currell for assisting in McCullough's escape. Currell's story and McCullough's note just didn't ring true. It did not seem possible that one man with a saw blade could have cut through the bars in the time that McCullough would have had while Currell was supposedly unconscious. The bars had black-stained butter, soap, and chewing gum on them. In all likelihood, McCullough had been at work on the bars for several nights, and had used those substances to hide the cut marks from the other death watch guards. Moreover, the jail's physician said that Veronal was a mild sedative, and that its effects would be counteracted by coffee.

On the very morning of McCullough's escape, Toronto's *Daily Star* and *Telegram* received letters in McCullough's handwriting, explaining that the guards were in no way responsible for breakout. The letter to the *Star* said, in part:

> I will explain part of my escape to you so that you may find out the truth and not put the blame for it on any of these men who were my keepers, for it is not their fault. The Veronal sleeping powder which I introduced into the night guard's coffee was given to me by a prisoner who came to the jail for that very purpose, and after the guard had gone to sleep I pulled the saw up through the window by means of a string, and was able to cut the bars in about one hour and 40 minutes.

This attempt to clear Currell of blame only convinced Cronin and others that he was in on the escape. McCullough's letter addressed the people from the Western Congregational Church who had believed so strongly in his conversion, and who had been working so hard to have his sentence commuted. He assured them that he had not broken faith with them or God. His escape, he said, was God's miraculous answer to his prayers for mercy. Furthermore, he said that for him to have stayed to be executed would have been "suicide," which was against God's law.

Reverend Nelles felt betrayed. Robinette was exasperated. He believed he had the federal government on the verge of granting McCullough executive clemency, and now all his hard work had been for nought.

The chase was on immediately. News of the escape went to cities across the country, especially border towns where McCullough might try to slip into the United States. Uniformed officers and plainclothes detectives scoured Toronto. Railway police scrutinized every man boarding a train at Union Station. By early afternoon the provincial government was offering a reward of $1,000 for information leading to McCullough's recapture. That was an extraordinarily large reward for the time — more than the average worker earned in a year. Officials were sure that sooner or later someone would cash in.

Meanwhile, W.W. Dunlop and the mayor of Toronto, Tommy Church, wanted to know what the hell had been going on at the Don Jail. What about these reports that McCullough had been receiving unauthorized packages? Chief Turnkey Addy laid the blame at Sheriff Mowat's door. The sheriff directed it right back to Addy.

In his interview with Currell, Dunlop was astonished to learn that the man had been acting as a go-between for McCullough and a young woman named Vera de Lavelle. He had carried letters for them, and had delivered boxes of chocolates from Vera to McCullough. Currell had even taken Vera home to meet his wife and children. Vera's description matched that of the mysterious woman who had tried to visit McCullough and who had been seen in Riverdale Park. Police had no doubt that she had been involved in the jailbreak. They traced her to a boarding house on Trinity Square. The landlady said she did have a boarder named Vera, but she had not seen her since the night of Frank McCullough's escape.

After a few days passed with no sign of McCullough, the newspapers all agreed that he was probably no longer in Toronto, and in all likelihood had crossed the border. Nonetheless, detectives kept looking into tips that he had been seen in various parts of the city. Currell continued to deny that he had helped McCullough escape, and officials squabbled about whether or not taxpayers' money should be spent to beef up security in the Don Jail. The window through which McCullough had escaped was bricked up. Then, on April 22, Detective Cronin spotted Vera de Lavelle walking along Queen Street, and arrested her.

Vera's introduction into the plot turned the one-dimensional account of an escaped killer into a story worthy of the pulp fiction press that was so popular at the time. But this was a (mostly) true drama about an outlaw and his lady love. People followed the developments daily in the newspapers. It was, in fact, the hottest story in town. The public seemed to forget that behind it all lay the murder of police officer.

Vera said she had met McCullough at a dance, and it was love at first sight. They were going to be married. The next thing Vera knew, Frank was in jail, charged with murder. She did not believe for a moment that he was guilty.

By means of a letter smuggled out of the jail, McCullough told Vera that Ernest Currell could be trusted. She began to send Frank letters and boxes of chocolates through Currell. One of those boxes of chocolates contained saws.

On the night that Frank broke out, Vera said, she met him in Riverdale Park, during the rainstorm. "That was the last time I saw him, in the park. He just kissed me and said, 'I am going, dear, and when I arrive at my destination I will write to you.' Then he turned and went towards the north."

Vera said she had no idea where Frank had gone. After they parted company in the park, she claimed that she had been afraid to go back to her room on Trinity Square, because she thought the police would be looking for her. "You know how the police think some very funny things sometimes," she observed. Vera said that until Detective Cronin picked her up, she had been wandering around the city, sleeping in empty houses.

There was now a swell of public sympathy for Frank McCullough, and it was not entirely due to the melodramatic tale of ill-starred lovers. During the war years, there had been growing resentment toward those who were considered "aliens" and "slackers." The "aliens" were European immigrants who had not joined the Canadian army (in fact, they were barred from enlisting). They were seen as opportunists, who took the jobs of men fighting overseas and did not relinquish them when the soldiers returned home. "Slackers" were Canadian born men who had not enlisted and, in the eyes of the public, stayed home to make money while others fought for king and country. Police officers like Frank Williams were lumped in with the slackers in spite of the fact that they performed an essential service at home.

In August 1918, Toronto was torn by three days of violence when returned soldiers rioted. Driven to fury by unemployment, the incompetence of government bureaucrats, and the feeling that their sacrifices were being ignored, the men destroyed several "foreign" owned restaurants on Yonge Street. City authorities responded by sending squads of club-wielding police into the mobs. The rioting soldiers fought back with bricks. In the violent confrontations, many of the soldiers who were clubbed to the ground and beaten bloody were veterans who had lost arms and legs in France. Innocent civilians — men, women, and children, inadvertently caught up in the chaos — were also struck down by police clubs. When it was all over, not a single policeman was held accountable for use of excessive force.

In the spring of 1919, the citizens of Toronto still remembered what they perceived to be a battle between the heroes of the war and the club-swinging slackers of the Toronto Police Department. They also recalled that according to the newspapers, Detective Frank Williams had been beating Frank McCullough with his billy club when McCullough shot him. Wasn't McCullough simply defending himself? They did not know that the man whom they were turning into a folk hero was a deserter from the United States army.

In Toronto and other Ontario communities, and even in other provinces, law-abiding citizens expressed their sympathy for McCullough and said they hoped he would get away. No one, said his admirers, would be so low as to turn him in for the $1,000 reward. But someone did!

On the morning of May 8, acting on a very guarded tip, Detective Bart Cronin and three other detectives named Tuft, Silverthorn, and Armstrong, went to a boarding house at 78 Bathurst Street. It was a rundown, two and a half storey red brick building, just around the corner from the livery stable where McCullough had shot Williams. Cronin and Tuft went in the front door, while Silverthorn and Armstrong took positions in the alley behind the house. The officers all had their guns drawn.

McCullough's hideout was a shabby, three dollar a week, second floor room, and he had the bad luck to be in when Cronin came calling. He heard footsteps in the hall, grabbed his boots and ran to the window. Just as Cronin burst through the door, McCullough raised the sash and jumped. One of his flailing feet shattered a window as he fell. McCullough hit the ground about twenty feet below, and that was as far as he got. He found himself covered by the guns of Silverthorn and Armstrong. He looked up, and saw Cronin and Tuft pointing guns at him from the window. "I've got nothing on me!" McCullough cried.

As the fugitive was taken into custody once more, Cronin said, "Well, McCullough, I'm glad we didn't have to shoot you." McCullough replied, "Well, I wish you had. You just got me a day too soon, that's all."

The police eventually learned that McCullough and Vera had rented the room as husband and wife. The landlady was an eighty-year-old Irish woman, who was completely deaf and had no idea her boarder was Canada's most wanted man. She said he spent most of his time in his room, but often went out to buy ice cream. "He was a really polite young fellow, and seemed quite nice."

McCullough and Vera needed money to get out of Toronto. He had gone to a place where he'd stashed some cash and loot from his burglaries, only to find it had been cleaned out, probably by his pal Albert Johnson. Vera had been cadging money and food from friends. Evidently, several members of the Western Congregational Church contributed, without the knowledge of Reverend Nelles. Then Vera was arrested, and Frank was on his own.

From his window, McCullough had actually seen Detective Cronin searching the neighbourhood, and he knew it was only a matter of time before his hideout was discovered. Realizing that he would have to make his run for freedom without Vera, he stole a bicycle, some money and jewellery, and a telephone lineman's tools and uniform. He was going to cycle from Toronto to Montreal, disguised as a lineman, then cross the border to New York. Cronin barged in on him the day before his planned departure.

Many people had seen McCullough entering and leaving the Bathurst Street boarding house, and knew who he was, but who tipped the police was never revealed to the public. The reward was claimed by a lawyer on behalf of a client. The police agreed to that arrangement for the protection of the informant. Toronto might not have been a very safe place for the squealer who handed McCullough over to the cops.

McCullough was back in the death cell of the Don Jail. Follis and Amory were again on death watch in the daytime, but a stern war vet, Sergeant R.F. Eyre, had replaced Currell for the night shift. There would be no more smuggled food. Gone were the toaster and coffee pot. No more card games; no horseplay in the corridor. But the ongoing tale of doomed romance was not over.

Frank McCullough and Vera de Lavelle were now prisoners in the same jail. They were not permitted to see each other or communicate directly. Nonetheless, they found a way to express their undying love — as well as play on the sympathies of the public — through the newspapers. Frank and Vera's love letters, delivered to the papers by their lawyers, touched many a sentimental heart; especially Vera's pledge that if Frank's death sentence should be commuted, she would wait for him.

On May 15, Vera was sentenced to seven years in prison for aiding an escaped criminal. Frank, who was still on the lam on May 2, the day he was supposed to hang, had his execution rescheduled for June 13, a Friday. On May 29, while hanging out laundry in the jailyard, Vera used a painter's ladder to go over the wall and escape.

Once again the city was in an uproar. The general public was delighted over Vera's escape. The newspapers gleefully ridiculed the jail's administration. Mayor Tommy Church said, "It's not a jail at all — it's simply a stop-over place." W.W. Dunlop called the Don a "picnickish jail." There should have been a shake up of the administration, beginning with Sheriff Mowat. Instead, two matrons were fired.

The police searched everywhere, but could find no trace of Vera. If anyone had seen her or knew where she was hiding, they weren't talking. A week after the escape, Vera's lawyer delivered a letter to the *Daily Star.*

Addressed to Frank, the letter was meant to wring the hearts of the public. Vera wrote that she escaped because she could not bear to be in the jail on June 13. She said she would be willing to take Frank's place, if it were possible. She wished that people could see Frank's good side, as she could. Then she came to what was probably the most important part of the letter:

> I will close, and last of all, should you get a reprieve, I will in all cases do my sentence, and after I get through I will write to you, as I could never forsake you. Now, dear, be brave, even for my sake. God bless you.
> I am, with love,
> Your Vera

Vera's open letter moved thousands of people to sign petitions pleading for a commutation. People wrote letters to the editor supporting that plea. However, not everyone was in favour of McCullough escaping the noose. One letter that appeared in the *Daily Star* came from a reader who believed that all the young women who were petitioning for McCullough were misguided.

> Let those girls put their brothers in Detective Williams'
> place, and see how it would sting them. It is a down-right
> shame to see such a promising young man as Detective
> Williams shot down by such a scoundrel.

The official who had to decide whether McCullough should hang or be imprisoned for life was Arthur Meighen, the Acting Minister of Justice and a future prime minister of Canada. He knew of the petitions and was well aware that public sentiment lay heavily in McCullough's favour. He had listened to Robinette and Nelles plead for McCullough's life. Meighen stated, for the record, "The responsibility of deciding on the fate of McCullough is one of the most anxious that I have ever been compelled to undertake."

In the end, Meighen's feelings were the same as those of the *Daily Star* reader whose letter was a reminder that Frank Williams' death had been untimely and tragic. He saw no reason why the law should not take its course. Frank McCullough had been tried and sentenced, and now he would hang.

The night before the execution, thousands of people gathered in Riverdale Park. They watched McCullough's window, and cheered whenever he made an appearance. They sang hymns and chanted, "Reprieve! Reprieve!" Doris Mytton was there. So was Vera. She had managed to have a final letter of farewell delivered to Frank. Now, in disguise, she was part of the death vigil.

Returned soldiers made up about half of the crowd outside the Don Jail, and almost to a man they sympathized with McCullough. Authorities were fearful of an attack on the jail, so they sent police out to clear the park and adjacent streets. The result was yet another battle, with bricks, stones, glass bottles, and billy clubs. The violence did not end until three o'clock on the morning of Friday the thirteenth.

The newspapers said that Frank McCullough went to his death "like a man." He refused morphine, and said he hoped his example would deter other young men from crime. Arthur Ellis, the hangman, made a quick, efficient job of it, and McCullough's neck was broken when he dropped. Then Ellis was whisked out of the Don Jail in a police wagon. As the vehicle pushed through the crowd, angry people shouted abuse and pounded on the hood and roof.

McCullough's body was buried in the jailyard's murderers' row, where the remains of other executed men had been interred. Ernest Currell was tried for assisting in McCullough's escape, but due to insufficient evidence he was not convicted. Frederick Mowat stayed on as the Sheriff of Toronto until 1923, but two weeks after McCullough's execution the province decided to appoint a governor to administer the Don Jail

Vera de Lavelle gave herself up to the police, but she did not serve the seven years in prison to which she had been sentenced. The authorities had endured enough of the bad publicity surrounding the McCullough case, and they did not want to make a martyr of her. Vera served four months, was released, and then vanished from history. The drama that had started with the murder of Acting Detective Frank Williams, during what should have been a routine arrest, and which had shaken Toronto the Good for the better part of a year, was gradually forgotten.

12

Guarding inmates in a penal or correctional institution has always been a potentially dangerous job. In Canada's prisons and jails, thirty-seven guards and other corrections workers are known to have been killed on duty, the greatest number of them in federal institutions. Some were murdered by hardened criminals in desperate escape attempts. Others were victims of the explosive violence that can erupt when tensions within prison walls reach a breaking point, or when one individual snaps. In the most commonly held perception of a prison guard murder, the victim is male and the killer is a tough con with nothing to lose. However, the case of one correctional employee's violent death goes entirely against that stereotype.

The Toronto Municipal Jail Farm for Women, located on Dufferin Street in Vaughan Township, north of the city, held forty-seven inmates on the night of May 24, 1925. Four of them were locked in cells in the isolation wing at the back of the main building. There were four cells, two on either side of the corridor. The prisoners, each alone behind the iron door of her cell, were officially in the isolation wing for medical reasons. But three of them knew that they were really there as punishment.

Jeanette (Jennie) McMinn had been sentenced to two years for being "incorrigible." On that May 24, her sentence had expired and she'd expected to be released. But Major W.J. Morrison, the prison superintendent, said that for health related reasons she would not be set free. Jennie was ordered to her usual work detail. Defiant, she'd refused to work.

Isabel Prouse, alias Ruby Smith, was serving an indefinite term for a breach of the Medical Health Act. A few days earlier she, too, had refused to work. Now she was doing a stint in the isolation wing on a diet of bread and water, an unpleasant break from the usual fare of porridge and syrup.

That morning, Bessie Carroll, serving an indefinite term for vagrancy, had been insolent to Margaret Carson, the general superintendent. For that indiscretion, Bessie was given five days in solitary on bread and water. Gladys Palmer, in jail for reasons unknown, was apparently the only person in the solitary wing for actual medical reasons. Gladys was twenty years old. Isabel was twenty-one. Jennie and Bessie were both just sixteen.

Little is known of these girls' lives before what was to be a most fateful day for them. Jennie McMinn's mother lived in Toronto, but Jennie was evidently on the streets when she wasn't in jail. Bessie Carroll had lost her mother at the age of eight. She lived with her father, who apparently abused her and had her confined because she wouldn't go to school. While in jail, she was told that her father had beaten up a married man she'd been running around with. Bessie responded, "Which one?" Isabel Prouse was born in Courtice, near Oshawa, but apparently her mother was now in Kapuscasing.

There was no guard in the corridor of the isolation wing. The lone matron on duty, sixty-three-year-old Margaret Mick, was in her office at the end of the corridor, with the door closed. Jennie, Isabel, and Bessie were talking to each other, using the small transoms in their cell doors. These openings, through which food trays were passed, had covers that were supposed to be locked at night. On this evening they were not. Just in case Matron Mick overheard them, the three girls spoke in pig Latin. Gladys Palmer, lying on her bunk, understood every word.

"I am going to make my getaway tonight," Jennie McMinn said.

Bessie Carroll responded, "I'm with you."

"I'd like to go, too," said Isabel Prouse, "but I might get cold feet."

Jennie McMinn stood just five foot one, and was of a petite build. Using a stool, she climbed up to the transom, which was only about the size of a telephone directory. She managed to wriggle her body through. In the corridor she took from her blue prison garb two dinner knives that she'd pilfered from the dining room. The latches for the cell doors were bolted to wooden frames. Jennie used the knives to dig away at the wood around the bolt securing Bessie Carroll's door. All the while she cast anxious glances toward the door at the end of the corridor, fearful that at any moment it would open and Matron Mick would catch her. Finally, the bolt came free and Bessie was out. The two teenagers went to work on Isabel Prouse's door.

When Isabel was free of her cell the three went to Gladys Palmer's door and asked in hushed tones if she wanted to go with them. Gladys said she did not. The others contemptuously called her a "stoolie" and told her to keep her mouth shut.

The girls still had to get out of the building, and Matron Mick had the key. Jennie McMinn had a plan for dealing with her. The girls tore some of their bedsheets into strips. Then one of them stood on a stool and unscrewed the single lightbulb from the ceiling. With the corridor in darkness, Bessie Carroll began to shout for Matron Mick. She said a pipe was leaking and water was running into her cell. As Bessie shouted, she and Jennie positioned themselves by the office door with a blanket stretched between them.

At two hundred pounds, Margaret Mick was a big woman. A widow with one married daughter, she had been making her own living for many years. Mrs. Mick was a veteran prison matron who had served in institutions all over Ontario. Far from the stereotypical domineering prison matron of film and fiction, Margaret Mick seems to have been regarded as a firm but fair woman. She was well-liked by staff and most inmates wherever she worked. Even so, her daughter and son-in-law had recently expressed concern about her working alone on the night shift. Her daughter had been tormented by a series of bad dreams in which terrible things happened to her mother. Margaret dismissed her daughter's worries as groundless. The majority of the women and girls at the jail farm liked her. And even at sixty-three, she could handle the ones who didn't.

Shortly before midnight on May 24, Matron Mick put her lunch on the table in her small office. Before she could eat a bite, she heard Bessie Carroll shouting from her cell — something about leaking water. Margaret Mick got up from her desk, walked to the door and opened it ... to darkness!

The matron had just started to cry out something about the light, when a blanket was thrown over her head. Ordinarily, Margaret Mick could easily subdue a violent inmate — even two. But three were too many for her, especially when she was blinded and netted. She struggled, but her attackers dragged her to the floor.

Mrs. Mick cried out, "Oh my God!" Then she felt a knee pressing into her chest and a pair of hands around her throat. Thumbs and fingers dug deep, crushing her windpipe. Finally the hands let go.

Matron Mick's face was still covered, but she heard a voice tell her to be still. "You care about your daughter, don't you?"

Mrs. Mick gasped, "Yes. I'd do anything for her." She couldn't say anything more. Inside her throat she was hemorrhaging. Margaret Mick was dying.

Jessie and Bessie used the torn bedsheets to tie Matron Mick's hands to the water pipes that ran along either side of the corridor. Then they bound her feet together. Isabel couldn't help with this work. She said she was too weak from her days on bread and water. When the unconscious matron was secure, the girls took her keys.

Margaret Mick was still breathing. In their desperation to escape, the young women were probably not even aware of how seriously she was hurt. Bessie put a pillow under Matron Mick's head, kissed her, and left a cup of water beside her. She thought when the matron came to she would be able to untie herself, and would want a drink.

Gladys Palmer could not see what was happening in the corridor, but she heard everything. As she cringed in her cell she heard Mrs. Mick's groans. Then one of the girls said, "Now you've done it!" Another asked, "What will we do?"

Terrified that the others would use Matron Mick's keys to open her cell door, Gladys fainted. When she regained consciousness, the corridor outside her door was silent. She did not know that the matron was dead on the floor.

Using Mrs. Mick's keys, the escapees left the building. They crossed the lawn in the darkness and climbed over a fence. After they'd put some distance between themselves and the farm, they tried to hitch a ride into Toronto. The first cars passed them by, but finally one stopped. In it were Leonard Swales and William Norton, both twenty. They agreed to give the girls a lift. Not until the three piled into the car and the young men saw their prison uniforms did they realize that the girls had run away from the jail farm.

The girls said they were looking for a place to spend the night and asked to be taken to a certain address where one of them had a friend. When they arrived there, however, the friend took one look at the uniforms and would not admit the girls into the house. The girls then asked to be driven to the home of a friend of Bessie's, Edith Garrod. Edith wouldn't take the jailbreakers in either, but she did give each of them a change of clothes so they could get out of the prison garb.

Now the girls asked to taken to Fort York. The old buildings there were used for storage at the time, and they knew of a place they could crawl into to sleep. William Norton had been nervous about having the escapees in the car, but he just couldn't leave them to sleep in a drafty old warehouse. He gallantly took them to his home.

The girls told William's stepmother, Maude Poole, that they had just been released from the jail farm and had nowhere to go. Maude took them in for the night and made up beds for them in a downstairs room. Not until they were at the breakfast table the next morning did the girls tell her they had run away from the prison. They said they'd tied up the matron, but "She's all right."

Maude knew she should call the police, but she couldn't bring herself to turn the girls in. Instead, she watched them get into the car with William and his eighteen-year-old brother James. The boys were taking the girls to Bowmanville, where one of them said she had a relative they could stay with. None of them were aware that at that very moment, Jennie McMinn, Isabel Prouse, and Bessie Carroll were wanted for murder.

At 6:30 on the morning of May 25, matrons Lillian Prince and Florence Thierry entered the isolation wing and found Margaret Mick's body, feet bound and hands tied to the plumbing. Bruise marks were on her throat and her face was almost black. The three empty cells pretty well told the story. Gladys Palmer tearfully filled in the details.

The Bowmanville relative turned the girls away. As the Norton brothers were driving them back to Toronto, Isabel and Bessie asked if they could stop in Oshawa. They wanted to look around the town. The two agreed to meet the brothers and Jennie in front of the fire hall later, but they failed to appear. Bessie and Isabel evidently wanted to ditch Jennie.

The boys took Jennie back to Toronto and dropped her at the home of an uncle. Then they drove home, thinking they'd seen the last of the jail farm girls. The Norton brothers and their friend Leonard Swales had never run afoul of the law in their lives. They were about to find themselves in very deep trouble indeed.

When Jennie told her uncle she had run away from the jail farm, he immediately took her to the nearest police station and turned her in. There she learned to her horror that Margaret Mick was dead, and she was under arrest for murder. Jennie's spur of the moment jailbreak, done as a lark, had suddenly become a nightmare. Between bouts of hysterical weeping, she told the police everything that had happened from the time she fled the jail up to that moment. Edith Garrod, Maude Poole, Leonard Swales, and William and James Norton were all arrested on charges of aiding and abetting fugitives. Maude said she only did what any mother would have done.

Upon learning that Bessie and Isabel had parted company from Jennie in Oshawa, the police concentrated their search there, as well as in Kingston, where one of the girls had relatives. Mr. F. Carroll, Bessie's father, went to Oshawa to help the police find his daughter. He told reporters she was a silly girl looking for excitement.

The police did not have to search for long, because Isabel and Bessie made no attempt to either run or hide. In Oshawa they "waltzed around town," as one newspaper put it, as though they hadn't a care in the world. Even after they saw a newspaper headline about Margaret Mick's death and Jennie's arrest, they did not seem to comprehend the seriousness of their situation. The day after they gave Jennie the slip, Isabel and Bessie watched a baseball game with some friends they'd met. Then they went to a Chinese restaurant. As they were leaving the restaurant, Bessie's father saw them from across the street. He immediately pointed Bessie out to the detective and two constables who were with him. When Bessie saw her father approach, she began to cry and pleaded with him not to strike her.

When the two were arrested on a charge of murder, the true nature of the trouble they were in struck home. They wept. They said they didn't mean to hurt Mrs. Mick. They said she was alive when they left her. Each of them denied putting her hands around the matron's throat, but it didn't matter who had done the actual strangling. In the eyes of the law all three were equally responsible.

The girls were returned to the jail farm where they were to be held pending trial. Bail was denied. To those who observed the three accused murderers — the jail staff, reporters sent to interview them, and the morbidly curious who gawked at them through a window — the girls' behaviour ran the gamut from remorseful to defiant. One reporter said they were "inclined to be saucy." Another said they often wept and wondered aloud what would happen to them. One of the girls was overheard saying, "Well, they can't hang us anyway, we are too young for that." At other times they laughed and giggled like schoolgirls. On one of their trips to court for a preliminary hearing, Jennie stuck her tongue out at a crowd of spectators.

Courtesy Toronto Daily Star

Jennie McMinn's mother visited her, and the newspapers reported a "pathetic" reunion between Isabel Prouse and her mother, who had come to Toronto from Kapuskasing. Neither mother seems to have been

Left to right: Bessie Carroll, age sixteen; Jennie McMinn, age sixteen; and Isabel Prouse, age twenty-one, in Toronto Police Court following the murder of Matron Margaret Mick at the Toronto Municipal Jail Farm for Women.

interviewed by the press. Mr. Carroll told the Toronto *Daily Star* that his daughter had less of an excuse than the others, because she had a home to go to and they didn't.

Meanwhile, Margaret Mick was buried in her hometown of Waterdown, Ontario. Letters of condolence poured into the family home and the jail farm office. Many were from former inmates — women who said that Matron Mick's kindness to them had helped them turn their lives around. Mrs. Mick's grieving daughter told the press that the family had planned a surprise party for her sixty-fourth birthday on June 1.

Jennie, Bessie, and Isabel were arraigned on a charge of murder. On the advice of their counsel they pleaded guilty to the lesser charge of manslaughter, and were sentenced to five years each. Their lawyer argued that they should be returned to the prison farm, but the magistrate decided that only a prison term could cure them of their "immoral habits." Bessie sobbed out loud when he announced they would be going to the Kingston Penitentiary. For aiding fugitives, Leonard Swales and William Norton each got a month in jail. James Norton got off with a suspended sentence.

The three girls entered the grim prison world on October 24, 1925. A little over three years later, on Christmas Day, 1928, they were released on parole. Within a week, Jennie and Bessie were back in a Toronto jail, charged with stealing clothing and jewelry. Because they had violated their parole, Jennie and Bessie had to serve out the rest of their sentences. They seem to have been sent to separate institutions in order to keep them apart, as they were considered to be a bad influence on each other. Jennie McMinn's name appeared in the papers one more time in 1933, when she was arrested in Toronto for vagrancy. After that the record is silent on the teenage killers of Matron Mick.

13

THE MAD TRAPPER:
MURDER IN THE ARCTIC

The saga of the Mad Trapper of Rat River has become a classic of both Canadian crime and the Canadian Arctic. Countless retellings of the story appear in articles, books, and even a largely fictitious Hollywood movie starring Charles Bronson. The mysterious trapper has been depicted as everything from a mad dog killer, to a freedom fighter battling police oppression. In his own time, he was seen as both a murderous outlaw and an outlaw hero. One thing was certain: Mounted Police constables who went after the Mad Trapper soon found themselves in the line of fire.

On December 31, 1931, during the long night of the Arctic winter, four men approached a remote cabin on the banks of the Rat River in the North-West Territories, not far from the Yukon border. They were RCMP constables Alfred King and R.G. McDowell, and special constables Joe Bernard and Lazarus Sittichinli. These men had travelled by dogsled for a day and a half, through subzero temperatures, to question the lone inhabitant of the cabin. His name was said to be Albert Johnson, but no one really knew who he was. The man was a loner who spoke to almost nobody.

Local Natives had complained to the police that Johnson, who was a stranger to them, had been encroaching on their legal trapping grounds.

He was springing their traps and hanging them in trees. He evidently considered all of the furs in that part of the country to be his.

Constable King, the commanding officer, knew that his men were cold and hungry. They wanted to take care of this routine business as quickly as possible so that they could go on to Fort McPherson to attend a New Year's party. Nonetheless, King told the men to be cautious.

Johnson, or whatever his real name was, had not gone unnoticed by the RCMP. He was a strange man who shunned human company. On his rare visits to settlements to buy supplies, he always paid in cash. The few people who spoke to him found him taciturn and sullen. They said he had cold blue eyes and a slight Scandinavian accent.

The RCMP had to keep tabs on everybody in Arctic frontier communities for reasons of general safety. Johnson had always been evasive when they questioned him. From all appearances he was an expert woodsman, and not a *cheechako* (newcomer to the Arctic). If he wanted to live alone in an isolated eight by ten foot cabin, that was his business, but now he had broken the law by interfering with legitimate trappers. There was no record that Johnson himself even had a trapper's license.

King had been to Johnson's cabin three days earlier. Johnson had looked at him through the window, but would not open the door. This was very odd, as RCMP constables were usually welcome visitors throughout the region. On that occasion, King had no warrant to enter the cabin uninvited, and had been obliged to go to Aklavik, eighty miles away, to get one.

Now King had a warrant. Smoke was billowing from the cabin's chimney, so he knew Johnson was inside. King walked up to the cabin while his men waited at the riverside. He called out, identifying himself as a police officer. King said he had a warrant. If necessary, he would force the door open. No reply came from the cabin.

King stood at the door and shouted, "Are you there, Mr. Johnson?" Still there was only silence. Then King knocked on the door. The quiet was shattered as a gun roared inside the cabin. A bullet smashed through the wooden door, hitting King in the chest. The Mountie fell backwards, bleeding in the snow.

King crawled away from the cabin while his men opened fire, trying to keep the gunman down. Their first priority was to get King to Aklavik before his wound and the bitter cold killed him. Dodging a few shots that the trapper took at them, the men pulled King to cover. Then they lashed him to the sled and made the run to Aklavik in record time. A doctor in the tiny Aklavik hospital saved King's life. Another RCMP constable would not be so lucky.

On January 9, 1932, RCMP Inspector A.N. Eames led a nine man posse of policemen, civilian volunteers, and a Native guide to Johnson's cabin. One of the constables was Edgar Millen, a native of Belfast, Ireland. Known to his friends as Spike, thirty-year-old Millen was a twelve-year veteran of the Force. He had an adventurous nature, and had volunteered for duty in the Arctic in 1923. Millen was very popular with his fellow constables and with the local people. He was the only man in the posse who had ever spoken to Johnson, having met him once at Fort McPherson. On that occasion, Millen had told Johnson he would have to purchase a license if he intended to do any trapping.

Eames wanted to get this business over with quickly. The posse had met with delays on the trail, and food for the men and dogs was already running low. The temperature was dropping quickly. These were not good conditions for a lengthy siege. Eames called on Johnson to surrender. He said that King had not died, so there would be no murder charge. Johnson did not say a word. He answered with his guns.

The police had no way of knowing how well Johnson had prepared for them. He had turned his tiny cabin into a bunker from which he could hold off a small army. He had dug a rifle-pit in the floor, providing himself with maximum protection and a good firing position. He had cut loopholes in all four walls, so he could shoot in any direction and not have to expose himself to gunfire by shooting from the window. The thick log walls were solid protection from bullets. He had warmth and food.

The police, however, were out in the biting cold. The men and dogs had to consume large quantities of food to keep up body heat. The Mounties could not rush the cabin without making themselves targets. With the temperature at -50°F (-45°C), they had just a day or two to breach Johnson's defences.

The posse attacked the cabin several times, but was driven back by gunfire. During one rush, two constables reached the door and attempted to break it in. They managed to jar it slightly open before a hail of lead from a rifle and a shotgun forced them to run for cover. In another attack they used flares, hoping to blind Johnson, but that tactic also failed. Finally, Eames decided to use dynamite. The sticks of explosive were frozen and had to be thawed out over an open fire; a very touchy job indeed. But soon the men were tossing them at the cabin, trying to blow open the door or knock down a wall. The solid little cabin withstood the blasts with only minor damage.

A civilian volunteer named Knut Lang dashed up close enough to the building to hurl a stick of dynamite onto the roof. The explosion ripped open a hole and knocked down the smokestack. Moments later, Lang was running for cover, with bullets whistling around him.

Eames could not keep his men in the field much longer. As a last resort, he lashed his remaining sticks of dynamite together to make a four-pound bomb. He lit the fuse and hurled the dynamite at the cabin. The explosion lifted the roof and partially caved in the walls.

Inspector Eames was sure that Johnson must now be dead, injured, or at least stunned by the blast. He and a civilian volunteer named Karl Gardlund approached the cabin. Gardlund carried a flashlight so that they'd be able to find whatever was left of Johnson in the smoking ruins.

Amazingly, Johnson was not dead. He was not injured. If he'd been stunned, the effect was fleeting. No sooner had Eames and Gardlund reached the open door of the wrecked cabin than a shot rang out, and the flashlight was ripped from Gardlund's hand. The two men beat another hasty retreat to the river.

So far, Eames's party had not suffered any casualties. But the crushing cold and dwindling supplies — and the fact that Johnson was still capable of shooting at any man who went near the cabin — left Eames with no choice but to go back to Aklavik. Another rush on the cabin would be futile and might cost lives. If Johnson tried to flee before the Mounties returned, they would soon pick up his trail.

The Mounties now had a lot of questions for which they had no answers. Why had Johnson shot King? Why had he stayed in his cabin, instead of making a run for it? What was the reason for this senseless stand against the law? Just who was this man?

The outside world soon learned about the shooting of King and the subsequent gunfight between Johnson and the posse. The media, with its flair for sensationalism, dubbed the gunman "The Mad Trapper of Rat River." The name sold newspapers and drew people to the news broadcasts on their radios. The thrilling tale of one man against an entire police force in the wild Canadian north was a real-life drama that soon had the attention of the nation, and beyond. The Great Depression had crippled the world economy, and people were losing their jobs and their homes. They looked upon police as the protectors of the wealthy. Even though Inspector Eames told the press that the so-called "demented trapper" was, in fact, "shrewd and resolute" and "a tough and desperate character," there were many who sympathized with Johnson as an underdog, and hoped he would get away. Such people conveniently overlooked the fact that Johnson had gunned King down without provocation or warning.

On January 14, Constable Millen and Karl Gardlund returned to the cabin. Johnson was gone. When they examined the ruined cabin, they were amazed that Johnson had come out of it alive. They went through the wreckage and searched all around the grounds. They found nothing that would offer a clue as to his identity. A heavy snowfall had covered up Johnson's trail, so they did not know which direction he had gone.

The chase that was to make Johnson a legend, while he drew his pursuers to the limits of their resourcefulness and endurance, began on January 16. The force of RCMP officers, civilian volunteers, Native trackers, and two men from the Royal Canadian Corps of Signals at Aklavik, was better prepared than the first posse had been. They had homemade bombs and a portable radio. Inspector Eames was in charge again, with Millen as second in command. They set up a base nine miles east of Johnson's cabin. Then white and Native trackers began the painstaking task of systematically searching the frozen wilderness for Johnson's trail.

By January 21, the men still had not found a trace of the fugitive. Eames again faced a supply problem, and had to take most of the posse back to Aklavik. That allowed him to leave four men with a ten day supply of food to continue the search. This smaller posse, led by Constable

Millen, included Karl Gardlund, Sergeant R.F. Riddell of the Corps of Signals, and a civilian named Noel Verville.

With no clue as to which direction to take, Millen acted on a hunch and led his men up the Rat River. The going was difficult because of drifting snow, bitter cold, and short hours of daylight. There was also the possibility that if Johnson *had* gone this way, he could be waiting in ambush almost anywhere.

The men came upon a food cache and decided to lay an ambush of their own. They left the cache untouched, and hid to keep watch on it. If Johnson was in the vicinity, he did not risk approaching the cache. Half frozen after hours of lying motionless in the deadly cold, the manhunters gave up the vigil.

On January 28, the searchers were running short of food. Millen was about to call off the hunt and head back to Aklavik, when Sergeant Riddell found the faintest trace of a two-day-old trail. Now turning back was out of the question. The posse followed the trail, lost it, and then found it again. Millen was starting to realize that his quarry was an exceptionally skilled woodsman, who seemed to possess almost superhuman stamina.

Johnson walked a zigzag pattern that allowed him to double back and watch his own back trail without being seen by his pursuers. That meant he had to cover, on snowshoes and carrying a loaded backpack, twice the distance that they did by dogsled, and still stay ahead of them. In temperatures that froze men to the bone, he could build only small fires under the cover of snowbanks. He travelled on ridges, where snow was packed and a trail hard to find. He crossed creeks only on glare ice, leaving no marks. Because he could not risk using his rifle to bring down large animals for food, he had to take the time to snare small game like squirrels and rabbits. Yet Johnson made his way across country that veteran Arctic travellers thought almost impassable, and managed to leave a trail that baffled the men chasing him.

Millen's party was camped far up the Rat River, having apparently lost the trail again, when a Native trapper approached them and said he had heard a gunshot in the Bear River region. Millen decided it was worth investigating. Johnson might have thought he had put enough distance between himself and the police to risk shooting a caribou.

The men found tracks that they presumed to be Johnson's near the Bear River. They followed them back to the Rat River, and then up a creek that was a tributary of the Rat. Along the way they came across the remains of a butchered caribou. On a ridge running parallel to the creek, they lost the trail again. Then they saw smoke rising above the trees. They had found Johnson's camp! It was now January 30.

The posse moved in quietly. Millen couldn't believe his good luck. Johnson had camped with a cliff at his back. There was no way out for him. The wily trapper had grown careless at last!

The men could not see Johnson, but they could hear him whistling as he apparently tended to some camp chores. They had to use extreme caution, knowing that Johnson would not hesitate to shoot if he suspected trouble. Riddell and Gardlund managed to creep up to positions near the camp's perimeter, only fifteen yards from Johnson. Millen and Verville stealthily moved in along the creek bed. Then one of them slipped and made a noise.

Instantly, Johnson grabbed his Savage 30-30 rifle. He saw Millen and shot at him. Millen and Verville dropped to the ground and shot back. Johnson suddenly leaped across his campfire for the cover of a fallen tree. As he did so, Gardlund, known to be good with a rifle, fired a round at him. Johnson landed on the other side of the tree and seemed to collapse. Gardlund was sure he had hit him.

Millen called to Johnson to surrender, and got no reply. He thought the trapper could be dead or wounded, but he might also be playing possum. None of the men dared leave cover in case Johnson came up shooting. But again, lying motionless in the bitter cold was almost as dangerous as rushing a gunman. Two hours passed, and neither a sound nor a sign of movement came from behind the fallen tree. Soon it would be dark. Millen decided that if Johnson was still alive, he might use the darkness to escape yet again. Against the advice of the others, Millen said he was going over to see if the man was dead or alive.

Riddell and Millen walked toward the fallen tree while Gardlund and Verville covered them. They hadn't gone six paces when Riddell cried, "Watch it!" He dove over an embankment for cover as a shot rang out and a bullet whistled over his head. Millen dropped to one knee and fired, just as the trapper took a shot at him. Both men missed. Millen fired and missed again. Then Johnson squeezed off two fast shots. Millen suddenly stood up, spun around, dropped his rifle, and fell face first in the snow. While Verville and Riddell kept Johnson's head down with a barrage of bullets, Gardlund crawled out, tied Millen's bootlaces together, and used them to drag him to cover. Constable Edgar Millen was dead from a bullet that went right through his heart.

The surviving members of the posse returned to a camp they had established nearby, and found that Sergeant Earl Hersey of the Corps of Signals and a Native guide had arrived from Aklavik with a sled load of supplies. They decided to send Sergeant Riddell back to Aklavik to report Millen's death. Now Johnson *was* wanted for murder, and the Mounties would spare no effort to run him to earth. When Gardlund, Hersey, and Verville returned to the scene of the gunfight the next day, Johnson was gone again. He had scaled the sheer cliff behind his camp by chopping hand holes in the ice with an axe.

In Aklavik, Inspector Eames had to concede that the RCMP was dealing with an exceptionally tough criminal, and would have to take extraordinary measures. A killer was on the loose, and the reputation of Canada's vaunted police force was on the line. The whole world was watching the Mounties fail to run down a lone gunman, who had been on the run for a month in the midst of the Arctic winter. The longer the Mad Trapper evaded capture, the greater the criticism directed at the Force. It also increased Johnson's chances of crossing the border into Alaska and disappearing for good.

Eames called for more volunteers and requested the use of a search plane. This would be the first time the RCMP would conduct a search from the air, and many people scoffed at the idea. But Eames knew that the plane would be useful, not only in searching for Johnson (or his trail), but also in ferrying supplies to men on the ground.

Eames led a new posse out of Aklavik on February 2. His party included Sittichinli and Riddell, now veterans of the Mad Trapper's one-man war with the RCMP. They went to the site of Millen's murder and once again began the frustrating task of searching for Johnson's trail. Meanwhile, W.R. "Wop" May, pilot of a Bellanca monoplane, joined the search.

Wop May was already a legend in Canadian aviation. During the First World War he had been the target of the famed Red Baron, when another Canadian pilot, Roy Brown, shot the German ace down. May went on to distinguish himself as a fighter pilot. Since then, he had become one of Canada's most celebrated northern bush pilots. In 1919, May had assisted the Edmonton Police Department with the pursuit and capture of John Guddard Larson, wanted for the murder of Constable William Nixon. This was the first recorded instance of police using a plane to help apprehend a suspect.

May landed at Aklavik on February 5. Two days later he ferried the first load of supplies to Eames's men in the field. Had it not been for May's work in the Bellanca, often flying under difficult conditions, the Mad Trapper might well have escaped to American territory and become lost among the trappers and prospectors there. Among other things, from the air May could examine the false trails Johnson left to confuse his pursuers, and spare the men on the ground the time and effort required to investigate them.

For several days, manhunters roamed across the frozen wilderness trying to pick up Johnson's trail. The killer seemed to have vanished. He'd been on the run for almost six weeks, living on scanty rations and snowshoeing his way across hostile terrain, sometimes in the midst of blizzards that kept even the Natives confined to their camps.

Not until February 12, did the police get a lead. What they heard was almost too incredible to believe. Snowshoe tracks, thought to be Johnson's, had been seen near Lapierre House on the Yukon side of the Richardson Mountains. The Richardsons are a northeastern extension of the Rockies, rising to 6,500 feet. Above the treeline they are bare, windswept rock. The passes were dangerous at the best of times, and thought to be impossible to cross in winter. Natives who were familiar with the Richardsons said no man, Native or white, could cross those ranges alone in the winter. But Johnson had done it, alone and after weeks of an exhausting run from the police.

The Mounties' sense of awe at this accomplishment was matched only by their determination to catch Johnson. He might have bested them in woodsmanship, but now their technological advantage came into play. On February 13, Wop May flew Eames, Gardlund, Riddell, and

Constable William Carter to Lapierre House. Meanwhile, an expedition was sent to cross the Richardsons through Rat Pass, which might have been the route Johnson had taken. Led by Constable Sid May (no relation to Wop May), this party included Sergeant Hersey and civilian volunteers Lazarus Sittichinli, John Moses, Frank Jackson, Constant Ethier, Peter Alexie, and Joe Verville (brother of Noel).

After landing his passengers, Wop May took to the air again to search for Johnson's trail. He found it, and then lost it in the tracks of a herd of Caribou. The clever outlaw was still using every trick in the book, but before disappearing in the caribou path, the trail indicated to May that Johnson was heading toward the Eagle River.

On February 14, heavy fog limited May's flying time to just one hour, but that was enough for him to spot Johnson's trail on the Eagle River, twenty miles upstream from its confluence with the Bell River. Johnson was evidently heading for a tributary of the Yukon River that would put him within striking distance of the Alaska border.

The next day, Constable Sid May's party reached Lapierre House. Eames's men had already set out on foot for the Eagle River. Constable May and his group quickly caught up on their dogsleds. The combined force of twelve men headed up the Eagle River valley, taking shortcuts across land between the stream's numerous bends to make up time. Fog had again grounded the Bellanca, but the men made spruce tree arrows on the ground to show Wop May the direction they had taken.

On February 17, the fog lifted and Wop May was in the air again. He followed the posse's markers, and had a bird's eye view of the climactic encounter between the Mad Trapper and the police. Albert Johnson had finally come to the end of his trail.

Johnson had been moving upriver, but then had backtracked. He might have been trying to circle behind his pursuers, or he might have thought sets of ski trails had been made by policemen, when, in fact, they'd been made by two local trappers. This was the Mad Trapper's first mistake, and it proved fatal.

On a hairpin turn of the Eagle River, Johnson found himself in plain view of the advance men of the posse. Sergeant Hersey was in the lead. He, Sid May, and Joe Verville immediately opened fire. While the bullets

Courtesy Glenbow Archives

The Mad Trapper of Rat River, in death. The killer of Constable Edgar Millen was known as Albert Johnson, but his real identity remains a mystery to this day.

whizzed around him, Johnson ran as fast as he could in homemade snowshoes. He went just a few yards, then stopped, turned, and fired one shot at Hersey, who was shooting from a half-kneeling position. The bullet struck Hersey in the elbow, deflected to his knee, then deflected again to his chest. Hersey was not mortally wounded, but he was in extreme pain and out of the fight.

Constable Sid May thought Hersey had been killed. He signalled to the men who had come running at the sound of gunfire. They broke into two groups and took positions along the riverbanks on both sides of Johnson. The Mounties and their men had Johnson in a three-way crossfire. Johnson threw himself down, pulled off his backpack, shoved it in front of him for protection, and continued to fire from a prone position.

Eames wanted to take Johnson alive, if possible. Three times he called on him to surrender. Each time Johnson replied with bullets. The Inspector did not want any more casualties. He told his men to return fire. Six bullets found their target, one of them smashing through Johnson's spine. The Mad Trapper was dead. Wop May swung low over the body, and signalled to Eames that the fight was over.

The mystery of the Mad Trapper has never been conclusively solved. There was no identification on the body, and the fingerprints did not match any the RCMP or the FBI had on file. There have been many theories as to who he was and why he shot Constable King and then led the RCMP on a gruelling Arctic chase. Some suggest that he was already guilty of murder, and was afraid that the police had found him out. This could indeed be the case, but the only person the Mad Trapper is known for certain to have killed was Constable Edgar Millen. A cairn on Millen Creek, in the North-West Territories, marks the spot where the Mountie died.

14

THE NEWFOUNDLAND RANGERS: "MORE PEACE THAN POLICE"

The story of the Newfoundland Rangers is one of the undiscovered treasures in the lore of Newfoundland and Labrador; undiscovered, that is, by most of the people in the rest of Canada. Of course, during the period that the Newfoundland Ranger Force existed, 1935 to 1950, Newfoundland was not yet a part of Canada. But when Newfoundland and Labrador joined Canadian Confederation in 1949, its rich and dramatic story was added to the tapestry of Canadian history. Moreover, many of the men serving with the Rangers at that time were welcomed into the ranks of the RCMP. During the fifteen years of the Ranger Force's existence, three of its officers died in the line of duty.

The Newfoundland Ranger Force was instituted in 1935, when the former colony was under the administration of a Commission of Government that sat in St. John's and reported to London, England. In urban centres like St. John's, the Newfoundland Constabulary was responsible for law enforcement and keeping the peace. However, a large portion of Newfoundland's population lived in tiny outports or in a few communities in the rugged interior. The Rangers were to be the official link between these isolated places and the capital.

Although the Rangers were empowered to investigate crimes and make arrests, their duties lay far beyond those of the Newfoundland Constabulary. The Rangers were, in many instances, the only government representative the people of a small community would ever see. Therefore, the Ranger wore many hats. He was a policeman and a truant officer, customs collector and wreck commissioner, fisheries officer and game warden. He took in applications for relief (welfare), and tracked down moonshine stills. The Ranger inspected logging camps, fought forest fires, and supervised the construction of roads, wharves, and breakwaters. If a mentally ill person had to be taken to a hospital in St. John's, it was the Ranger's job to get the individual there safe and sound. Under the Commission, Newfoundlanders living in the outports had no democratically elected representatives in St. John's, so the Rangers represented the interests of those citizens. The Rangers were trained in first aid and in rescue work. They organized adult education courses. In an emergency, they could even extract bad teeth.

At the outset, because nobody in Newfoundland had any experience in training men for such a diversified job, the training of the first Rangers was undertaken by officers from Canada's RCMP. In fact, the Ranger's khaki uniform very much resembled that of the RCMP. The Rangers' structure of command was modelled after that of the RCMP, making the Rangers a paramilitary organization. The officers were armed with .38 calibre Colt revolvers and .303 Lee Enfield rifles, but as one Ranger put it, "We were peace officers, putting more emphasis on peace than police."

Of course, the Rangers conducted many of their patrols by sea, sailing from outport to outport. They also used the train that crossed Newfoundland at that time. Otherwise, land patrols were done by hiking, dogsledding, and snowshoeing across some of the roughest country to be found anywhere. Roads, if they existed at all, were primitive. One such patrol overland proved fatal to Danny Corcoran, the first Newfoundland Ranger to die in the line of duty.

Danny Corcoran was a native of St. John's, and was among the original thirty who completed the Ranger training course. As a member of the St. John's Hiking Club, Corcoran had gone on forty mile cross-country hikes, and was considered to be a long distance walker with stamina and experience. In the autumn of 1935, he was posted to the community

Danny Corcoran of the Newfoundland Rangers, in the summer of 1935. The following spring, Ranger Corcoran died after trying to cross Newfoundland's Great Northern Peninsula alone, on foot, while investigating reports of caribou poachers.

Courtesy The Rooms Provincial Archives, St. John's C6-31

of Harbour Deep, on the east coat of Newfoundland's Great Northern Peninsula. This was a very isolated community, five days by sea from St. John's. Between Harbour Deep and the west coast of the peninsula lay the Long Range Mountains, actually the northernmost extension of the Appalachians.

Early in March 1936, Corcoran received reports of caribou poachers. He decided to hike across the peninsula alone to see if he could catch them at it. He expected to meet fellow Ranger John Nichols at Port Saunders, on the west coast. The distance from Harbour Deep to Port Saunders was about sixty miles, as the crow flies. The actual trail overland was much farther. Corcoran thought the trip would take him at least two days.

John Nichols was in Flower Cove when he received a telegram, delivered to him from Port Saunders, that Corcoran was snowshoeing across the peninsula. When Nichols returned to Port Saunders, he spoke to two trappers who had met Corcoran on the trail. They had told him that Nichols was not in Port Saunders, but was on patrol farther north. Corcoran decided to return to Harbour Deep. Days passed, and he did not show up.

John Nichols organized a search party. The men swept the country inland, from Port Saunders up to the plateau of the Long Range Mountains. They found no trace of Ranger Corcoran. Another search was made from the eastern side of the peninsula. Almost a month after he had been reported missing, Danny Corcoran was found. He was lying in the snow, with his feet in a pool of meltwater. He was alive, but just barely.

Corcoran had started back to Harbour Deep, but had experienced one of the worst accidents that can happen to a person in a wilderness setting in very cold weather. While crossing a frozen brook, he broke through the ice and got his feet wet. He also lost some of his equipment, and was unable to make a fire. That night the temperature dropped and Corcoran's feet froze. Ranger Danny Corcoran now faced a grim battle for survival that would last almost twenty days. He crawled on his hands and knees, practically wearing his hands to the bone, in a courageous attempt to reach Harbour Deep. Then he found himself stranded on a point of land between two rivers, unable to cross the water because of breaking ice. That was where the search party found him, too weak to move another inch.

The rescuers took Corcoran by dogsled to White Bay on the peninsula's eastern coast. Then they placed him in a local clergyman's boat for the trip to St. Anthony at the northern tip of the peninsula. Because of ice conditions, that voyage took seven brutal days. A doctor in St. Anthony amputated both of Corcoran's feet, but found that he had contracted tetanus. The doctor wired the General Hospital in St. John's for antitoxin. The medication was put on a single-engine plane to be rushed to St. Anthony, but luck was not on Danny Corcoran's side. Bad weather forced the pilot down. Danny Corcoran died on April 7, 1936, three days before the antitoxin finally arrived in St. Anthony. He was buried in Mount Carmel Cemetery in St. John's. Danny Corcoran's tragic story is the subject of a novel, *Will Anyone Search For Danny,* by Newfoundland author Earl B. Pilgrim.

The second Newfoundland Ranger to perish while on duty was Michael Greene. Born in Placentia Bay in 1914, Greene had been a member of the Newfoundland Constabulary before joining the Rangers. Officers from the Constabulary were always welcomed by the Ranger Force because they were experienced policemen who could be counted upon to provide leadership for the young men who graduated from Ranger training.

On March 5, 1939, Greene was on patrol in a horse-drawn sleigh, near Lamaline on the Burin Peninsula. He was crossing a frozen pond when the ice broke. Greene managed to climb out of the frigid water. He dragged himself across the ice for about one hundred yards, before he succumbed to shock and exposure.

The last Newfoundland Ranger to be killed on duty was Michael Collins. He was born in Lamaline in 1917, and served in the Royal Navy during the Second World War. For a while, it seemed as though Collins led a charmed life. Twice he survived torpedo attacks on ships to which he'd been posted. He was finally invalidated out of the service.

Collins joined the Rangers in February 1946, and soon after had another brush with death. He was on a boat with two other Rangers, conducting inspections along the south and west coasts of Newfoundland, when the vessel's engine exploded. No one was killed, but Collins was seriously burned and the boat was disabled. Fortunately, another vessel showed up to lend assistance.

Michael Collins' luck ran out on August 7, 1946, just six months after he'd joined the Rangers. He was driving a motorcycle near Stephenville, with another Ranger in the sidecar. The bike went off the road, and Collins was killed. His passenger suffered barely a scratch.

In 1950, after Newfoundland and Labrador entered Confederation as Canada's tenth province, The Newfoundland Rangers were disbanded. The Rangers' duties were taken over by the RCMP, and many Rangers transferred to the Mounties. The legend of the Newfoundland Rangers is still kept alive by the Newfoundland Ranger Force Association.

15

— CHARLES R. MILLAR:
THE REGINA RIOT

In times of social unrest, some elements of a population will see the police as the enemy. The uniformed, armed police officer, empowered by the state to arrest and detain, using force if necessary, has been seen at times as the protector of the wealthy and powerful, and the oppressor of the poor. At various times in Canadian history, police were, in fact, used to break up strikes and disperse protesters. They were used to spy upon and harass persons and organizations whose political views were not acceptable to those in power. Quite likely, there were individual officers in such situations who obeyed orders reluctantly, believing that the people they had been sent out to disperse or arrest actually had just cause.

More often, however, the police in these situations did their jobs enthusiastically, and with the belief that they were doing the right thing. They usually accepted as truth the official line that the people they were being sent to confront were radical agitators, communist subversives, or just troublemaking rabble. To the average police officer, the troublemakers were a threat to all that was decent about Canada, and therefore had to be stopped. Such was the attitude of the Regina Police Department and the RCMP on July 1, 1935, when they clashed with the On To Ottawa Trekkers.

The Great Depression — that era so accurately called the dirty thirties — was the worst economic period in Canadian history. Factories closed and unemployment skyrocketed. Agricultural prices plummeted, and farmers became destitute. In the eyes of many, the Conservative government of Richard Bedford Bennett did little to ease the plight of ordinary Canadians. Bennett himself was a millionaire, and subscribed to the prevailing belief that a healthy young man who didn't have a job was just lazy. There was always work to be found *somewhere*.

Bennett's response to rising anger and discontent among the growing throngs of unemployed was to beef up the RCMP with more men, equip them with riot gear, and pass legislation that gave police broad powers when dealing with "subversives." He also installed Major General James Howden MacBrien as Commissioner of the RCMP. MacBrien was a disciplinarian who believed that all Canadian boys should receive military training from the age of six. He shared Bennett's hatred of anything that smacked of socialism. He saw himself and the RCMP as bastions against godless Communism.

Among those particularly hard hit by the worsening economic crisis, and the Tory government's ineffective policies, were unemployed single males. Their steadily growing ranks included boys barely into their teens, and veterans of the Great War. Deemed ineligible for even the meager relief that was begrudgingly handed out to other people in dire straits, these "transients," as they were called, wandered across the country looking for work and handouts of food and clothing. Bennett and MacBrien considered them the most dangerous of all, because they were certain alien Communist agents were filling their heads with un-Canadian ideas.

Bennett's solution to this problem was to have the Department of National Defence set up "relief camps." The first ones opened in October 1932. In these camps, single men would work in return for food, clothing, shelter, and twenty cents a day. At first the idea was applauded, especially since Bennett promised that the camps would be only a temporary necessity.

Soon, however, the DND relief camps were being denounced as "slave camps." They were run by army officers with strict military discipline. Many of them were in isolated locations. Most of the work involved monotonous, back-breaking labour, done with hand tools because the government would not provide machinery. Many of the make-work projects were practically useless. Life in the camps was humiliating and demoralizing. The men felt they were being treated like convicts. By the spring of 1935 these "temporary" camps were still in full operation, with no end in sight for the men forced by desperation to go to them. In British Columbia, hundreds of frustrated workers walked out of the camps and descended on Vancouver to begin a protest that would come to be called the On To Ottawa Trek. They were going to ride the tops of boxcars all the way to the capital and present their case to Prime Minister Bennett personally.

On June 3, more than 800 Trekkers rode the rails out of Vancouver. As they travelled east their numbers increased to almost 2,000. On Bennett's orders they were stopped at Regina on June 14. What followed was one of the most violent confrontations in Canadian labour history.

Bennett agreed to meet with eight of the Trek leaders in Ottawa, while the rest of the protesters camped in Regina's Exhibition grounds, closely watched by the RCMP. The meeting that took place in Ottawa on June 22, quickly deteriorated into a shouting match and accomplished nothing. The Trek leaders returned to Regina.

Some of the Trekkers attempted to continue their journey east by car, but the RCMP turned their convoy back. The Trek leaders finally agreed to disband and leave Regina. However, the RCMP blocked all routes out of the city and said the men would have to go to a camp being set up for them at Lumsden, fifteen miles northwest of Regina, to be "processed."

The Trekkers suspected that the "camp" was a trap. They believed Bennett had agreed to the Ottawa meeting, not because he really intended to negotiate in good faith, but to give the police time to prepare for a major confrontation. The leaders called for a rally to be held in Regina's Market Square on July 1, at 8:00 p.m.

Commissioner MacBrien had been anxiously awaiting permission to serve warrants on the Trek leaders. As the Trekkers were organizing their rally, he got the go ahead to arrest them. Unfortunately, senior RCMP officers picked the worst possible time and place to make those arrests: the Market Square rally!

The rally began at eight o'clock, as scheduled. The leaders used a flatbed truck as a platform. Within minutes, plainclothes RCMP officers were mingling with the crowd, and truckloads of RCMP and city police were converging on the square. At 8:17, RCMP Inspector Walter Mortimer gave a shrill blast on his whistle, and the police charged into the crowd.

Accounts as to just what happened are contradictory. Many witnesses claimed the police used billy clubs to strike down anyone within reach. The police denied hitting anyone. No doubt, many of the people who were hurt sustained injuries in the mad rush to get out of the way of the police. In any event, the square was quickly cleared, but the police managed to grab only two of the seven men for whom they had warrants.

People running from the police in the square ran into other police formations, and these officers did use excessive force; even plainclothes officers reported being clubbed down by uniformed officers. The police fired guns over the heads of the people, waded into crowds with swinging clubs, and fired tear gas. The men began to fight back, hurling rocks and bottles at the police, and picking up anything that could be used as a weapon. Downtown Regina resembled a war zone, as violence surged through the streets. Many local men joined the Trekkers in the battle against the police. The police did not have shields, and therefore had no protection from the barrage of objects being thrown at them.

As the Regina city police poured into the square, Detective Charles Millar watched from a window of the police station, where he was being held in reserve. Scottish-born Millar had been with the Regina Police Department since 1920, and had been promoted to detective in 1929. He was a veteran of the Great War and was highly respected by fellow officers. In 1927, his wife had died giving birth to their daughter, Margaret.

While watching the dramatic action in the square, Millar saw two officers who appeared to be in trouble. He rushed outside to help them. Millar was dressed in a plainclothes suit. He had a leather billy club and his service revolver in his coat pocket. The officers were apparently able to take care of themselves, because something else quickly drew Millar's attention.

A steamroller was parked near the fire hall, and a group of men were attempting to break into the machine's tool box, no doubt looking for items to use as weapons. Millar ran over and tried to drive them off. There was a skirmish, and Millar fell to his knees after being struck on the shoulder and forehead with a shovel. Then, someone wielding a piece of cordwood smashed him in the head from behind. Millar collapsed with a fractured skull and massive brain damage.

An RCMP constable who was at the scene later reported, "There seemed to be a rumble over near that steam roller ... something similar to a rugby match ... men piled up on the top of another."

Another RCMP officer, E.A. Wakefield, who was also in plainclothes, was in front of the fire hall when he saw Millar struck down. He rushed to the detective's aid, but he too was hit on the head and knocked unconscious. City Policeman Alex Hill now went to help Millar. He was photographed trying to lift the fallen detective by the armpits, moments before he himself was dazed by a blow. Finally, City Constable R. Anderson was able to drag Millar into a police garage where other casualties awaited aid. When he was finally taken in a

Courtesy Saskatchewan Archives Board #R-B171-1

The Regina Riot: City police constable Alex Hill can be seen (centre) trying to lift the mortally wounded Detective Charles Millar. Moments after this picture was taken, Hill was also struck down.

patrol car to Regina's General Hospital, Millar was pronounced dead on arrival.

News of Millar's death spread through the ranks of embattled police officers. They knew that eight-year-old Margaret Millar was now an orphan. The police unleashed their fury on the rioters. The Trekkers and their supporters, who had believed from the very beginning that the police were out to break bones and crack heads, responded in kind.

By the time the fighting ended early in the morning of July 2, thirty-nine police officers had been injured. Police arrested 120 people during the riot. How many civilians were injured is not known, because those who went to the hospital for treatment were also arrested. Many people were treated in private homes. The number of civilian injuries was probably in the hundreds. Reports from the time state that no civilians were killed. However, years later evidence was uncovered that indicated hospital records were altered to conceal the fact that one civilian did, in fact, die as a result of injuries received during the riot.

The din of the riot had barely died away before newsboys were on the street shouting out the headline news of Detective Millar's death. Little Margaret heard them. She had not yet been told that her father had died. "That is my daddy," she said, and then cried. Saskatchewan Premier Jimmy Gardiner angrily blamed the Bennett government and the police for the riot, which had caused heavy damage in downtown Regina. He arranged for the Trekkers to be transported out of the city — and Saskatchewan — without going to the camp at Lumsden.

Charles Millar's funeral was the largest Regina had ever seen up to that time. A reward of $2,000 was offered for information leading to the arrest of those responsible for his death. Arthur "Slim" Evans, a Trek leader, accused RCMP officers of beating Millar to death. But Evans was nowhere near the scene at the time, and there was absolutely no evidence that police officers were responsible. Many people who claimed to have witnessed the assault came forward with descriptions of three men, but no one was ever charged. The case was officially closed in 1939.

Prime Minister Bennett and Commissioner MacBrien were satisfied that the police had struck a severe blow against Communism, but there was a loud public outcry over what had happened in Regina.

Politicians and journalists questioned the wisdom of the police attempting to arrest the Trek leaders in such a potentially volatile setting as the rally, when the men could have been quietly picked up at another time. They wanted to know why the Riot Act had not been read, and why the people at the rally had not been told to disperse before the police went charging in. Charles Millar's death, they argued, had been totally avoidable.

In a federal election later that year, William Lyon Mackenzie King's Liberals swept Bennett's Conservatives from power in a landslide. One of King's first acts was to dismantle the relief camps. His government began to investigate other ways to deal with the unemployment problem, such as unemployment insurance and a minimum wage. Relics from the Regina Riot are on exhibit in the Saskatchewan Provincial Archives.

16

DEADLY OCTOBER: ─────────────
FOUR OFFICERS SLAIN

In October 1935, a spree of violence that began in Manitoba, and ended almost 800 miles away in Alberta, made front page news across Canada. It was a short-lived melodrama that gave Canadians a taste of the kind of lawlessness that had so recently been visited upon the United States by the likes of Bonnie and Clyde and the Barker Gang. The three young men responsible for the bloody crime wave were all sons of hard-working, law-abiding Russian Doukhobors; a strict Christian sect whose followers abstain from such worldly vices as alcohol and tobacco, and who embrace pacifism. The young men's parents had fled religious persecution in their homeland, to settle on farms near the Saskatchewan towns of Pelly and Arran. All of the young men were Canadian born. Of the three, only one had ever been in trouble with the law, and that had been over a relatively minor charge of stealing grain. Yet, in a series of events that bewilders Canadian crime historians to this day, the three youths killed four police officers. That was the largest Canadian police-killing of the twentieth century.

On the evening of Saturday, September 28, 1935, two young men, armed and masked, entered the Smith and Fawcett General Store in the Manitoba village of Benito, just across the provincial border from Arran. When proprietor W.R. Fawcett refused their demand for money, one of the bandits struck him over the head with a pistol. Seconds later, Fawcett's partner Smith, and Smith's son Oscar, arrived at the store. The robbers fled, with Oscar right behind them. Oscar caught one of the thugs, but was slugged to the ground with a pistol. He saw the pair escape in an old car driven by a third man. The vehicle had no license plates.

Smith reported the attempted robbery to William Wainwright, the fifty-year-old constable of Benito. With assistance from the nearby RCMP station at Swan River, Wainwright searched the crime scene, but found no clues. However, he suspected that the same gang was responsible for several robberies that had occurred in the area.

At about 12:30 a.m. on October 5, Wainwright spotted an unlicensed car that matched the description Smith had given him. He pulled the car over to speak to the four well-dressed young men inside. They were John Kalmakoff, twenty-one; Joe Posnikoff, twenty; Peter Woiken, eighteen; and a youth named Paul Bogarra. Wainwright searched the car, but did not find any weapons. Satisfied that they were not the culprits he was looking for, he let them go on their way with just a warning about driving without a license plate.

However, about three hours later Wainwright apparently had second thoughts on the matter. He located the car again, just as the youths were dropping a couple of girls off at a farmhouse after a local dance. After talking to the young men, Wainwright decided to let Bogarra go, but told the other three they would have to go with him to his office in Benito. Bogarra drove off, and the others got into Wainwright's car. Apparently, he did not search them.

From his office, Wainwright called the Swan River RCMP post. He had no jail in which to hold the suspects, and wanted to take them to Pelly, Saskatchewan, about twenty miles away. The police station there had a jail, and Wainwright also thought the trio might have been involved in a recent robbery in that community. Wainwright wanted an RCMP officer to assist him in transporting Posnikoff, Kalmakoff, and Woiken. Half an hour later, Constable John G. Shaw arrived at Benito. Shaw, thirty-eight, was a decorated veteran of the Great War, having served with the British Expeditionary Force and the Royal Flying Corps. He was a former member of the Manitoba Provincial Police, and had been a Mountie for three years.

The two officers and their suspects left Benito in Shaw's unmarked police car, a Chevrolet sedan. The policemen sat up front, and the Doukhobor youths in the back. Evidently, the suspects still had not been searched. Perhaps Shaw assumed that Wainwright had already done that. Whatever the reason for the oversight, it proved fatal. The car never made it to Pelly.

When Wainwright and Shaw did not return to Benito or Swan River by noon on October 5, the Mounties organized a local search for the missing car. They were unaware that by that time it was heading west across Saskatchewan. The whereabouts of the two police officers remained a mystery until October 7.

That Monday morning, a Doukhobor farmer named John Kollenchuk was driving his wagon along the dirt road between Arran and Pelly. His team of horses suddenly became skittish and would not go any farther. Kollenchuk got down to investigate. In a slough about fifty feet from the road he found the bodies of John Shaw and William Wainwright.

After the shaken farmer reported his grisly discovery, and police had recovered the bodies, RCMP Assistant Commissioner Thomas Dann of the Swan River post received an anonymous tip that he should speak to Paul Bogarra. The youth told him about Wainwright's confrontation with Kalmakoff, Woiken, and Posnikoff. Dann now had the names of suspects. He tried to reconstruct what had happened in the police car.

At a place where the winding road suddenly straightened out the prisoners had attacked the officers. Wainwright had a stab wound in the back of his neck and slashes on his head. Shaw, who had been driving, had slashes on his right cheek and right hand. One of the prisoners managed to get hold of Wainwright's .38 service revolver, and shot him through the left eye. Another already had a .32 pistol, which he used to shoot Shaw in the back of the head three times. The car went off the road and into a ditch. The killers rifled the victims' pockets, then dragged the bodies out of the car and dumped them in the slough. They pushed the car out of the ditch and fled. Autopsies indicated that Shaw died instantly, but Wainwright lived for several hours. Wainwright left behind a widow and four adult children. Shaw was engaged to be married.

On Monday afternoon, William Pereluk told police that the three fugitives had stopped at his farm about ten miles northwest of Pelly, at about 10:30 on Saturday morning and asked for something to eat (not uncommon in those days). As Pereluk made them a meal, they told him that they were detectives searching for the killers of two police officers. This was two days before the bodies were found. Pereluk thought their story sounded fishy, but he didn't want to provoke them. All three had revolvers — one in a police belt — and one had a large hunting knife. He could also tell that they had been drinking.

When the three were ready to leave, Pereluk walked with them to their car. He saw a jug of moonshine on the floor and stains on the front seat. The young men told him they were heading south to investigate along the American border. This might have been a ruse to trick the police, in case Pereluk spoke to them, because they did not head for the border. There is no explanation for why Pereluk waited two days before giving this information to the police.

Assistant Commissioner Dann was certain that the young killers would head straight for the United States. However, once the story was spread by radio news reports and in the papers, he learned that they were heading west on Highway 49. They had bought gas in Preeceville, Saskatchewan, and then, amazingly, they had attended a Saturday night dance in the little community of Ketchen. They even had dates, young women who no doubt would have been horrified if they had known their escorts had murdered two policemen less than twenty-four hours earlier. Just as amazingly, the killers still had Constable Shaw's car. More experienced criminals would have ditched it and stolen another vehicle.

Shortly after 7:00 p.m. on October 7, the killers stopped at a gas station in the small town of Exshaw, Alberta, about twelve miles east of Canmore. The proprietor, Roy Zeller, thought it odd that the "rough looking" youths in the car wanted only one gallon of gas. They were, in fact, running low on the money they had taken from the dead policemen. When Zeller asked where they were going, one of them replied, "Anywhere." He also noted that the car was rather banged up, as though they had rolled it.

Inside, Zeller's wife Lucille had the radio on. While her husband was putting gas in the car, she heard a news bulletin about the hunt for three suspected killers. The bulletin gave the license plate number of the stolen car. Lucille looked out the window and saw that very car at the gas pump. She went outside just as the car pulled away. Lucille immediately called the RCMP station at Canmore. A little later, a waitress at a diner in Canmore noted that three young male customers seemed to have barely enough money to pay for their inexpensive meals.

The killers left Canmore and headed for Banff National Park. Earlier in the day they had attempted to enter the park through the east gate. When the officer on duty, Tom Staples, told them there was a $2 admission charge, they said they didn't have any money. Staples thought it odd that three young men in a car with Manitoba plates should arrive at the park dead broke. He began to question them about the car. Instead of answering, they turned around and drove away. Staples found this all very suspicious and called the RCMP in Banff.

In desperate need of money, the fugitives decided to try their hands at highway robbery. They pulled over to the side of the road and used flashlights to wave down the first car to come along. The vehicle was driven by C.T. Scott of Calgary, who was on his way to Banff with his wife. Thinking someone was having car trouble, Scott pulled over to give assistance, but when he saw the three men walking toward his car, he didn't like the look of them. Scott quickly stuffed $85 that he had in his pocket into the car seat.

One of the men asked Scott if he could spare some gasoline. Scott replied that if they could get it out of his tank, they could have it. Suddenly Joe Posnikoff pointed a gun at Scott's head. On the passenger side, John Kalmakoff covered Mrs. Scott with his gun. They ordered the couple out of the car. One of them went through Scott's pockets and found $10. They asked if he had anymore money, and Scott said no. Posnikoff pointed his revolver directly at Scott's head and said, "If there is, you know what it means." Then the bandits took Scott's watch.

With the frightened couple standing at the side of the road, the three youths began to argue in a mixture of Russian and broken English. The Scotts couldn't understand much of what was said, but they were certain the robbers were debating whether or not to kill them. Finally, one of the men gave Scott back his watch and told him and his wife that they could go. The couple continued on the road to Banff. When Scott looked in the rear view mirror, he was surprised to see the Chevrolet following him.

Meanwhile, police from the RCMP detachments in both Canmore and Banff were heading for the east gate of the national park. Constable Grey Campbell at Banff had received Tom Staples' call. He and the other officer on duty, Constable George "Scotty" Harrison, had been joined by two off-duty policemen who happened to be in the station when the call came in: Sergeant Thomas Wallace and Constable George Combe. These men were not yet aware that the occupants of the Chevy with the Manitoba plates were wanted for murder. The call with that information came into the station just after they left. A Constable named Bonner and Police Magistrate R.S. Hawke were coming from Canmore.

A short distance east of the east gate, the Mounties from Banff set up a roadblock so that they could check all vehicles heading for the park. It was not long before they saw the headlights of two approaching cars, one only about twelve yards behind the other. The first was the Scotts' car. As Constable Combe looked in the driver's window and then waved him through, Scott said, "The bandit car is right behind."

As soon as the young men in the second car saw the police they opened fire. Caught in the full glare of the car's headlights, the officers were easy targets. Constable Harrison, who was nearest to the killers, was shot in the throat. Before he fell he managed to shoot out the Chevy's headlights. Constable Wallace had been walking toward the suspect car when he was shot in the chest. He returned fire as he staggered back to the police car. There he asked Constable Combe for some ammunition, and then collapsed.

The stretch of road on which this was taking place was under construction, and all the activity raised a cloud of dust. That and the darkness made visibility very poor. Constables Combe and Campbell heard the shots and then saw the car lights go out. The next thing they knew, Wallace emerged from the dust, walking backwards and firing his gun. Campbell later wrote in his report:

> Just as I stooped to pick up Sergt. Wallace a heavy set
> man pounded through the dust running west. Const.

Combe was immediately to my rear and started firing at this running figure that passed on the north side of the car, thus covering my actions in attempting to get Sergt. Wallace into the car. Const. Combe joined me and after getting Sergt. Wallace into the back seat we saw a figure lying under the engine of the Manitoba car with his hands waving. We could not distinguish the object for a few seconds but when we recognized the uniform of the struggling figure we ran over. It was Cst. Harrison who was lying in a pool of blood, badly injured.

By this time, the three gunmen had abandoned their car and fled into the bush. They continued to fire at Campbell and Combe, who were trying to help Harrison. The two Mounties shot back. The gun duel was still going on when Constable Bonner and Magistrate Hawke arrived. They drew their weapons and laid down a barrage of fire to keep the bandits' heads down while Campbell and Combe got Harrison to the police car. Campbell rushed the wounded men to the hospital in Canmore. Because of the serious nature of their injuries, the men were taken by ambulance to a larger hospital in Calgary.

In spite of the doctors' efforts, both officers died the next day. Sergeant Wallace, thirty-nine, had been a sniper with the Gordon Highlanders in the Great War. He had been a police officer in Alberta for fourteen years, and a Mountie for three. Earlier in the year, Wallace had been with the Mounted Police contingent that battled the On to Ottawa Trekkers in Regina. He left a widow, but no children. Constable Harrison, twenty-nine, was a native of Scotland. He had been with the Mounted Police for four years, the length of time he had been in Canada. He had become engaged the previous July.

After leaving the wounded men at the hospital, Campbell raced back to the scene of the gun battle. Combe, Bonner, and Hawke were still exchanging fire with the killers in the bush. When Campbell returned, the policemen spread out to outflank the bandits.

There was a brief lull in the gunfire. Then, as he peered into the darkness, Combe saw a movement in the bush. He snapped on his

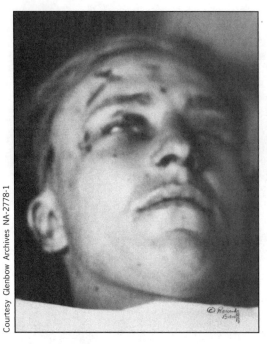

Courtesy Glenbow Archives NA-2778-1

Joe Posnikoff, leader of the Doukhbour bandits, in death.

flashlight, and the beam caught Joe Posnikoff holding a pistol. Combe fired immediately and hit Posnikoff in the head, killing him on the spot. The gun Combe took from the dead man's hand was Wainwright's .38 Colt service revolver.

The other gunmen fled deeper into the bush. The officers did not attempt to pursue them in the darkness. At daylight, Inspector A.G. Birch arrived from Banff with more constables and about sixty armed civilian volunteers. Among the reinforcements were Sergeant John Cawsey with Dale, his tracking dog, and Park Warden Bill Neish. A former RCMP officer, Neish had a reputation as a marksman.

Inspector Birch divided the manhunters into small groups for a systematic search of the bush. He left a pair of men to patrol the road in case the fugitives tried to cross it. A heavy snow was falling, but Dale picked up a scent.

For a few hours the fugitives managed to stay ahead of the posse, but with the dog on their trail they must have felt the hunters closing in. At about 10:00 a.m., the men watching the road saw Kalmakoff and Woiken break from cover and dash across the road. They told Birch, who quickly assembled a party to go after them. This group included Neish and fellow Park Warden Howard Leacock.

The fugitives had been seen entering the bush at a place called Seven Mile Hill. At about 10:30, the hunters carefully began to search that area. They had not gone very far up the hill when Leacock saw a man moving through the trees. He shouted, "Halt!" Two bullets whizzed past his head in reply.

Courtesy Glenbow Archives NA-2778-4

Funeral procession in Calgary for Sergeant T.S. Wallace and Constable G.C. Harrison.

Bill Neish dropped to one knee and squinted down the site of his rifle. Through the brush he could see the glint of a gun. He gave the man one more chance, calling on him to surrender. The answer was another shot. Neish coolly squeezed off two shots. The man — Peter Woiken — screamed and fell, writhing on the ground in agony.

Leacock and Neish had barely started moving forward, when Leacock suddenly saw the barrel of a gun pointing at him across a rotten log. He dove for cover as yet another bullet whistled over his head. Neish dropped to the ground, too. The shooter had taken cover behind the decayed log, which Neish knew would not stop a bullet. He had a good idea just where the man was. Firing from the prone position, Neish put a bullet right through the log. John Kalmakoff cried out when the slug tore into his stomach. He and Woiken both died later that day in the Banff hospital.

The slain officers were all buried with military honours. John Kalmakoff's family buried his remains in an unmarked grave on their farm. The families of Peter Woiken and Joe Posnikoff did not claim their bodies, and the people of Banff and Canmore did not want the cop-killers buried in local cemeteries. The bodies were finally interred in an unmarked grave in a cemetery in Morley, Alberta.

The carnage of that deadly October in 1935 was not matched until March of 2005, when four RCMP officers were murdered near Mayerthorpe, Alberta. The failure of professional police officers to search the prisoners for weapons still defies explanation. As for the reasons behind the killings: the fugitives fired on the Mounties in Alberta because they were already guilty of murder, and knew that if captured they would probably hang. But before they murdered Wainwright and Shaw, they were only suspected of being involved in a series of petty robberies. The young killers died leaving unanswered the question that was in everybody's mind. Why?

17

JOHN LEWIS:
RED RYAN'S LAST HOLDUP

May 23, 1936, would turn out to be a landmark date in the annals of Canadian crime. It would also be the last day in the life of Constable John Lewis, a member of the thirteen-man police force in the small city of Sarnia, Ontario.

Even by the standards of the time, the Sarnia police department was undermanned and not properly equipped. The officers carried .32 Colt revolvers; mere popguns compared to the deadly artillery favoured by armed bandits. Their department did not even own a bulletproof vest.

There had been recommendations to expand the police force and upgrade equipment, but with the country in the grip of the Great Depression the money was simply not available. Sarnia's municipal government didn't give high priority to such an expense. After all, what could happen in the quiet community of 18,000 to justify fitting the police out like big city cops? None of the constables had ever been obliged to draw his gun in the line of duty. That was about to change, because on May 25, Red Ryan came to town.

Norman "Red" Ryan has been called "the Canadian Jesse James." According to Ryan biographer Peter McSherry, author of *The Big Red Fox,* the dramatic image of Ryan as an arch-criminal and a master of bank robbery was largely a creation of the media. Born in Toronto in 1895, Ryan was in trouble with the law all his life. In 1921 he landed in the Kingston Penitentiary for the third time, having pulled several bush-league bank robberies. Ryan might also have been responsible for the murder of an Australian sailor named Albert Slade. Toronto Chief of Police Samuel Dickson described Ryan as a "vicious, dangerous and resourceful thief."

In September 1923, Ryan and four other inmates made a spectacular escape from the prison. Ryan pulled another string of armed robberies in Canada and the United States. In December he was captured by police in Minneapolis and transported back to Kingston.

Ryan now faced a lifetime behind bars. As the years passed, he

seemed to change. He told one and all that he deeply regretted the errors of his past and that, given the chance, he would make up for them. He advised younger convicts to mend their ways. Ryan became a nurse in the prison infirmary, and an altar boy in the prison chapel. Newspaper articles began telling the wonderful story of the "new" Red Ryan. Bad men *could* be reformed, the journalists said. Soon they were arguing the case for Ryan's parole. Father Wilfred Kingsley, the prison chaplain, had nothing but praise for Ryan, and strongly recommended him for parole.

Norman "Red" Ryan following his release from prison. The supposedly reformed bandit was leading a double life.

Courtesy Metropolitan Toronto Police Museum

The press made Ryan a celebrity. People jumped onto the "parole Ryan" bandwagon. One of those who took up the cause was Agnes McPhail, social reformer and Canada's first female Member of Parliament. Prime Minister R.B. Bennett went to the penitentiary to meet Ryan in person, and agreed to help him. A year later, in July 1935, Ryan was paroled. He said that he was "retired from the banking business for good."

Red Ryan became a champion for prison reform, speaking at picnics, bazaars, and sporting events on the need for rehabilitation instead of strict punishment. He also lectured on the theme of "crime does not pay." He once stated, "If I ever go in for crime again, I deserve to be shot."

Ryan was given a job as a car salesman in Toronto, and he moonlighted as doorman at the Nealan House Hotel on King Street. An admirer, Dr. Oswald Withrow, was writing a biography that was almost guaranteed to be a bestseller, with Ryan sharing in the royalties.

Red Ryan had it made. He had a car, a wardrobe of fine suits, and a host of influential and respectable friends. Everywhere he went, people wanted to shake his hand. Nobody suspected that the new Red Ryan was secretly in partnership with a thief and burglar named Harry Checkley, and another paroled convict named Edward McMullen, whom the warden of the Kingston Pen had called the most dangerous man in the prison. Ryan's cheering public did not for a moment connect him with a rash of bank robberies in Ontario and Quebec. Nor did any suspicion fall on Ryan when on February 29, 1936, thieves killed a Markham automobile dealer named Edward Stonehouse — and seriously wounded his son — in an unsuccessful attempt to steal a high-powered car. After all, Red Ryan was a reformed man. He even offered to help the police track down the villains who had murdered Stonehouse. Ryan went on living this double life … until May 23.

On that day, Ryan and Checkley drove from Toronto to Sarnia in a stolen car with stolen and doctored plates. Their target was the Sarnia liquor store. Since it was the Saturday of the Victoria Day long weekend, the bandits had calculated that by closing time the store would be fat with money, and would be much easier pickings than a bank.

The liquor store was on the main street of downtown Sarnia, only a block from the police station. It was on the second floor, and had separate entrance and exit doors at street level, divided by a wall. The customer entered the IN door, went up a flight of stairs to a landing, and made a right turn into the store area, which was about thirty-five feet long. Like all Ontario liquor stores of the time, the interior of the one in Sarnia somewhat resembled the layout of a bank. The customer had to go to a wicket on a long counter, and place his order with a clerk. The clerk then went into a storeroom at the back to get the bottle. Having made his purchase, the customer went down the exit stairs to the OUT door.

Just before 6:00 p.m., the end of the business day, Ryan and Checkley parked their car around the corner from the liquor store and walked down an alleyway toward the target. They were dressed in railway workers' clothes. Ryan had dyed his red hair brown. In their pockets the bandits had masks, goggles, and guns. Ryan carried a .45 Colt automatic and a .38 Ivor Johnson revolver. Checkley had a Smith & Wesson and an Ivor Johnson, both .38s. They entered the building and then locked the IN door. No last minute customers would be able to come up behind them. Then they began to don masks and goggles.

Evidently, Ryan's plan was to wait at the bottom of the stairs until most of the customers had made their purchases and left through the exit. Then, he and Checkley would dash up the stairs, and surprise the staff and the few remaining customers. They would grab the money, and then probably force the people down a stairway to the building's cellar. With the people locked up, the bandits would go down the stairs to the OUT door, and onto the street. Anyone watching would think they were just a couple of working men leaving the liquor store. They would be well on their way to Toronto before anyone could raise an alarm.

The heist did not go as Ryan had planned. A customer on the sales floor happened to look down the stairwell, and saw the two men putting on masks and goggles. At the same time, Checkley saw *him* and realized they would have to make their move immediately. He charged up the stairs yelling, "All right, come on!" Ryan dashed up right behind him.

The robbers burst into the store, each with guns in both hands. Checkley cried, "Stick 'em up!" The twenty-plus people in the store were too startled to know what to do, but when Checkley snapped, "Come on, I mean it! This is a holdup!" they quickly raised their hands.

Manager D.A. MacDonald, who had been in charge of the store for only two days, thought at first that he was the victim of a prank. He knew it was the real thing when the smaller gunman made the customers face the back wall with their hands raised, and then the bigger man (Ryan) vaulted over the counter to get at the cash drawers. Ryan told the four employees to turn around and not look at him. Then he stuffed his pockets with money from two drawers. He evidently did not know that just a few feet way was an unlocked safe with more than $1,000 in it.

While Ryan was looting the cash drawers and Checkley was waving his pistols at the staff and customers, two men — one of them named Geoffrey Garvey — arrived at the entrance door and found it locked. They were surprised, because it was not quite six o'clock. Not to be denied their weekend bottles of spirits, they went in the OUT door and sneaked up the exit stairs. As they reached the landing, they saw people with their hands in the air, being covered by a man with a gun. Garvey's companion cried out, "It's a holdup!" Neither Checkley nor Ryan seemed to have heard, but MacDonald and one of his clerks saw the two men in the exit stairwell and exchanged glances with Garvey. As Garvey stated later, "I said to myself this is no place for me." The two retreated down the stairs as quietly as they had come up. When they reached the street, Garvey ran across the road to a taxi stand, where a driver immediately called the police.

The phone rang in the Sarnia Police Station at 5:58 p.m., just as the officers were having a change of shift. Detective Frank McGirr and Sergeant William Simpkins were just about to go off-duty. Constable John Lewis and Sergeant George Smith were about to start their shift. That meant there were four officers available to respond to the alarm, instead of the usual two. McGirr, Simpkins, Lewis, and Smith piled into a patrol car for the short dash to the liquor store.

Lewis had barely set foot inside the police station when the robbery call came in. Just minutes earlier he had left his modest Nelson Street home, saying goodbye to his wife Vera, and his children, ten-year-old Donna and eight-year-old Jack. Lewis, thirty-three, had been with the Sarnia police for seven years. Four years earlier he had been commended for capturing two burglars. Fellow officers said that if a situation got rough, Lewis was a "scrapper." He had a reputation as an easygoing man, and was known as "the policeman with the long, slow step." But there was nothing slow about Lewis in the moments after the police car pulled up in front of the Sarnia liquor store.

Inside the store, Ryan and Checkley had no idea that police were on the way. Checkley, addressing Ryan as "Alex," shouted to him to grab a couple of bottles. Ryan either didn't hear him, or ignored the request. He asked Checkley if the door was "all right," and Checkley said it was. Then Ryan said, "Come on, let's go. I've got it all."

Ryan began to herd the customers toward the back of the store, possibly intending to force them down a stairway to the cellar. Then he heard a noise from the exit stairway. He turned, with two guns at the ready to deal with whoever came through the door.

When the patrol car screeched to a halt in front of the liquor store, the officers jumped out and Simpkins went straight to the IN door, which was locked. Lewis, McGirr, and Smith went through the OUT door and then up the stairs, with Lewis in the lead. Lewis had his gun in his hand when he reached the landing and started to turn left into the store. Suddenly, he was confronted by a big man with two guns pointed directly at him. Lewis could have fired, but he hesitated. The customers were directly behind the robber. If Lewis fired and missed, he might hit an innocent person.

Lewis's hesitation cost him his life, because Ryan didn't hesitate for an instant. Ryan fired his Colt automatic four times at point-blank range. Lewis was almost lucky. One bullet was deflected by a metal button on his tunic. Two more struck a hunting and fishing regulations book in his pocket. But the fourth bullet pierced his chest and severed an artery near his heart. Lewis collapsed without firing a shot.

From the stairwell came shouts of "Police!" and "Duck!" Staff and customers dove for the floor and scurried for whatever cover they could find. McGirr and Smith entered the store right after Lewis. Ryan fired again, his bullet clipping McGirr's clothing without actually touching the officer. Now there were no customers standing directly behind Ryan, so McGirr and Smith returned fire. A bullet struck Ryan in the left arm.

With escape through the exit stairwell blocked, Ryan retreated to the top of the entrance stairway, leaving a trail of blood on the floor. Checkley was already there, apparently confused and panicked by the sudden appearance of police. Before the bandits could take cover in the stairwell, McGirr and Smith fired again. One or both of the robbers must have been hit, because later the police would be unable to find bullet holes in the wall there.

Simpkins had started up the stairs after the other officers, but when he realized the bandits were going down the IN stairs, he hurried back down to make sure they did not escape through the entrance. McGirr and Smith heard the sound of someone — probably Ryan — falling down the stairs. They hurried to the top of the stairwell and took turns looking around the corner to shoot down at the outlaws. Lewis staggered to his feet and tried to join in the gun battle, but was unable to go more than a few steps.

Ryan and Checkley were now in a trap. With one hand, Ryan struggled to open the door he himself had locked just minutes earlier. With the other hand, he fired his gun up the stairwell until he was out

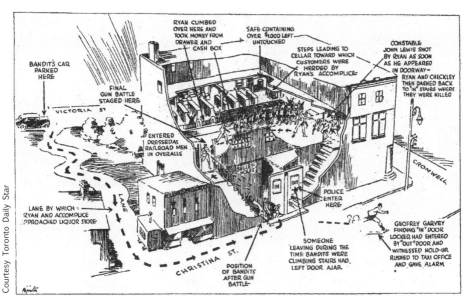

Courtesy Toronto Daily Star

Shootout in Sarnia: artist's conception of the liquor store robbery that re-sulted in the deaths of Red Ryan, Harry Checkley, and Sarnia Police Con-stable John Lewis.

of ammo. Then he pulled the other gun and began to shoot again. From a position about halfway up the stairs, Checkley also fired a few shots. Suddenly Checkley cried, "I give up!" He dropped his guns and then collapsed. By now, Ryan was slumped against the door. When ordered to throw his guns up the stairs he did so. The robbery had lasted no more than three minutes. The gunfight, from first shot to last, had spanned about thirty seconds. The total loot in Ryan's pockets was $394.

Constable Lewis and the two bandits were rushed to hospital by ambulance. Checkley, shot once in the chest, was pronounced dead on arrival. Ryan, wounded in the arm and ankle, and with a bullet in his head, died at about 7:50 p.m. without regaining consciousness.

Lewis died at about 6:45 p.m., minutes after his wife arrived at the hospital. He was conscious when she got there, and spoke to her. Later, she would not disclose his dying words to the *Toronto Star*. Those words, said Vera Lewis, were for her ears alone. However, she told a reporter for the *Sarnia Canadian Observer* that her husband's last words were, "I'll soon be with Mr. Rhodes." This was in reference to Reverend A.H. Rhodes, a family friend whose funeral Lewis had attended just the day before.

In an article in which she was likened to the heroine in Alfred Lord Tennyson's classic poem, "Home They Brought Her Warrior Dead," Vera told a *Toronto Star* reporter, "Of course John would do that," when told that her husband had been the first one to go through the door to confront the robbers. "It just wouldn't have been John if he hadn't been first. He was doing his duty. He wouldn't have thought of doing anything else."

Frank McGirr told the *Star*:

> The instant Ryan opened fire right on top of Lewis, we knew it was their lives or ours, and we made up our minds to shoot it out to the death. We mightn't have been so rough with them if we hadn't seen Lewis shot down. It was no time to hesitate with one of our own men knocked off almost before the shooting started. Right there I made up my mind that neither of them would get away, though it cost me my life to stop them.

Constable Lewis was given a hero's funeral, and was praised by Sarnia Chief of Police William J. Lannin as the finest officer on the force. More than 2,500 people filed past the slain policeman's coffin. A procession of 150 cars followed the hearse that carried the body to the cemetery in the nearby village of Blackwell, where Lewis had grown up.

Although the whole town mourned the fallen hero, the community nonetheless took pride in the fact that the Sarnia police had taken down the infamous Red Ryan. An editorial in the *Sarnia Canadian Observer* reflected local feelings.

> That efficient action by the Sarnia officers is one of the best performances of its kind ever accomplished by a police department in Canada under circumstances where quick thinking and quick actions undoubtedly saved their own lives and those of a number of customers who were in the store at the time, for their first fusillade of bullets after their colleague had been shot laid both marauders low and prevented further damage on their part.

For the late Red Ryan, the Canadian public expressed nothing but extreme disappointment and disgust. The police had no idea who the dead bandits were until Detective McGirr found Ryan's driver's license in his pants pocket. The news hit like a thunderbolt. The man who had so recently been held up as a shining example of prison reform and rehabilitation was now seen as a fraud who had betrayed everyone from his closest friends to the Canadian public in general. Soon, fingers were being pointed at all of the people who had vouched for Ryan's parole, blaming them for Constable Lewis's death. On May 28, another killing occurred that would also be laid to the charge of the advocates of prison reform. On that day, Edward McMullen, Ryan's partner and fellow parolee, shot and killed a United States Customs officer while trying to cross from British Columbia to the state of Washington. McMullen was also mortally wounded in that incident. The Red Ryan scandal probably set the cause of prison reform back at least ten years.

In 1942, McGirr, Simpkins, Lewis, and Smith were named as recipients of the King's Police Medal. This award was instituted by King Edward VII in 1909, and was considered the civilian equivalent of the military Victoria Cross. John Lewis was the first of only three Canadian police officers to be awarded the medal posthumously.

18

EDMUND TONG: ——————————
LAST DAYS OF THE BOYD GANG

Sergeant of Detectives Edmund "Eddie" Tong, of the Toronto Police Department, could have been the inspiration for the tough, streetwise cop who was a stock character in the film noir melodramas of the 1940s and 1950s. With his stocky build and well-worn fedora and overcoat, he certainly looked the part. Nicknamed "the Chinaman" because of his unusual name and his jet black hair, Tong knew the streets of Toronto, and the people — good and bad — who lived on them, better than any other policeman in the city. Fellow officers who had worked with Tong said they never saw him pull his gun, but that he was more than capable of handling himself in a rough situation. The punks of the Toronto underworld knew better than to mess with the Chinaman.

Like the hardboiled cops in the movies, Tong was a tough guy with a soft heart. People on the street who were down on their luck knew that Eddie was an easy touch for a few bucks. "Go get something to eat," Tong would say, as he slipped a guy a five dollar bill. It wasn't that Tong had a lot of money to spare; he was a married man, devoted to his wife Evelyn. He had a daughter, Margaret, who had chronic health problems, and a son, Raymond. But Tong knew that little favours often resulted in valuable information when he was working on a case.

Edmund Tong was from Leeds, England. He immigrated to Canada in 1926, at the age of twenty-one, and joined the Toronto Police Department three years later. He did not remain in uniform for long. His superiors saw that he had a talent for picking up clues, and in 1933, Tong was promoted to acting plainclothes detective. He became detective sergeant in 1938, and a full sergeant of detectives in 1940.

Over the years, Tong developed a long list of informants. Whenever a crime occurred, he knew who was likely to know something about it. Many of the hoodlums on Toronto's streets had served jail time thanks to Tong, but they respected him. When they were released on parole, they would invite him to their "coming out" parties. Sometimes he would accept, just to see who was there. He never drank with the crooks. He would go into the bars favoured by gangsters and their henchmen, and they would call out to him as though to a good buddy, but Tong was not fooled into thinking any of these criminals were his friends.

Sometimes his fellow policemen complained that Tong would not share his informants. Tong had a good reason for keeping the names to himself: he did not trust other officers to be as discreet as he was. If word got out on the street that an individual had been talking to a cop, that person would be in danger of underworld retribution; the informants would no longer trust the Chinaman.

Thanks to his keen eye for clues and his painstakingly cultivated pool of snitches, Tong became one of the most effective officers on the Toronto police force. Among his many successes were the capture of Donald "Mickey" MacDonald, a notorious hoodlum who had hijacked $40,000 worth of liquor; and the breakup of the infamous Polka Dot Gang. This was a five-man band of armed robbers who distinguished themselves by wearing bandanas with bright red polka dots. In September 1951, after there had been a bank robbery in the town of St. David's, Ontario, Tong found the clue that put him on the trail of the bandit, a man named Frank Miller, whom Tong traced to Minneapolis. Tong was also instrumental in solving numerous homicides, including the sensational "Silk Stocking Murder" of Lila Adams, in Toronto's Cabbagetown district. Years after that case had been closed, a *Toronto Star* reporter said the murder might have remained one of Canadian crime's great mysteries had it not been for the work of Detective Edmund Tong. By the summer of 1951, Tong was a living legend. In July of that summer, the Chinaman first encountered the man who would ultimately play a key role in his fate.

Lennie Jackson (real name Leonard Stone) was a Toronto-born felon who first got in trouble with the law at the age of sixteen. He had ridden the rails as a hobo, and earned the nickname Tough Lennie because of his prowess as a street brawler. He joined the Canadian army in 1939, but was discharged due to a combination of health problems and numerous breaches of discipline. In 1944, he joined the merchant navy, and was aboard the freighter *Idefjord* when she was torpedoed by a German U-boat. The vessel did not sink, but that brush with death was enough for Jackson. When he got back to Canada he quit the merchant marine.

Jackson went back to travelling around the country in boxcars, looking for excitement and the occasional job. In the summer or fall of 1946, while attempting to hop a freight in the Toronto railyards, Jackson slipped. A wheel cut off his left foot. Jackson was fitted with an artificial foot, which he learned to master so well that few people knew about it, unless they were told. Nonetheless, Jackson considered himself handicapped, and was bitter. Lennie Jackson always presented himself as friendly and polite, but beneath that exterior he was a troubled, brooding young man who thought life had dealt him a bad hand. People who knew him would often comment on the "intense look" in Jackson's eyes.

Jackson liked money and the things it could buy, but he had only a grade eight education, and was not qualified for anything more than menial jobs. Such work was monotonous, and Jackson had a low tolerance for boredom. His future didn't look very promising. He took a job as a waiter at the Horseshoe Tavern in Toronto. The Horseshoe was a popular hangout for local criminals. It wasn't long before Tough Lennie found an exciting way to make fast money.

On February 27, 1951, Lennie Jackson and another man robbed the Canadian Bank of Commerce in the town of Pickering, just east of Toronto. Over the next few months, Jackson and his pals hit banks in the small Ontario communities of Colborne, Mitchell, and Woodbridge. On July 10, they paid a return visit to the Woodbridge bank. The total haul from these stickups was almost $30,000.

Now Tough Lennie was rolling in dough. He quit his job at the Horseshoe Tavern and bought a 1949 metallic blue Oldsmobile Rocket. Jackson wasn't the brightest of crooks, and didn't realize that his sudden show of wealth would draw the attention of the many underworld spies of Detective Edmund Tong.

Tong had been on the case since Jackson's first bank robbery. He'd been leaning on his informants to come up with some leads. Tong had arrested a few suspects, but it wasn't until July 30 that he got the tip that directed him to Lennie Jackson.

Tong and three other officers went to a room Jackson kept in a boarding house on Roncesvalles Avenue. There, they came face to face with Tough Lennie. Tong and Jackson fought, and Lennie found that he was no match for the Chinaman. Jackson was proud of his reputation as a hard case, and being bested by a cop did not sit well with him. Sometime after the arrest Jackson allegedly warned Tong, "You better watch out. You're going to get it," — or words to that effect.

Jackson was locked up in the Don Jail. He'd been there a little over two months when, in mid-October, a new prisoner was lodged in the cell next to his. This man's name was Edwin Alonzo Boyd. He and Jackson had a lot in common. Both were native born Torontonians. Boyd, in fact, was the son of a Toronto policeman. Both had hoboed their way around the country. Both had served in the army during the war — though Boyd had a more impressive military career and was a trained commando — and both men liked to rob banks.

Boyd, who was eight years older than Jackson, had been in minor scrapes with the law as a youth. Then he was caught attempting to burglarize a gas station and did two and a half years in prison. After the war, Boyd got a job as a streetcar driver in Toronto, but like Jackson he craved money and excitement. According to a story Boyd told many years later, he read a newspaper account about an autistic youth who held up a bank just by walking in and demanding money. Boyd decided he had found his calling.

Between September 9, 1949, and October 16, 1951, Boyd knocked off seven banks in the Toronto area. He usually operated alone, but on the last two robberies he had a partner named Howard Gault. The seventh holdup was bungled, and Gault was captured. He quickly ratted on Boyd.

While Boyd and Lennie Jackson were becoming acquainted, another hoodlum landed in their wing of the Don Jail. This was Willie "the Clown" Jackson (no relation to Lennie), a twenty-five-year-old car thief and mugger, who liked to tell jokes. He was awaiting transport to the Kingston Penitentiary to do a seven-year stretch for robbery with violence.

Soon the three bandits were plotting an escape. Lennie Jackson's artificial foot was attached to his leg by a leather brace (now on display in the Metropolitan Toronto Police Museum). Amazingly, no one had thought to search it when Jackson was processed into the jail. Hidden inside were several hacksaw blades.

Over the next few weeks, Boyd and the two Jacksons cut through the century-old bars that stood between them and freedom. On the night of November 4, using ladders made from bedsheets, they went over the wall and escaped. At that point, none of their names were well-known to the public. But the Boyd Gang would soon be as notorious in Canada as the Dillinger Gang had been in the Unites States, seventeen years earlier.

As is usually the case with "celebrity criminals," the media played a major role in turning common hoodlums into nationally known figures — even folk heroes. The *Toronto Star* and the *Toronto Telegram* were engaged in a newspaper war. Each tried to outdo the other in coming up with sensational stories to sell papers. The breakout of the "Boyd Gang" practically begged for exploitation.

Soon the escapees began robbing banks. Lennie Jackson was quite likely the brains of the outfit, but Edwin Alonzo Boyd had a catchier name and the good looks of a Hollywood star. He was more charismatic than Jackson, and his dramatic leaps over bank counters made for riveting copy. Jocko Thomas, a veteran crime reporter for the *Star*, was probably more responsible than any other reporter for making the Boyd Gang the most notorious outlaws in Canadian history.

On the night of the escape, the jailbreakers were hidden by Steve Suchan (real name Valentine Lesso). Suchan, twenty-three, was a native of Czechoslovakia who had come to Canada at the age of eight. He was an accomplished violinist, but was never able to earn a living as a musician.

Suchan had difficulty holding onto jobs. He was working as a doorman at Toronto's prestigious King Edward Hotel when he met Lennie Jackson in 1951. Soon, he was robbing banks with Tough Lennie. Suchan liked this line of work, because carrying a gun made him feel like a big shot. He was delighted when he and Lennie stole several firearms, including four Thompson submachine guns, from the military base at Camp Borden, north of Toronto.

In spite of their mutual friendship with Lennie Jackson, Boyd and Suchan did not like each other. Suchan did not want Boyd and Willie teaming up with him and Lennie to begin with. Then he became jealous when the newspapers began calling them the *Boyd* Gang. For his part, Boyd thought Suchan was conceited. "Suchan wanted to be the important one next to Len," Boyd said years later. "Lennie and Willie would listen to me, but not Suchan."

Personality conflicts notwithstanding, the men all needed money. On November 20, they hit the Bank of Toronto at Dundas and Boustead for $4,300, and got away in a stolen car. They were disappointed with the take, so nine days later they raided the Royal Bank on Laird Drive. This time the gang got away with over $46,000! The biggest bank robbery, to date, in Toronto history.

On December 18, Willie Jackson was arrested in a Montreal restaurant. He would not tell the police anything about the other gang members. Willie the Clown was sent straight to the Kingston Pen.

The loss of Willie Jackson did not slow the gang down, and the robberies continued: $10,000 from a bank in Scarborough, $24,000 from a bank in downtown Toronto. The public, who generally detested the banks, seemed thrilled to have a "criminal mastermind" like Edwin Alonzo Boyd in the usually staid city of Toronto the Good. But Chief of Police John Chisholm was under pressure from Mayor Allan Lamport to put a stop to the crime wave. One of the detectives out on the street trying to pick up leads on the Boyd Gang was, of course, Sergeant Edmund Tong.

Among the many people Tong pried for information was Lennie Jackson's half-sister, Mary Mitchell. She was also embroiled in a love triangle that included Steve Suchan and a woman named Anna Camero. Mitchell was in Tong's office several times. She told her brother and

Suchan that she spoke to Tong only to see if she could get information out of *him* about the hunt for the Boyd Gang. On one occasion, however, in an attempt to get Camero out of the way, she gave Tong a description of Camero's car, and the licence plate number, and said it was being used to transport stolen goods to Montreal. Later, she told Suchan and Jackson that Tong had tortured her to get that information by burning her breasts with a lit cigarette. She showed them the burn marks to prove it.

Edwin Boyd did not believe Mary Mitchell's story; nor did other police officers when they heard it. Those who saw the burn marks said they were superficial and were probably self-inflicted. Officers who had seen Mitchell leave Tong's office on several occasions said she was always smiling when she came out. Nobody believed that Edmund Tong would stoop to torturing a woman. Nobody, that is, except Suchan and Jackson. They believed Mitchell, and they were furious. They set up a papier mâché dummy, with a plaster head, in Camero's basement, and used it for target practice with a couple of air pistols.

On the morning of March 6, 1952, Suchan and Jackson borrowed Camero's 1951 black Monarch sedan. Quite likely they intended to rob a bank. Two days earlier Boyd, who had grown mistrustful of both of them, had knocked off a bank without their help. Instead, he had done the job with two other accomplices. Suchan and Jackson evidently had decided that if Boyd could rob a bank without them, they could pull a raid without him. They knew that Mary Mitchell had brought Camero's car to police attention, but dismissed any thoughts of risk.

The police were, in fact, watching the black Monarch. Tong and his partner, Detective Sergeant Roy Perry, had been keeping it under surveillance for several days. With the most recent Boyd robbery still fresh in the news, Tong was anxious to pursue any lead that might result in an arrest.

Roy Perry did not know who owned the car. Tong, ever protective of his informants, had told him only that the Monarch "is sometimes driven by someone other than the owner." Perry did not see *anyone* drive the black car until that fateful March day.

At about 1:00 p.m., Perry and Tong were in an unmarked patrol car driving North on Roncevalles Avenue. Usually Tong drove, but this time Perry was at the wheel. Tong had just grabbed a quick lunch in a restaurant. Perry hadn't been hungry, and so had gone on a little patrol through the neighbourhood. He had seen a man he knew wave and call to him, but decided he didn't want to speak to that person at that particular moment, and so kept driving. Had Perry stopped to talk to the man, he would have picked Tong up a few minutes later, and the fatal confrontation might never have happened.

As it was, the black Monarch pulled out of Wright Avenue and onto Roncevalles a few vehicles ahead of the patrol car. Tong spotted the Monarch and told Perry to follow it. The Monarch turned off Roncevalles and took side streets to get to Dundas Street West. This allowed the detectives to get close enough to confirm the license plate number and see that the car was occupied by two men. They did not know who the suspects were.

At the intersection of College and Lansdowne, the driver, Suchan, had to slow down as he approached cars stopped for a red light. Perry pulled the police car alongside, three or four feet from the Monarch. Tong wound down his window and said, "Pull over to the curb, boys." He might not have recognized Suchan, whom he had never met personally. He might not have recognized Jackson either; he had grown a moustache, was wearing horn-rimmed glasses, and was somewhat blocked from view by Suchan. Quite likely Tong did not, or he would have drawn his gun.

The cars stopped, with the police vehicle slightly to the rear of the Monarch. The traffic light had turned green, and cars swung out to move past them on the left. Suchan and Jackson reached for their guns.

On any other day, Perry would have been the one to get out of the car and confront the suspects, but this time it was Tong who opened the door and stepped onto the road. He approached the Monarch until he was about three feet from the driver's door. Then he hesitated and started to turn to the right. Perhaps he saw the .45 Smith & Wesson revolver in Suchan's hand. Suchan fired and the detective fell, face down on the pavement.

No sooner had the Chinaman hit the ground than Suchan opened fire on the police car. The first bullet pierced the windshield and whizzed by Perry's ear. Perry had left his service revolver in his desk at the station. He quickly raised his right arm to protect his head as he tried to get out of the car. That instinctive action undoubtedly saved his life, as a bullet struck his arm. Perry later said, "It was like being hit with a red hot sledge hammer … They never gave us a chance. They just opened fire at point-blank range."

As Suchan blasted away at the police, Jackson jumped out of the passenger side of the Monarch and pulled his revolver. He would later testify that he didn't fire a shot. Perry and other witnesses would give conflicting testimony as to whether or not Jackson shot at the police car. When Suchan rammed the shift into first gear and the Monarch began to move forward, Jackson scrambled back into the car.

In the patrol car, Perry was on the verge of blacking out from pain and loss of blood. He managed to call for help on his radio. "Hurry," he said. "We've been shot." He saw the Monarch roar away and lose itself in traffic. Suchan and Jackson soon ditched the car and fled the neighbourhood in a taxi.

Ambulances rushed Tong and Perry to Toronto General Hospital. Perry's wounds were not life-threatening, but Tong's condition was critical. Suchan's bullet had struck him in the left side of the chest, punctured both lungs and severed his spine. If by some miracle Tong lived, he would be paralyzed.

The police did not take long to name the gunmen as members of the Boyd Gang. From his hospital bed, Tong identified Suchan from a photograph. Public opinion turned decidedly against the bandits as news of the brutal shooting hit the streets. Mayor Lamport angrily demanded an end to the gang's "reign of terror," and offered a $2,000 reward for information leading to an arrest.

Sergeant of Detectives Edmund "Eddie" Tong was on the trail of the notorious Boyd Gang when he was shot down on a Toronto street on March 6, 1952. Tong died on March 23. Two gang members were hanged for the murder.

Courtesy Metropolitan Toronto Police Museum

Chief Chisholm had 1,000 officers turning Toronto inside out to find Suchan, Jackson, and Boyd.

Police searched Anna Camero's house, where they found guns, ammunition, and the dummy that Suchan and Jackson had used for target practice. They also found information that led them to two other Toronto addresses where they turned up even more clues, including the address of a residence Suchan used in Montreal.

Tong was too weak for the doctors to risk surgery to remove the bullet. They kept him alive with massive blood transfusions. When a call went out for blood donors, Tong's fellow officers responded admirably.

Tong drifted in and out of consciousness. He was awake the morning after the shooting when his wife Evelyn; son Raymond, thirteen; and daughter Margaret, twenty-one, were allowed into his room. Evelyn asked, "How do you feel, dear?"

Tong managed a feeble chuckle and said, "I feel fine today and so do all the hoodlums." Evelyn reminded him that it was Raymond's birthday. The *Star* and the *Telegram* ran daily reports on Tong's condition and on the family's courageous struggle to bear up under such trying circumstances. The papers milked the story for full sentimental value.

At the time of the shooting, Edwin Boyd was in a movie theatre. When he learned that Detective Tong had been shot, he had a strong suspicion that Suchan and Jackson were involved. He was furious when, the next day, his picture was on the front page of the *Star*. The accompanying article named Suchan and Jackson as the gunmen, and said they had been on their way to a rendezvous with Boyd to rob a bank when they were stopped by Tong and Perry. The story went on to say that Boyd had helped them escape from the scene of the crime. Boyd holed up in a Toronto boarding house, venturing outdoors only after dark.

Suchan and Jackson fled to Hamilton, then stole a car and drove to Montreal. Both men had apartments there, a little more than a block apart. When Suchan went to his apartment building on Côte-des-Neiges, he did not know that the Toronto police had learned of his Montreal address, as well as the alias under which he rented the place. That information was immediately passed on to the Montreal police. On the afternoon of March 7, Suchan left his apartment to sell a car for some much-needed cash, and have supper in a restaurant. While he was gone the police arrived and set up an ambush. When Suchan returned he was confronted by Sergeant Albert Dauphin, one of four detectives waiting in the apartment. Suchan had three guns on him, including the Smith & Wesson he had used to shoot Tong and Perry. That was the weapon he pulled as soon as he saw the Montreal cop. Dauphin didn't give him a chance to use it. He fired three shots from his .38 service revolver, hitting Suchan in the chest, abdomen, and arm. Suchan fell, and then tried to raise his gun and fire, but was unable to do so. The gun dropped to the floor and Dauphin kicked it out of reach. Then he and another officer took the other two guns they found on the suspect.

Suchan sneered, "You guys are poor shots. Why don't you finish me? What are you waiting for? No one will know the difference."

Dauphin replied, "We want to keep you alive for the Toronto police. You won't be shooting anymore cops." Suchan later denied that he had pulled a gun on Dauphin.

While Suchan was recovering in Montreal's Queen Elizabeth Hospital, Edmund Tong had taken a turn for the worse in Toronto. The hunt continued for Boyd and Jackson. On Tuesday, March 11, the Montreal police found Tough Lennie.

A neighbour in Jackson's Lincoln Avenue apartment building had recognized his picture in the paper and informed the police. Just after five o'clock that evening, more than a dozen constables and detectives took up positions in and around Jackson's building. With them was Detective Jack Gillespie of the Toronto police, who knew Jackson by sight.

Jackson's pregnant wife, Ann, was in the apartment with him, but when he realized the police were closing in, he decided to shoot it out. He had a Tommy gun, but had not been able to assemble it, so he blazed away at the police with a pair of pistols. Gillespie, who was nearest to Jackson when the gunfight started, emptied his service revolver at him and hit him in the abdomen, the right hand, and twice in the left arm. "Wyatt Earp couldn't do better than that," Gillespie said later.

Injured though he was, and holding his left hand over the bullet hole in his abdomen, Jackson continued to fight, shooting and reloading with his bleeding right hand. All the while, Ann screamed

Newspaper artist's conception of the Montreal gunfight in which police captured the Boyd Gang's "Tough Lennie" Jackson.

hysterically for him to stop. Tough Lennie ignored her, shouting repeatedly at the police, "*Tabernac!* Come and get me!"

Gillespie and other officers in the corridor fired through the apartment door. Officers outside sniped at the window. They fired tear gas into the apartment and soon Jackson and Ann were choking on it. Still, Jackson refused to surrender. Two hundred constables were called in to hold back the huge crowd that was gathering in the street.

The gun battle raged for half an hour. Then Ann screamed at Jackson, "Stop shooting! Think of the baby!"

At that Jackson said, "Okay," and dropped his gun on the floor. The only policeman injured was Gillespie. One of Jackson's bullets had struck a wall close to the detective's head, and a fragment of flying plaster had cut him at the corner of one eye.

Jackson was taken to Montreal General Hospital. The bullet in his abdomen had not caused any serious internal injuries. Jackson would live to stand trial. He told Gillespie he did not know where Edwin Boyd was. He became indignant when Gillespie referred to Boyd as the gang's "leader." He also told the officer, "I'll get out again."

Now only Boyd was left. Toronto police got a lead on him by means of a newspaper ad through which he tried to sell a car. They traced him to a house on Heath Street and staked the place out. Sergeant Adolphus Payne, in charge of the operation, did not want another shootout. He waited until just before dawn on the morning of Saturday, March 15, to move in.

Payne had a key that would unlock the back door of the house, and he knew the layout of the interior. Boyd would most likely be sleeping in one of the three upstairs bedrooms. Payne and two other officers quietly entered the house and crept up the stairs. Sixty constables had the building surrounded. Boyd was asleep when Payne burst into his room. The first thing the bandit knew, Payne had him pinned to the bed with a revolver pointed at his head. The detective said, "It's Payne! You son-of-a-bitch, if you grab your gun, I'll blow your head off!"

Boyd did not resist. Had he been given the opportunity, he probably would have. There were five loaded pistols within easy reach of his bed. Police also found — in addition to a satchel containing $25,000 — a letter addressed to the editor of the *Toronto Star*, in which Boyd warned police to keep out of his way if they wanted to avoid bloodshed.

As soon as Mayor Lamport was informed of Boyd's capture, he rushed to the scene to take advantage of the photo opportunity. Boyd said to him, "I didn't think it would take something like this to meet your worship. Shall I smile?"

Lamport replied, "In the trouble you're in, you'd better not. You can be thankful you're alive. You're in the land of a fine police force."

Boyd looked at the officers around him and said, "Yes. You fellows did a fine job."

Police Inspector John Nimmo phoned Evelyn Tong and told her Boyd had been captured. "My husband is avenged at last," she said. "I couldn't rest until all those men were taken in. I am so glad the police have been successful but I am terribly worried because my husband was not too well yesterday. He moaned all day and it made me afraid. If only he would get better everything would be wonderful."

That same day, Detective Tong was told of Boyd's arrest. He managed a weak smile and said, "Good." He had been slipping in and out of comas.

By March 21, Lennie Jackson had recovered enough from his wounds to be moved from the Montreal hospital to the Don Jail. Guards took care to put him in a cell that was nowhere near Boyd's. This time they examined the artificial foot, and found hacksaw blades hidden in the leather brace.

At 12:23 a.m., on Sunday, March 23, Edmund Tong died. Evelyn, who had been in with their children to see him only hours earlier, was devastated. She had thought he was recovering. "It should never have happened to him," she wept. "He was a good man and never hurt anyone in his life."

On Wednesday, March 26, thousands of mourners lined the streets for Tong's funeral procession, which consisted of more than one hundred vehicles. The Little Church of the Nativity on Monarch Park Avenue, was filled to capacity. Tong was buried with full honours in Pine Hills Cemetery.

Chief Chisholm said in his eulogy,

> I cannot speak too highly of the courage, initiative and devotion to duty displayed by the late Sergeant of Detectives Edmund Tong, who gave his life in the execution of his duty. Cheerful at all times and in all circumstances, he was admired by citizens and police alike.

In the Ontario Legislature, Attorney General Dana Porter also paid tribute to Tong.

> His cases and arrests read like a rogues' gallery, with almost every prominent criminal listed. Murders, holdups, shootings, big robberies — Tong got them all. He cultivated underworld contacts and was known by criminals everywhere. Though many criminals feared and hated him, others admired and respected him. For Eddie Tong was fair. He never lost his head or used bad judgment. He was kind and considerate to those who deserved it. He was hard and tough with others — those who usually ended up in Kingston Penitentiary.

Lennie Jackson and Steve Suchan now faced a murder charge. Even though Suchan had done the actual shooting, Jackson was considered an accomplice and therefore equally responsible. Boyd had nothing to do with the shooting, but faced a long list of charges for bank robbery, escaping custody, car theft, and illegal possession of firearms. Willie Jackson, whose involvement in Boyd Gang robberies had only recently been discovered, was transferred from the Kingston Pen to the Don Jail, to be tried in Toronto for those crimes.

Once Suchan had recovered sufficiently from his wounds, he was moved to the Don Jail. Guards uncovered an escape plot that Lennie Jackson had cooked up, so he was moved from his cell to one in the same wing as Boyd, Suchan, and Willie Jackson. This was considered the most secure part of the jail. After the big jailbreak the previous year, the new governor, Thomas Brand, had introduced new measures to make this part of the jail "escape proof." As it turned out, they weren't enough.

Using a homemade key and a smuggled hacksaw blade, the four bandits broke out of the Don Jail in the early morning hours of September 8. The uproar that followed was monumental. A $26,000 reward was offered for information leading to their recapture. An enraged Mayor Lamport wanted to know if the jail was being run by "morons." Thomas Brand and seven guards who had been on duty at the time of the escape were suspended, and Ontario Provincial Police constables were sent to the jail to beef up security. The first three pages of the *Toronto Star* were full of nothing but stories about the escape of the notorious Boyd Gang. The newspaper reported that every police officer in Ontario had instructions to "shoot to kill." The widowed Evelyn Tong said the escape was "a disgrace to the city." The new CBLT television station began its broadcasting program with a feature about the jailbreak. Throughout Toronto, and its suburbs, bank managers wondered who would be hit first.

Meanwhile, the escapees were trudging through the bush and ravines of the Don Valley, just trying to keep out of sight. Lennie Jackson had a tin cup on the stump of his leg, because the guards had taken away his artificial foot. After spending a night in the bush, they found shelter in an abandoned barn in North York. They decided to stay there for a few days while they figured out what to do next. They got food by raiding nearby vegetable gardens at night. They were seen, however, and the police were tipped off. On September 16, police surrounded the barn and captured the whole gang without a fight.

Steve Suchan and Lennie Jackson were convicted of the murder of Edmund Tong and sentenced to death. They were hanged together in the Don Jail on December 16, 1952. Willie Jackson was sentenced to thirty years in Kingston.

Edwin Boyd was sentenced to eight life sentences. He was paroled in 1966, and lived in British Columbia under an assumed name until his death in May 2002. Boyd told biographer Brian Valee that it was not fair that Lennie Jackson was hanged along with Suchan, when Suchan had fired the fatal shot. He thought Jackson should have had enough sense to keep clear of Suchan. Perhaps Boyd should have kept away from Suchan, too. His career as a bank robber was finished the moment Suchan shot Edmund Tong.

19

LAKE SIMCOE TRAGEDY: ————
A PHANTOM AFFAIR

Just before midnight on Saturday, June 7, 1958, five RCMP officers climbed into a fourteen foot boat with a thirty-five horsepower outboard motor at Paradise Beach, two miles west of Jackson's Point on Lake Simcoe, in Southern Ontario. The officer in charge was Corporal Herbert M. Smart, thirty-three, a native of Toronto and a fifteen-year veteran of the force. When he left his home that Saturday afternoon, Corporal Smart told his wife Rita, and daughters Patricia and Susan, that he would probably be back late. With him in that boat were Constable George H.E. Ransom of Melville, Saskatchewan; Constable Maurice Melnychuk of Prince George, British Columbia; Constable Glen F. Farough of Stocton, Manitoba; and Constable David M. Perry of Vancouver. Constable Perry was nineteen years old. The other three were twenty-one. Smart, Farough, and Perry worked out of the RCMP station in Orillia. Ransom and Melnychuk had been sent up from Toronto. All five men were wearing their uniform trousers, but civilian jackets. Thus, anyone they approached in their boat would not immediately recognize them as police.

At the time that the officers launched their boat, the lake was calm. However, at about 12:30, a sudden squall blew in, whipping up four foot waves. Then, at about three o'clock Sunday morning, a severe electrical storm lit up the skies over Lake Simcoe. Dawn came, and the five officers had not reported back to Orillia. The car that they had driven to Paradise Beach in was still parked there.

While eight planes searched from the air, RCMP and Ontario Provincial Police boats, assisted by civilian craft, criss-crossed the surface of the lake. At about 11:00 a.m., Donald Thompson of Toronto, out for a day of fishing, came upon the missing men's capsized boat, half a mile west of Georgina Island. Thompson later told a reporter for the *Toronto Star*:

> It was upside down in the water with only the bow showing. I examined it but couldn't tell if there was anything under it or not. Nothing was floating about. I saw there was nothing I could do so I made a note of the license number and continued on to Pefferlaw to report it.

When Thompson docked he saw a Mountie patrol car parked nearby, and he told the officers about the capsized boat. He took them out to the site, but the boat had been found by other fishermen, who towed it to Georgina Island. When police inspected the boat they found that it had plenty of gasoline, the running lights were still on, and the windshield was broken. The throttle was in the "full speed" position.

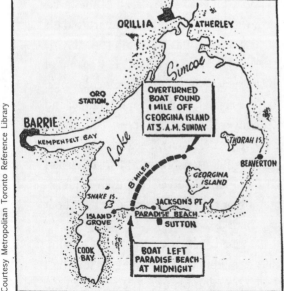

Map of Lake Simcoe, showing route taken by the five RCMP officers who drowned on the night of June 7, 1958. The RCMP denied that the men were out to catch Native residents of Georgina Island in illegal possession of alcohol.

Some residents of the island said they had seen the running lights of a boat heading south shortly after midnight, but they had no way of knowing if it was the Mountie patrol.

Not long after the boat was found, the Mounties' worst fears were realized. A mile west of Georgina Island searchers recovered the body of Corporal Smart. A life jacket was around his neck, as though he'd been trying to put it on when the boat capsized. The search continued until nightfall, but nothing was found except some seat cushions, a life jacket, and a coat. Over the next few weeks the other four bodies were recovered, all in the vicinity of Georgina Island. The last one found was that of Constable Ransom, on July 9.

The press had two direct questions for RCMP officials: what caused the accident, and what were the men doing out on the lake at night? Of course, with no surviving witnesses, people could only speculate as to what happened out on the dark water. Did the boat capsize during the squall, or did the men meet disaster during the electrical storm? Dr. Smirle Lawson, the Supervising Coroner for Ontario, flatly stated that the boat was overloaded, that it was not designed to carry five adults. However, Inspector K.W. Lockwood of the RCMP Marine Division in Toronto said the boat was "quite adequate for five men. The boat had all the safety devices and government approved life preserving equipment," he told the *Toronto Star*. He said the boat had often been used on Georgian Bay, and had survived many Lake Simcoe storms.

As to what the officers were doing that night, Inspector W. G. Fraser would say only that it was a "routine patrol." Reporters would not accept that. It was not "routine," they said, for a patrol to be on the lake in the middle of the night. Nor was it usual for officers from Toronto to be involved. Why were the officers wearing civilian jackets instead of regulation tunics? The press speculated that the patrol was in fact a liquor raid. Georgina Island is a Native reserve where alcohol was forbidden at the time, and that night the inhabitants were having a wedding celebration. Were the constables on their way to catch the islanders in illegal possession of alcohol? Inspector Fraser said they were not.

The questions were raised again at an inquest held in Pefferlaw on June 24, and several other interesting points were revealed. Constable

Farough, who was actually driving the boat, was an excellent boater, with plenty of experience on the water, but he had never taken a boat out after dark. Farough and Ransom were both top notch swimmers, with bronze medals from the Royal Lifesaving Society. Corporal Smart had twenty-nine hours of swimming training, but no badge or official recognition as a strong swimmer. Constable Perry was believed to be a better than average swimmer, and no one knew if Constable Melnychuk could swim well or not.

A report from an earlier mission, written in Corporal Smart's handwriting, indicated that on the night in question, the officers were, in fact, on a liquor raid. Smart's report told of attempting to reach Georgina Island to enforce the Indian Act regulation concerning alcohol, but being driven back by a storm. On the night the five Mounties were lost, two other officers were in a patrol car at Paradise Beach, with a walkie-talkie. The men in the boat were under orders to maintain radio silence, but had a walkie-talkie in case they ran into trouble. When the storm blew in and the officers in the car did not hear anything from the men in the boat, they assumed their colleagues had taken shelter on the island. Still, senior RCMP officials said the men were on a "routine" patrol. The *Toronto Star* called it a "phantom affair."

The manufacturer of the patrol boat brought attention to a plaque on the boat that stated its capacity was 975 pounds. Inspector Fraser said he and his fellow officers had thought that weight limit did not include the motor, when in fact it did. The combined weight of the five men, their equipment (guns, etc), and the motor was 1,110 pounds, well over the limit.

The inquest concluded that the accident had been caused by an overloaded boat. It was also determined that the life jackets the Mounties had been using were of inferior quality. As a result, the RCMP upgraded its equipment, and changes were made in Canada's boating regulations. On June 7, 2008, the families and friends of the five drowned Mounties gathered outside the RCMP detachment in Newmarket to commemorate the fiftieth anniversary of the largest single-incident loss of life in the history of the Force.

20

JACQUES MESRINE: ────────────
THE FOREST RANGER MURDERS

Conservation officers, who are also called game wardens and forest rangers, are responsible for enforcing laws and regulations designed to protect Canada's natural resources, flora, and wildlife. The work can be dangerous, and is often carried out in remote areas. Conservation officers have lost their lives through drowning, plane crashes, and natural disasters. They have died in forest fires, car accidents, and animal-related incidents.

Poachers and others engaged in illegal activities in the forests can make the conservation officer's job especially hazardous. A poacher might be a farmer who kills a deer out of season just to put meat in his own freezer, but poachers can also be hunters who work for organized crime, providing syndicates with meat, pelts, animal parts, and even live animals. The fact that poachers are usually armed makes a confrontation with them potentially deadly. Several Canadian conservation officers have been slain in the line of duty.

On July 5, 1930, Game Warden Dennis Greenwood was shot to death by a poacher at Canal Flats, British Columbia. Another British Columbia Game Warden, Albert Farey, was killed near Lillooet on October 4, 1932, when a poacher shot him in the back twice. Nova Scotia Forest Ranger Arthur Eisenhaur died on December 12, 1931, after being assaulted by four men near Kearney Lake. On May 12, 1967, Manitoba Conservation Officer William McLeod died of complications that resulted from a wound he received when a drunken trapper shot him in the leg. Quebec Game Warden Luc Guindon came upon a poacher's lair near Sainte-Agathe-des-Monts on October 10, 1989. He was killed when an arrow shot from a crossbow struck him in the chest.

In September 1972, the murders of two Quebec forest rangers caught the attention of the entire country, but not because the unfortunate men were the first Quebec conservation officers to be murdered in the line of duty. Rather, the media attention was due to the identity of one of the killers; he was one of the most notorious desperadoes of the post-Second World War twentieth century.

A native of France, Jacques Mesrine was three years old in 1940, when his country fell to the Nazis. Four years later, he was eyewitness to the massacre of helpless French civilians by retreating German soldiers. He also saw the brutal revenge that the French took on countrymen who had collaborated with the Nazis. After the war, Mesrine's family returned to their middle class lifestyle in Paris. In spite of his parents' best efforts, Mesrine became a juvenile delinquent. He was expelled from one school after another. He kept bad company. As a youth, he could not hold onto a job.

Mesrine served a stint in the French army, and volunteered to go to Algeria, where rebels were fighting to throw off the yoke of France. Mesrine enjoyed the excitement of armed combat. He found he had no qualms about killing, and was decorated three times.

However, Mesrine did not like military discipline. When his term of service was up, he returned to civilian life. He took with him some valuable skills learned in war, and a .45 automatic pistol that he kept illegally. He briefly tried to earn a living as a salesman, grew bored with it, and turned to crime.

Mesrine began his criminal career as a burglar. That was lucrative, but not as exciting as he'd hoped it would be. In 1961, Mesrine became involved with the *L'Organisation de l'Armée Secrète*. The OAS was a militaristic terrorist group determined to keep Algeria under French rule, despite President Charles de Gaulle's attempts to seek a political solution to the Algerian crisis. As an OAS mercenary, Mesrine was quite likely a gunman, weapons smuggler, and extortionist. He enhanced his knowledge of firearms. He learned how to tap into the underworld network of forgers and thieves who could provide false or stolen passports and other important documents, and who could connect him with the kingpins of the criminal world. The OAS taught Mesrine to communicate in codes, and a bagful of tricks that would help him avoid arrest. Because the members of the OAS saw themselves, and not de Gaulle, as the true French patriots, Mesrine learned to be contemptuous of legal authority. He took genuine pride in being an outlaw.

Algeria became independent in 1962. Even so, the OAS continued to engage in treasonous operations against the French government. Mesrine freelanced for them between robberies. In 1965, he was arrested for breaking into the home of the governor of Palma, in Mallorca. Sentenced to thirty-six months in prison, he was paroled after serving just eighteen. At the time of his arrest he was married and had three children. The marriage did not last long after his release from prison, because he continued with his criminal ways.

For a few years, Mesrine and his girlfriend Jeanne Schneider, a prostitute and small-time thief, lived the high life of casinos and fine hotels. Their money came from extortion, burglaries, and armed robberies. Schneider sometimes assisted Mesrine with the holdups. The OAS training helped Mesrine stay a jump ahead of the police, but in 1968, at the age of thirty, he decided it was time to get out of France for a while. He and Jeanne flew to Montreal.

In March 1969, a Montreal textile millionaire named Georges Deslauriers hired Mesrine and Schneider as his chauffeur and housekeeper. Deslauriers had a beautiful estate in Saint-Hilaire, on the outskirts of Montreal. His new servants were provided with a small house on the property. The millionaire was delighted to learn that the chauffeur was also an excellent cook. Moreover, the fellow had a talent for entertaining guests with card tricks and amusing stories.

Mesrine and Schneider were pleased that their boss stayed at the estate only on weekends. He needed crutches to get around, and when he was there he required a lot of personal assistance. His absence during the week gave Mesrine and Schneider time to enjoy the beautiful Canadian countryside, and to establish contacts in the Montreal underworld. However, their stay at the Deslauriers estate came to an abrupt end after just a few months. Jeanne had a violent argument with Georges' beloved old gardener. She and Mesrine were dismissed.

Mesrine had never intended to go straight for good, but getting fired stung his pride. He decided to kidnap Georges Deslauriers and hold him for ransom. When he and Schneider had the money, they would fly to Venezuela. Mesrine recruited a young Montreal hoodlum named Michel Dupont to help with the job.

Just a few nights after they'd been fired, Mesrine and Schneider broke into Deslauriers' house when the old man was alone. They forced him to write a ransom note for $200,000 to his brother Marcel. The money was to be handed over to the kidnappers in a Sherbrooke Street subway station. If Marcel called the police, the note said, Georges would be killed.

The kidnappers hauled Deslauriers to a hideout. They took away his crutches and clothes, and then forced him to drink a large glass of drugged gin. The concoction was supposed to knock him out for hours. Mesrine delivered the ransom note to the Deslauriers Company office. Then he and Dupont went to the subway station to await Marcel, while Schneider stayed with the prisoner.

Marcel did not show up with the money. Schneider went out to see what was happening with Mesrine and Dupont, leaving Deslauriers unguarded. The "drug" they had given him turned out to be some harmless substance, and Deslauriers awoke from his gin-induced sleep. He found his clothes and his crutches, and escaped. The kidnappers had only $500 they'd taken from his wallet.

The gang fled Montreal. After a few days Dupont went his own way, and was soon picked up by the police. Mesrine and Schneider made it to Windsor, Ontario, where they crossed into the United States. They were heading for Texas, where Mesrine had established some criminal contacts. Unfortunately for them, Dupont knew of this plan, and told the police.

On July 16, Mesrine and Schneider were arrested in Texarkana, Arkansas. A week later they were flown back to Montreal. The Deslauriers kidnapping had made the newspapers, and a few reporters and photographers were waiting at Dorval airport. Mesrine thought he had become a celebrity criminal, in the order of Al Capone or John Dillinger.

At the Montreal headquarters of the Sûreté du Québec, the provincial police department, Mesrine and Schneider were charged with murder. During their flight from Montreal they had spent some time in Perce, at the Motel les Trois Soeurs. Witnesses had seen them in the company of the owner, an elderly, unmarried woman named Evelyne le Bouthillier; their fingerprints (which matched samples sent from France) were found in the motel. Sometime after Mesrine and Schneider left Perce, Bouthillier's body was found. She'd been strangled.

Mesrine would swear to his dying day that he had nothing to do with the murder. However, the details of his account of their stay in Perce changed every time he told it. He expressed indignation at the idea that he would murder a helpless old woman.

Mesrine and Schneider were transferred to the jail in Perce to await trial. On August 17, using a homemade knife, Mesrine overpowered a guard and then sprang Schneider from the women's wing. The pair escaped from the jail and fled into the forest, but nothing in Mesrine's experiences had prepared him for the Canadian woods. They soon became lost. When police recaptured them the next day, they were only two miles from the jail.

Due to the illness of a Crown prosecutor, Mesrine and Schneider did not go to trial for murder until January 18, 1971. They were acquitted on a technicality, much to the disgust of the presiding judge, but they were both sentenced to prison time for kidnapping and escaping custody. Schneider got five and a half years. Mesrine drew eleven years. He was locked in the maximum security wing of the newly constructed Saint Vincent de Paul Penitentiary at Laval. This was reputed to be Canada's most secure prison. Mesrine was about to prove otherwise.

In the prison inmate hierarchy, Mesrine was a big shot; an armed robber, kidnapper, and professional gunman who had already busted out of one Canadian jail. He had a swaggering charisma that appealed to other inmates. Among his admirers was twenty-eight-year-old Jean Paul Mercier, a violent man who was serving a twenty-four-year sentence for armed robbery, kidnapping, and attempted murder. He, too, had once pulled off a successful jailbreak, only to be recaptured a month later. Mesrine, Mercier, and a few other inmates decided to test the claim that Saint Vincent de Paul was escape-proof.

The escape was so simple it embarrassed the prison administration. On August 21, 1972, using a couple of pliers stolen from the workshop, Mesrine, Mercier, and four other men cut through the two perimeter fences surrounding the prison. One man was quickly recaptured, but the others got away in cars they hijacked on the highway. Mesrine had thumbed his nose at the cops again. His image of himself as a supercrook was growing.

The story of the brazen escape was plastered all over the newspapers, and the Canadian government was furious. Mesrine soon added to their exasperation. He and Mercier pulled three swift bank robberies, netting almost $30,000. This was operating money for a scheme Mesrine had cooked up to demonstrate to the world just what an extraordinary criminal he was. He and Mercier were going to free the rest of the convicts in the maximum security wing of Saint Vincent de Paul! They bought extra guns, rented several Montreal apartments for use as hideouts, and stocked them with food.

On September 3, armed with sawed-off shotguns, as well as the pistols they intended to toss over the fence to the prisoners in the exercise yard, Mesrine and Mercier headed for Saint Vincent de Paul in a blue Chevrolet. As they neared the prison, they could see that the number of guards had been increased. Then they realized that a police car was behind them, and another car full of armed guards was approaching from the front.

Mesrine immediately cut loose on the police car in the rear with his shotgun. The blast blew out the windshield, causing the vehicle to swerve into the ditch, injuring two officers. Mercier wheeled the Chevy around as the guards in the other car jumped out and sent a barrage of bullets after them. The outlaws made it back to Montreal, but Mercier had been hit in the leg and right arm. Mesrine's face had been grazed by a bullet.

The outrageous attempt to empty a prison of the country's most vicious criminals stunned the Canadian public and incensed law enforcement officials. Mesrine and Mercier had been recognized — they were now the most wanted men in Canada. Though the big prison break had failed, the publicity Mesrine was receiving swelled his ego.

On September 10, a week after the shootout, Mercier, his girlfriend Suzanne Francoeur, and Mesrine drove to a heavily forested area near the community of Saint-Louis-de-Blandford, about forty-five miles southwest of Quebec City. They were going to have a picnic, and the men wanted to practice their shooting. Mercier's arm was stiff from the bullet wound, and he thought a little target practice might loosen it up. They drove three miles down a dirt track called Chemin Petit Belgique, to a spot where they believed they could do their shooting undisturbed.

The three had a pleasant lunch. Mesrine and Mercier spent the afternoon blasting away at targets and congratulating each other on their marksmanship. At about 4:30 p.m., they got into their car to head back to Montreal. Soon after, as they made their way along the narrow track toward the Trans-Canada Highway, about a mile and a half distant they saw a purple pickup truck blocking the way. Two uniformed men stood there. Mesrine instantly thought they were police, but then he realized that they were actually forest rangers. A pair of Canadian yokels like these should present no problem for a criminal of his high caliber.

The men were in fact officers of the *Ministere des Ressources Naturelles et de la Faune Quebec* (Quebec Ministry of Natural Resources and Wildlife). Médéric Coté, age sixty-two, of Plessisville, was a twenty-three-year veteran of the department. Daveluyville resident Ernest Saint-Pierre, age fifty, had been with the department twelve years.

The two forest rangers had heard all the shooting, and had gone out from the ministry station in Plessisville to investigate. Before their encounter with Mesrine and Mercier, they were last seen drinking sodas in a Saint-Louis-De-Blandford restaurant at 3:15. Part of their job was to make sure hunters had the necessary licenses, and obeyed the regulations regarding guns and ammunition. Because they often had to deal with armed poachers, the rangers carried revolvers. Coté and Saint-Pierre also had a .308 calibre rifle in their truck. However, the truck was not equipped with a radio.

The car coming down the lane stopped, and the rangers asked the two men to get out and open the trunk. They did not recognize Mesrine and Mercier, whose pictures had been in the newspapers. Coté and Saint-Pierre must have been stunned when they saw the small arsenal that was in the trunk. Moreover, the guns were all loaded. Still, the rangers did not seem to realize that they were dealing with anything more than people in violation of hunting regulations. They told Mesrine and Mercier it was illegal to carry loaded guns in a car. Then they said the men would have to follow them to the station in Plessisville to see the senior warden.

Mesrine argued. He said they had only been doing some target shooting to get ready for hunting season. The officers insisted that the matter would have to be dealt with in the warden's office. Suddenly Coté recognized Mesrine. He gasped, "The escaped prisoners!"

If the rangers reached for their guns, they never had a chance to pull them from the holsters. In a flash, Mesrine pulled a pistol and shot Coté in the chest. Barely a heartbeat later, Mercier gunned down Saint-Pierre.

The killers went through the victims' pockets and took their revolvers. They found the rifle in the truck, but cast it aside. Then they seized the bodies by the feet, dragged them about 150 feet from the truck, and dumped them thirty feet into the bush. To be sure the men were dead, Mesrine shot each one in the head twice. They covered the bodies with branches and leaves, then got in the car and continued on to Montreal. Coté left behind two sons, aged sixteen and eight, and a thirteen-year-old daughter. Saint-Pierre had a twenty-three-year-old daughter.

Later, Mesrine would express no remorse over the murders. He said the forest rangers had just been "unlucky." Mesrine said he was saddened when he saw a newspaper photograph of one of Coté's sons weeping over his father's coffin, but he also said he wondered if the boy knew his father had the authority to kill in the name of the law.

The two rangers were scheduled to finish their shift at five o'clock, but there was no reason for anyone to feel alarmed when they did not arrive in town, as it was common for troubles on the job to cause a ranger to work overtime. Not even when Coté's wife called Inspector Denis Emond, the two rangers' superior officer, at eleven o'clock at night to report that her husband had not come home, did anyone suspect that anything was seriously wrong. But when there had still been no sign of the men by five o'clock the following morning, Emond called the Victoriaville detachment of the provincial police for assistance.

Coté and Saint-Pierre were known to have been investigating gunfire in the woods near Saint-Louis-de-Blandford, so police officers and forest rangers began searching there. At about 9:00 a.m., they found the truck. From there it was easy to follow the trail to the bodies under the pile of brush. Forest Ranger Claude Brunelle broke down and wept when he saw Saint-Pierre's body. Brunelle was supposed to have been Coté's partner on the day of the murder, but Saint-Pierre had switched shifts with him so that Brunelle could attend a wedding. "It was horrible," Brunelle said. "I took a look at Saint-Pierre and kept seeing my body in his place."

"It doesn't make sense, it doesn't make sense," Inspector Emond said over and over as the bodies were placed in an ambulance. "They were shot like dogs. But why? What did they see that was so important it had to be kept secret by killing two persons? They enjoyed their jobs and never thought or worried about long hours they might have to put in … They were good men, in and out of uniform." Autopsies would show that each man had been shot six times.

At first, the police thought the rangers had been the victims of poachers. Then they found the spot where the killers had done their practice shooting. The ground was littered with spent shotgun shells and bullet casings. A cardboard box that was full of holes had evidently been used as a target. Homicide detectives from Quebec City soon linked the killings to Mesrine and Mercier. A nationwide manhunt was launched, but the killers had gone no farther than Montreal. In fact, instead of lying low, the pair pulled a couple of bank robberies. Mesrine was a master of disguise, and he often dined in Montreal's best restaurants. When the public was critical of the police for being unable to capture him, Mesrine was known to speak in the officers' defence. After all, the cops were up against a brilliant man like him!

Nonetheless, Mesrine and Mercier thought it might be a good idea to get out of Canada. They had plenty of bank robbery loot to live well on, so they obtained passports and travelled first to New York City, and then to Venezuela. They planned to make Caracas their base for bank robbery raids in neighbouring South American countries and the United States, but they soon learned that Interpol was on their trail. Mercier returned to Canada, and Mesrine went back to France via Spain.

For Jean Paul Mercier, time was running short. On December 4, 1972, police arrested him in Montreal. He was tried and sentenced to two terms of life imprisonment for the murders of Coté and Saint-Pierre. Suzanne Francoeur was given prison time for being an accomplice.

Mercier's reputation as a criminal was never more than that of a vicious punk, but some of Mesrine's flamboyance must have rubbed off. He boasted that he would escape. On May 13, 1973, he did just that. He and four other men cut through an iron bar and scaled a wall to get out of Saint Vincent de Paul. Mercier was recaptured three weeks later, while taking a nap in a Montreal hideout. When he was returned to the prison, he snarled to the guards, "You won't hold me for a week."

It didn't happen as quickly as he had predicted, but Mercier did escape again. On October 23, 1974, he broke out of prison for the last time. Mercier and several accomplices were in the act of robbing a Montreal bank on October 31, when police moved in. In a blazing gun battle, Mercier was shot in the stomach and head. He died in hospital the next day.

In France, Jacques Mesrine achieved the status of celebrity criminal that he craved. His life was a series of bold robberies, dramatic arrests, and spectacular jailbreaks. His lawless exploits made headlines around the world. Journalists arranged secret meetings with Mesrine so he could tell readers his side of the story. He revelled in his notoriety and called himself a "gentleman bandit." Admirers saw him as a social rebel, and called him "the Robin Hood of the Paris streets," which he certainly was not.

Mesrine sent taunting letters to the police. In June 1978, he threatened to wage a one man guerilla war against France if the government did not close down top security prisons.

"If I have to go and train with the Palestinians, I'll go," Mesrine warned. "I will unleash a wave of violence such as France has never seen."

Mesrine's end came as suddenly and dramatically as one of his own bank raids. At 3:00 p.m. on November 2, 1979, he and his girlfriend, Sylvie Jeanjacquot, were in a brand new BMW. They had just left their apartment on a quiet Paris street. In a well-planned police operation, two trucks boxed the BMW in at the entrance to an intersection. Then policemen fired twenty brass coated, high velocity bullets into the car. The young woman was wounded, though not seriously. Jacques Mesrine was dead, his body riddled with sixteen bullets. The police officers cheerfully congratulated each other.

There would be an outcry from some quarters that Mesrine had been "executed" without being given a chance to surrender. Police officials defended their action by pointing out that Mesrine had hand grenades on him at the time of his death, and he had repeatedly said he would never again be taken alive.

When the police searched Mesrine's apartment they found a large cache of guns and ammunition, several bars of stolen gold, and a taped message. The recording was for Jeanjacquot, in the event of his death. Mesrine said, "perhaps we'll meet again … maybe in hell … I regret nothing."

Throughout France there were reports of people who had made a folk hero of Mesrine mourning the death of the man they called *Le Grand*. They toasted his memory with cognac. The sentiment was not shared by the people of the little Quebec communities of Plessisville and Daveluyville.

21

DEREK BURKHOLDER: A DOMESTIC DISPUTE

There is an old cliché that for police officers, domestic disputes are among the most potentially dangerous calls. Whether or not this observation originated with police officers is not known, but domestic disputes can be very unpredictable. Officers have been injured, and even killed, when seemingly routine situations in ordinary residences suddenly turn violent. The consequences can be devastating. Such a tragedy struck the town of Lunenburg, Nova Scotia, on June 14, 1996.

Derek Burkholder was born in Ontario, but grew up in New Brunswick. He joined the RCMP in 1966, and for the next twenty-nine years served in several different communities in Nova Scotia. In 1995, Sergeant Burkholder was placed in command of the small Mountie detachment in Lunenburg.

Everybody who knew Derek Burkholder liked him. He was involved with organizations like the Lion's Club, Big Brothers, and Big Sisters. He was devoted to his wife Frances, and their daughters Tammy and Tanya. Burkholder was also dedicated to police work.

On that fateful June morning all was well with the Burkholder family. Tammy had been married the previous September, and Tanya was to be married that summer. No one would have thought that a nightmare was about to descend.

Burkholder spent most of the morning doing paperwork in his Lunenburg office. Then he drove to nearby Bridgewater for a staff meeting. At about 11:30 a.m. he had an urgent call from Lunenburg; shots had been fired in a trailer community called Martins Brook. The mobile home in which the gunfire had occurred was the residence of Ronald Stevens, a man who did not have a serious criminal record, but was known to the police.

Stevens was an unemployed fisherman who had gotten into trouble with the law for illegal fishing. He was bad tempered, argumentative, and had few friends. Several years earlier he had joined Alcoholics Anonymous to fight a drinking problem, but he still used painkillers because of a bad back.

Sergeant Burkholder had dealt with Stevens on earlier occasions and had always been able to settle him down when he seemed to be losing control. Burkholder decided that he'd better handle the dispute at Martins Brook personally, because he thought Stevens would respond more positively to him than to another officer. When he left the Bridgewater police station, he indicated that he would not require assistance.

Other officers were concerned because shots had been fired, and decided to stay close in case of trouble. Constables Les Kakonyi and Gary White headed for Lunenburg in one car, and Corporal Rick Simmons followed in another. White called Burkholder on the radio and asked if he wanted them to meet him at Martins Brook. Burkholder told White to meet him at the Lunenburg station. Before he did anything else, Burkholder wanted to talk to Stevens' wife Rhonda. She was the one who had phoned in the complaint.

At the Lunenburg station Burkholder spoke to Mrs. Stevens on the phone. She told him that the night before she and Ronald had a big argument. In the morning he was still angry over a variety of issues and had taken a lot of prescription pills. She fled to a neighbour's after her husband threatened her and fired several shots inside the trailer.

Burkholder phoned Stevens so that he could get some idea of the man's mental state. Burkholder convinced Stevens that he wanted to talk to him, not about the shooting, but about an application for a Firearms Acquisition Certificate. Stevens agreed to meet Burkholder outside the trailer.

Burkholder told the other officers that he would go to the trailer alone in his unmarked car. He felt that a show of force by the police could escalate the situation. Kakonyi, White, Simmons, and Constable Roger Robbins were to wait nearby in two patrol cars. If Burkholder needed assistance, he would call them.

Sergeant Burkholder drove into Martins Brook alone. The other officers, who'd had reservations about the plan, waited anxiously in two cars at the bottom of a hill, out of sight of the trailer. At last, Burkholder called and told them to come ahead. Apparently, he had the situation in hand.

The two patrol cars pulled in behind Burkholder's unmarked car. Ronald Stevens was sitting in the front seat beside Sergeant Burkholder. In the report he wrote later, Constable Kakonyi noted that as he walked past the car, he wondered if Burkholder had searched Stevens. He assumed that he had.

Sergeant Burkholder was a professional police officer, and in all likelihood he did search Stevens for weapons. Stevens was wearing loose fitting jogging pants. Burkholder would have patted the pockets. However, he would not have touched the crotch area. If Stevens had concealed a handgun in the crotch of his underwear, Burkholder would have missed it.

Because there had been a report of gunfire, the Mounties were obliged to search the interior of the trailer. Both doors were locked, so they asked Stevens for the key. He said he didn't have it. Kakonyi found an open screen window, and Robbins crawled in through it.

Inside the trailer the constables found a small arsenal of guns and ammunition. The firearms included a loaded 12 gauge shotgun and a loaded .22 calibre pistol. There were numerous bullet holes in the ceiling, and cartridge casings on the floor.

Corporal Simmons went to speak to Rhonda Stevens and the neighbours. Constable Kakonyi left the trailer to get a camera from one of the patrol cars. He saw that Burkholder had moved Stevens from his unmarked car, and was putting him in the back seat of a patrol car. Kakonyi thought that there had been trouble, and he asked Burkholder what had happened. The sergeant said that Stevens was giving him a hard time, so he thought the patrol car would be a better place for him to continue taking Stevens' statement. Kakonyi asked if Burkholder needed help, and the sergeant said no. Kakonyi went back to the trailer with the camera. Meanwhile, Burkholder had given Simmons permission to leave. Simmons had found Rhonda Stevens, who was now in the trailer giving her statement to Constable White. Burkholder evidently thought everything was under control.

Ronald Stevens saw things differently. One officer had left. Three others were inside the trailer. He was alone in a patrol car with Sergeant Burkholder. And he had a gun.

Constable Kakonyi made one more trip out to the patrol car to get a yellow crayon for marking the bullet holes in the trailer. As he searched in the trunk, he noticed that the screen between the front and back seats was open. If the sergeant had felt anything was wrong, he would have closed it. Stevens and Burkholder were talking calmly, so it did not appear that there was anything to be unduly concerned about. Kakonyi went back into the trailer.

No one will ever know exactly what happened in the patrol car after that. All that is known for certain is that Stevens used a .38 handgun to shoot through the opening in the screen and put two bullets into Sergeant Burkholder's head. Burkholder must have seen something at the last moment and tried to deflect Stevens' aim, because powder burns were found on his right hand. The policemen in the trailer didn't hear a thing.

Constable White came out of the trailer to get some evidence bags from his car. As he approached the rear of the vehicle, he suddenly saw Stevens pointing a pistol at him through the rear window. Swearing, Stevens cried, "I'm gonna kill you!"

White dropped to the ground and crawled for cover. The driver's door of the car was partly open, and he could see Burkholder slumped over. White called to him and got no answer, then dashed for the trailer to alert the others. He burst through the back door and shouted, "He's got a gun!"

The officers told Rhonda Stevens to stay in the trailer. Then Kakonyi went out the front door and took cover behind a car about fifteen feet away. He aimed his gun across the hood. Constables White and Robbins left the trailer by the back door and took up positions that gave them a clear view of the patrol car. The officers did not know if Burkholder was dead or alive. They could see that Stevens was now in the front seat.

The Royal Canadian Mounted Police Cenotaph in Regina, Saskatchewan, pays homage to all Mounted Police officers who have fallen in the line of duty.

Kakonyi shouted several times, "Get out of the car with your hands up and drop the gun!"

He did not shoot, for fear of hitting Burkholder. Then Stevens opened the passenger door and fired a shot at Kakonyi. He missed. Somehow, the roof lights on the patrol car were suddenly activated. Kakonyi thought this was a signal for help from Burkholder. It *could* have been, but if the sergeant was already dead, Stevens must have inadvertently hit a switch.

Constable Kakonyi shot back, hitting Stevens in the right armpit. Then a shot fired by Constable White went through the windshield and hit Stevens in the chest. Stevens ended the gunfight by shooting himself in the head.

Sergeant Derek Burkholder was forty-nine years old. His sudden death was devastating to his family, and a shock to Nova Scotians. Never before in that province had a Mountie been slain in the line of duty. Burkholder was buried with full honours and the funeral was attended by 800 police officers from across Canada and the United States. In addressing the mourners, Reverend Alexander MacLean said, "Let us be clear that what happened did not have to happen. It was not the will of God, but the direct consequence of pent-up frustration, despair, malice, and rage-run-rampant in one dangerously disturbed man."

A brother of that "dangerously disturbed man" told the press, "Over the years he (Ronald Stevens) was kind of a radical ... well, maybe not a radical, he had his faults like we all have our faults."

There is now a Memorial Trust Fund in Derek Burkholder's name that provides scholarships for graduating high school students in Lunenburg County.

22

MAYERTHORPE: A NATIONAL TRAGEDY

On the morning of March 3, 2005, most Canadians had never heard of the little agricultural community of Mayerthorpe, about eighty-seven miles northwest of Edmonton. But before the day was out, the name of this Alberta town would be on the lips of every television and radio newscaster in the country. By the following day it was in headlines from St. John's, Newfoundland to Victoria, British Columbia. The name has been seared into the Canadian consciousness. What happened there is Canada's unfortunate equivalent of an American tragedy that occurred on June 17, 1933, when gunmen allegedly led by the notorious Pretty Boy Floyd murdered four law enforcement officers. But unlike the Kansas City Massacre, the slaughter in Mayerthorpe was not the work of gangsters. The four slain Mounted Police constables were the victims of a single disturbed and violent man.

James Michael Roszko hated cops. He had been in trouble with them since he was a teenager, and he blamed them, especially the Mounties, for all of his problems. Forty-six years old at the time of the massacre, Roszko had a criminal record dating back to February 1976, when he was convicted of breaking and entering, theft, and possession of stolen property — a rifle. He got off with a $150 fine and a year of probation.

Over the next seventeen years, Roszko had one run-in after another with the police, over matters of break and enter, theft, possession of stolen goods, making harassing phone calls, breach of probation, obstructing justice, uttering threats, assault, and traffic violations. Sometimes he was acquitted on technicalities. Other times he walked away with a suspended sentence or probation, or was made to pay a relatively small fine. In all, he spent only forty-five days in jail. Because of his criminal activities and drug use, James Roszko had become estranged from his father.

In 2000, Roszko was sentenced to two and a half years in prison for sexually assaulting a boy. The assaults began in 1983, when the victim was ten years old, and continued for almost seven years. Not until he was an adult did the victim step forward. He said that at the time the molestation was occurring, Roszko warned him not to tell anyone or "he'd beat the s___ out of him." When Roszko was released from prison he was placed under a ten-year firearms ban, but he purchased guns in the United States and smuggled them into Canada. He was often seen in possession of firearms on his property, but on the one occasion that police went out to confiscate an illegal gun, they could not find it.

There had been other charges against Roszko: assault with pepper spray, aggravated assault, pointing a firearm, using a firearm in the commission of an offence, and common assault, but somehow he was able to escape doing more time in jail. After the sexual assault conviction he was "flagged" as a potential dangerous offender, but was never actually classified as one. A psychiatric report on Roszko, released in 2000, recommended that he be kept locked up, but it was not acted on.

Everybody who had contact with Roszko knew that he was dangerous. He was a loner with a violent temper and a reputation as a bully. He ordered trespassers off his property at gunpoint, and it was widely rumoured that the place was booby-trapped. To further ensure his "privacy," Roszko laid spike belts to blow the tires of cars, and kept a pair of vicious rotweillers. Many times Roszko was pulled over for traffic violations, and on every occasion he was abusive and extremely abrasive. He consistently used foul language with police officers. According to one retired police officer, what angered Roszko most of all was getting ticketed for not wearing a seat belt.

Bailiffs who had to go to Roszko's farm because of his unpaid bills or outstanding loans were warned that he was "aggressive." In the summer of 1999, a bailiff had the unenviable task of seizing cattle and a truck from Roszko, whom the Agricultural Financial Services Corporation had sued for defaulting on a $40,000 loan. The bailiff had to go to the farm wearing body armour and with four Mounted Police constables to back her up. A veterinarian who was supposed to have accompanied her backed out at the last minute, saying it wasn't worth the risk. When the bailiff confronted Roszko, he claimed the truck and cattle she wanted were either gone or were the property of his mother. The bailiff left the farm with nothing. When she tried to talk to neighbours about Roszko, she found that people were afraid to say anything about him. One local resident would later make the observation that Roszko was "a ticking time bomb."

The backgrounds of the four constables whose names would be so unfortunately linked with Roszko's were dramatically different from his. These were all outgoing men who shared a love of life and challenges. They had a sense of civic duty that drew them to the RCMP.

Peter Schiemann, the twenty-five-year-old son of a Lutheran minister, was born in Pretrolia, Ontario. His family later moved to Alberta. Peter was a musician and an athlete. He graduated from Concordia College in Edmonton with a major in sociology. He passed his first RCMP exams in December 1999. In November 2000, Peter Schiemann was posted in Mayerthorpe.

Constable Leo Johnston, thirty-two, was from Lac La Biche, Alberta. His father was Métis, and his mother of Ukrainian descent. He had an identical twin brother named Lee, who was his constant companion when they were growing up. Both were motorcycle enthusiasts, and at the age of twenty they tried to join the Edmonton Police Department together. They were turned down because they were too young. In 1997, Lee applied to the RCMP. Leo was badly injured in a motorcycle accident, and took over a year to recover. In 2000, he followed Lee into the RCMP. He was posted to Mayerthorpe in 2001. On November 13, 2004, Leo married a young woman who had been serving as an auxiliary member of the RCMP for eight years.

Anthony Gordon, twenty-eight, was married and had one son. He was born in Edmonton, but grew up in Red Deer. Anthony applied for the RCMP in 2000, and excelled in his classes at the academy in Regina. After graduation, he was posted in Whitecourt, twenty-eight miles northwest of Mayerthorpe. He once played a key role in breaking up a cigarette theft ring. In the course of his work, Anthony met Peter Schiemann and Leo Johnston. Anthony and his wife had learned in October 2004 that they had a second child on the way.

Brock Myrol, twenty-nine, was born in Outlook, Saskatchewan, but he, too, grew up in Red Deer. After graduating from high school he spent ten years as a commercial security guard. Brock was highly skilled in various forms of martial arts, and won many trophies at major tournaments. He studied anthropology and biology at Red Deer College, and was an accomplished musician and songwriter. In 2004, he applied for the RCMP and began his training in Regina. Soon he was instructing other police cadets in martial arts. While still in training, Brock was engaged to be married. His first posting was Mayerthorpe, where he and his fiancé rented a house. This house would be Brock Myrol's home for only seventeen days.

The series of events that would result in one of the darkest days in the history of Canadian law enforcement began at about 3:00 p.m. on March 2. Two Edmonton bailiffs arrived at Roszko's property to seize a 2005 white Ford pickup truck on behalf of Kentwood Motors in Edmonton. The dealership had discovered irregularities in Roszko's credit background, and he had not responded to any attempts to contact him.

The bailiffs found the gates locked. One of them gave a blast on the horn. Roszko emerged from one of the outbuildings. One of the bailiffs called to him from the gate. Roszko shouted obscenities and then released his two guard dogs. The bailiff squirted a dog with pepper spray as he retreated to the safety of his vehicle. The other bailiff had already called the Mayerthorpe RCMP station for help.

Corporal James Martin received the bailiff's call at 3:20. Ten minutes later he arrived at the farm with Constables Peter Schiemann and Julie Letal. They were there to assist the bailiffs in serving their civil enforcement warrant, while "keeping the peace." By this time, Roszko had driven away in the white truck. Where he went and what he did during the next few hours would be a matter of considerable controversy and investigation.

The Mounties forced the gate open with a crowbar and began to search the property. They had to drive the dogs away with pepper spray. Roszko owned a three-quarter section of land (a section is one square mile), some of which he rented to neighbouring farmers. He lived in a compound that included a house trailer, three granaries, and an eighty by forty foot Quonset hut. Behind the hut was a pen for the dogs.

The officers entered the hut and saw that Roszko had been a very busy man. He had been running a stolen vehicle chop shop, and a marijuana grow op. There were two new, partially dismantled trucks and an array of bumpers, fenders, dashboards, and brand new tires. The constables found twenty-nine mature marijuana plants and several pots with seedlings growing in them. Corporal Martin returned to town to get a search warrant, leaving Schiemann and Letal behind in case Roszko came back.

Police cruisers were dispatched to patrol the region in search of Roszko and the white pickup. They found neither, but had a report from a group of people who had been horseback riding that a man in a white pickup had roared past them. He was driving erratically and had spooked the animals. The truck would eventually be found in a shed on the property of Roszko's aunt, near Cherhill, about twenty-one miles east of Roszko's farm. She would claim that he had put it there during the night, without her knowledge.

At 8:40 p.m., Corporal Martin returned from Mayerthorpe with a warrant and six more constables. By this time the bailiffs had left, after posting a copy of their seizure notice. The Mounties began a thorough search of the property. As the evening progressed they were joined by Sergeant Brian Pinder, the commanding officer of the Mayerthorpe detachment, and officers from Edmonton's RCMP "green team," who had a warrant to search for drugs.

The Mounties discovered enough evidence to lay a long list of charges on James Roszko. On the property were 280 marijuana plants, $8,000 worth of (stolen) cultivation equipment, a stolen Warmac generator for producing heat and light, a motorcycle with altered serial numbers, a pickup truck box full of automotive parts, and a cache of ammunition of assorted calibres. One particularly stunning find was a handwritten list of the names of all the RCMP constables from the Mayerthorpe, Whitecourt, and Evansburg detachments. Each name was accompanied by the call sign for the police car used by each individual, and the cellular telephone numbers assigned to each car. The police had suspected that Roszko was using police scanners, but were surprised that his information was so detailed. Considering what happened later, it was chilling.

Soon after midnight, two mechanics arrived with a tow truck to take away the stolen trucks and some of the automotive parts. They were provided with a police escort. Specialists from the RCMP auto theft section in Edmonton were expected in the morning. All of the officers left the site, except for two who stayed on guard duty. At 3:30 a.m., March 3, those officers were relieved by Anthony Gordon, who had come over from Whitecourt, and Leo Johnston from Mayerthorpe.

For a long time it was not known just how Roszko sneaked back to his compound and slipped into the Quonset hut. Undercover police would not learn until 2007, that Roszko had gone to the town of Barrhead to get assistance from Shawn Hennessey, his partner in the grow op enterprise. Hennessey and his brother-in-law, Dennis Cheeseman, would eventually be found guilty of driving Roszko to his property under cover of night, and providing him with a .300 Magnum Winchester rifle. Once Roszko was in the vicinity, it would not have been difficult for him to stealthily make his way across the fields and enter the compound unseen. He knew the terrain well. He wore socks over his boots to muffle the sound of his footsteps, and he had a white bedsheet with which to camouflage himself against the snowy fields.

Roszko was armed with the Winchester and a semi-automatic Beretta pistol when he crept back onto his property. He also had access to guns that he had hidden on the grounds or in the hut. One of the weapons he had was a Heckler and Koch .308 calibre automatic assault rifle. This gun had a twenty-round magazine, and could spray bullets like a machine gun.

No one will ever know just what was going on in Roszko's mind that night. Quite possibly the hatred and rage he'd held for police for so long drove him beyond the point of no return. He knew the police had found his chop shop and grow op. He was looking at jail time for sure. He didn't want to go back to jail, so why not go out in a blaze of violent glory and take a cop or two with him!

Shortly before nine o'clock, on the morning of March 3, Constables Schiemann and Myrol called on a veterinarian in Mayerthorpe for drugs to sedate the dogs, which were now in the pen at Roszko's compound. Schiemann was on his way to Edmonton to purchase camera equipment and office supplies. RCMP officers do not shop in uniform (it's considered inappropriate), so Schiemann was in civilian clothes and unarmed, though he was on duty. Having obtained the animal sedative, the constables drove to Roszko's compound. Soon after they arrived there, two auto theft specialists from Edmonton drove up: Constables Steve Vigor and Garrett Hoogestraat.

At not quite 10:00 a.m., Hoogestraat and Vigor were near the rear of the Quonset hut where they had parked their patrol car. They were pulling on coveralls to protect their clothing from the greasy auto parts. Gordon, Schiemann, Johnston, and Myrol had been talking near the dog pen, where one of them had just given the animals a piece of drugged meat. Now the four men walked around to the front of the hut and entered through the wide open front doors … straight into an ambush!

Moments after the officers walked into the Quonset hut, Constable Vigor heard a series of rapid-fire gunshots come from within. Though nobody would ever know exactly what happened in those few seconds, police were later able to reconstruct at least part of the scenario. When Gordon, Schiemann, Johnston, and Myrol walked through the doors, they had no idea Roszko was in there, hiding behind three large plastic containers in the corner, to the left of the entrance. Schiemann, Johnston, and Myrol moved toward the middle of the room, perhaps discussing Roszko's illegal operations. Gordon waited just inside the doorway.

Roszko struck without warning, giving the men no chance to defend themselves. He shot Gordon twice at near point-blank range, and then sprayed the other three with automatic fire. Johnston and Schiemann fell immediately. Myrol dove for the cover of two sheds at the rear of the hut, but was cut down before he could make it. The carnage had taken just a few seconds.

Corporal Vigor had been trained as an Emergency Response Team (ERT) member. When he heard the shooting, he drew his gun and ran toward the front of the Quonset hut. He hadn't gone far when Roszko came out of the hut. Roszko immediately opened fire on Vigor. He missed, but put two bullets into a patrol car behind the constable. Vigor shot back and hit Roszko in the thigh and the hand. The gunman limped back into the hut. In addition to the Heckler and Koch assault rifle, Roszko had the 300 Magnum rifle slung over his shoulder, and the Beretta pistol stuck in the waistband of his pants.

As Constable Hoogestraat covered him, Vigor called for backup. Neither of them heard the last shot inside the hut. James Roszko, having murdered four Mounties in cold blood, killed himself with a shot through the left side of his chest.

Due to the light and their positions, the two remaining officers could not see inside the hut. They did not know what had happened. They called out the names of the four constables, and got no reply. They did not know that the gunman was dead.

Soon, ERT teams arrived from Edmonton and Calgary. A police helicopter circled overhead. Three military vehicles, including an armoured ambulance, were dispatched from the Canadian Forces Base at Edmonton. At 2:00 p.m., a camera-equipped robot was sent into the hut. The pictures the robot sent back to its operators showed three constables and Roszko lying on the ground. Myrol's body was out of the camera's range. ERT members entered the hut and had their worst fears confirmed. All four constables were dead.

The nation was shocked. Not since the days of the North-West Mounted Police had four Mounties been killed by gunfire in a single violent episode. The Mayerthorpe Massacre raised many questions about police and court policies concerning individuals known to be extremely dangerous, and police procedure in the face of potentially dangerous situations.

The slain officers would be buried by their families with all due honours, but before any of the funerals were held, there was a magnificent memorial service in Edmonton. On the morning of March 10, to the sound of the pipes and drums, 5,000 red-coated Mounties, followed by

Courtesy Fallen Four Memorial Park, Mayerthorpe, Alberta

Monument to slain RCMP officers Peter Schiemann, Leo Johnston, Anthony Gordon, and Brock Myrol.

thousands of police officers from across Canada and the United States, marched to honour their fallen comrades.

In July 2008, hundreds of police officers and civilians attended the opening of Mayerthorpe Memorial Park, and the unveiling of statues of the four constables. The park, which is near the town's RCMP detachment, features a garden, a picnic area, and a visitor's centre. It is intended as a memorial to all Canadian law enforcement officers who died in the line of fire.

BIBLIOGRAPHY

Books

Atkin, Ronald. *Maintain the Right: The Early History of the North West Mounted Police.* Toronto: Macmillan, 1973

Berton, Pierre. *The Wild Frontier.* Toronto: McClelland & Stewart, 1978.

Butts, Edward, and Harold Horwood. *Pirates & Outlaws of Canada.* Toronto: Doubleday Canada, 1884. Reissued, Toronto: Lynx Images, 2003.

_____. *Bandits & Privateers: Canada in the age of Gunpowder.* Toronto: Doubleday Canada, 1987. Reissued, Halifax: Formac Publishing, 1988.

Butts, Edward. *True Canadian Unsolved Mysteries.* Toronto: Prospero Books, 2006.

_____. *True Stories of Canadian Battlefields.* Toronto: Prospero Books, 2007.

Dempsey, Hugh A. *Charcoal's World*. Saskatoon: Western Producer Prairie Books, 1978.

Fryer, Mary Beacock. *More Battlefields of Canada*. Toronto: Dundurn Press, 1993.

Graves, Donald E., ed. *More Fighting for Canada; Five Battles, 1760–1944*. Toronto: Robin Brass Studio, 2004.

Horwood, Harold. *The Newfoundland Ranger Force*. St. John's: Breakwater Books, 1986.

Johnson, Mark. *No Tears to the Gallows*. Toronto: McClelland & Stewart, 2000.

Kelly, Nora & William. *The Royal Canadian Mounted Police: A Century of History*. Edmonton: Hurtig Publishers, 1973.

Knuckle, Robert. *In the Line of Duty: From Fort Macleod to Mayerthorpe*. Renfrew, ON: General Store Publishing, 2005.

Lamb, Marjorie and Barry Pearson. *The Boyd Gang*. Toronto: Peter Martin Associates, 1976.

Larracey, Edward W. *Resurgo, The History of Moncton* (Vols 1–2). Moncton: City of Moncton, NB, 1990.

Liversedge, Ronald. *Recollections of the On To Ottawa Trek*. Toronto: McClelland & Stewart, 1973.

Machum, Lloyd. *A History of Moncton, Town & City, 1855–1965*. Moncton: City of Moncton, NB, 1965.

Macintyre, N. Carroll. *The Life & Adventures of Detective Peter Owen Carroll*. Antigonish: Sundown Publications, 1985.

McGahan, Peter. *Killers, Thieves, Tramps & Sinners.* Fredericton: Goose Lane Editions, 1989.

McGrath, Darrin, Robert Smith, Ches Parsons, and Norman Crane. *The Newfoundland Rangers.* St. John's: DRC Publishing, 2005.

McSherry, Peter. *The Big Red Fox: The Incredible Story of Norman "Red" Ryan.* Toronto: Dundurn Press, 1999.

Paterson, T.W. *Canadian Battles & Massacres.* Langley: Stagecoach Publishing, 1977.

Pfeifer, Jeffrey and Ken Leyton-Brown. *Death by Rope: an Anthology of Canadian Executions.* Regina: Centax Books, 2007.

Robin, Martin. *The Bad & the Lonely.* Toronto: James Lorimer & Co., 1976.

___. *The Saga of Red Ryan.* Saskatoon: Western Producer Prairie Books, 1982.

Schofield, Carey. *Mesrine: The Life & Death of a Supercrook.* Middlesex, U.K.: Penguin Books, 1980.

Thomas, Jocko. *From Police Headquarters: True Tales From the Big City Crime Beat.* Toronto: Stoddart Publishing, 1990.

Vallee, Brian. *Edwin Alonzo Boyd: The Story of the Notorious Boyd Gang.* Toronto: Doubleday Canada, 1997.

Waiser, Bill. *All Hell Can't Stop Us: The On-to-Ottawa Trek and Regina Riot.* Calgary: Fifth House, Ltd., 2003.

Periodicals

The author found source material in various issues from the archives of the following newspapers: *British Colonist, Calgary Herald, Halifax Chronical Herald, Montreal Gazette, Montreal Star, Sarnia Canadian Observer, Globe and Mail, Toronto Star, Winnipeg Free Press,* and *York Gazette*

Other Sources

"Alberta Online Encyclopedia." *www.albertasource.ca.*

"Canada Death Penalty Index." *http://members.shaw.ca/canada_legal_ history.*

"Dictionary of Canadian Biography." *www.biographi.ca/index-e.html.*

"Encyclopedia Saskatchewan." *www.esask.uregina.ca.*

"History of Constables and Policing in Pioneer York Toronto." *www. russianbooks.org/crime/cph11.htm.*

"History of Victoria's Police." *http://vicpd.ca/history.html.*

"Mayerthorpe, RCMP Tragedy: Bad Day at Barrhead." *The Fifth Estate, www.cbc.ca/fifth/baddayatbarrhead/timeline.html.*

"Newfoundland and Labrador Police and Peace Officers' Memorial Page." *www.policeandpeaceofficers.ca.*

"Newfoundland Rangers Homepage." *http://home.ca.inter.net/~elinorr.*

"Officer Down Memorial Page, Canada." *http://www.odmp.org/canada.*

"On to Ottawa: Regina Police Riot." *www.ontoottawa.ca/trek/trek_riot. html.*

"RCMP Veterans' Association." *http://rcmpvets.net/lastpost.htm.*

Taylor, Constable Scott. "Murder on the Prairies," Winnipeg Police Service. *www.winnipeg.ca/police/history/story23.stm.*

"Titillating and Terrorizing Toronto." *Torontoist Historicist, www. torontoist.com/2008/09/historicist_titillating_and_terrori.php.*

"VPD Memorial: Saluting the Heroes." *www.vancouverpolicemuseum.ca/ FallenOfficers.*

Wong, Gordon K. "Report on James Michael Roszko, Prosecution History." *www.assembly.ab.ca/lao/library/egovdocs/2005/aljag/152010.pdf.*

Also By Edward Butts

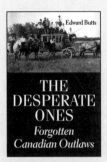

The Desperate Ones
Forgotten Canadian Outlaws
978-1-55002-610-8
$24.99

They were among Canada's most desperate criminals, yet their names have been all but forgotten in the annals of history — until now! In their day these lawless men made headline news. Author Edward Butts has rescued their stories from dusty newspaper pages and polished them up for today's readers in this fascinating volume.

Running With Dillinger
The Story of Red Hamilton and Other Forgotten Canadian Outlaws
978-1-55002-683-2
$24.99

Here are more remarkable true stories about Canadian crimes and criminals — most of them tales that have been buried for years. The stories begin in colonial Newfoundland, with robbery and murder committed by the notorious Power Gang, and continue on across the country where readers will meet the last two men to be hanged in Prince Edward Island, smugglers who made Lake Champlain a battleground, and John "Red" Hamilton, the Canadian-born member of the legendary Dillinger gang.

Of Related Interest

The Last to Die
Ronald Turpin, Arthur Lucas, and the End of Capital Punishment in Canada
by Robert Hoshowsky
978-1-55002-672-6
$24.99

They were the last two people executed in Canada, but surprisingly little was known about them. This is the first book to uncover the lives and deaths of Ronald Turpin, a Canadian criminal, and Arthur Lucas, a Detroit gangster. Featuring crime scene photos and never-before-published documents, this book uncovers what actually happened the night of the hangings and reveals the gruesome mistake that cost Arthur Lucas not only his life, but his head.

Available at your favourite bookseller.

 DUNDURN PRESS
www.dundurn.com

Tell us your story! What did you think of this book? Join the conversation at
www.definingcanada.ca/tell-your-story by telling us what you think